Where the trails are—bill williams

ASHLAND –MEDFORD AND BEYOND

How to find nearly 150 recreation trails located in or around the
Rogue River Valley, or on nearby public lands. The geographical
area covered in this book extends from near the California-Oregon
border, north to the Diamond Lake vicinity. Historical and map
information is included.

Cover design and art work by Bob Sisson

Bob

D1736165

Independent Printing Co. – 640 Tolman Cr. Road – Ashland, OR

i

ACKNOWLEDGEMENTS

This book became reality due to the contributions of many persons and agencies including:

U.S. FOREST SERVICE: Rogue River, Winema,and Umpqua National Forest Ranger District personnel. The forest recreation maps at the rear of the book and many historical notes were reproduced from Rogue River National Forest information.

OTHER SOURCES INCLUDE: U.S. Bureau of Land Management, U.S. Army Corps of Engineers, Boise Cascade Timber and Wood Products Group, Crater Lake National Park Staff, Jackson County & Medford Parks and Recreation Departments, The Nature Conservancy and Oregon Fish and Wildlife personnel.

AUDREY WILLIAMS: "Over the shoulder advice"
IVAN COLLVER, Ashland computer programmer, helpful guidance.

PLEASE NOTE: The emphasis of this book is to DESCRIBE HOW TO GET TO THE TRAILS AND WHAT EQUIPMENT TO BRING. Although known precautions are listed, the author cannot be responsible for trails that may be hard to follow due to reduced maintenance, abandonment, new roads,logging operations or any other unforeseen conditions. Check with the applicable agencies for the latest trail status.

First Edition c 1988 Bill Williams

Sixth Edition c 2001 Bill Williams   ISBN: 0-9622114-6-X

TABLE OF CONTENTS

Collings Mountain Trail

Bill says, "Leave things as you found them for others to enjoy."

INTRODUCTION

Southern Oregon is a paradise for outdoor enthusiasts! It provides year-round opportunities for hiking and backpacking, horseback riding, and a variety of winter sports! Southern Oregon has less rain than does most parts of the State, and if a person is careful in choosing where and when to go, it is possible to find trails where rain is at a minimum. It is also possible to locate areas above the fog and into the sunshine!

DURING THE WINTER MONTHS, the Applegate Valley and vicinity provide spectacular outdoor experiences! This is a great place to soak up some sunshine and enjoy the open views of the surrounding mountains, or to travel the trails along the Applegate River or Applegate Lake area.

Other favorite winter trails are those at Lost Creek Lake, Table Rocks, Roxy Ann Peak, or the beautiful Lower Rogue River Trail. Ashland generally lifts its head above the Rogue Valley winter fog, and the trails are less muddy due to granite soil.

Mt. Ashland is a favorite for winter sports and is complete with a ski lodge, ski rental facilities, rope tows, chair lifts and trails for cross-country skiing. Contact a Forest Ranger Station for locations of other cross-country ski trails in the Cascade Range.

IN LATE SPRING OR SUMMER, the trails at high elevations begin to open up, but above 7000 feet elevation the snow might not be gone until mid-July. The Pacific Crest National Scenic Trail in this area travels 31 miles through Crater Lake National Park before it continues south another 75 miles along the Cascade Range, crest of the Siskiyou Mountains and on to the Klamath River. This is but a portion of the Pacific Crest National Scenic Trail that extends 2500 miles from Canada to Mexico.

1

In addition to Crater Lake National Park, southern Oregon boasts several Wilderness Areas: The Rogue-Umpqua Divide, Sky Lakes, Mountain Lakes and Red Buttes. The summit of Mt. McLoughlin at 9495' elevation, is the highest point one can reach in the area covered by this book.

The author has hiked many of these trails during outings conducted by the Oregon-Idaho Conference of the United Methodist Church or by the Rogue Chapter of the Sierra Club. While along on these trips, it became obvious that a book was needed to help find the trailhead locations, because many road junction signs were damaged or missing. Maps are sometimes hard to follow or may need revision, and so an effort is made to present a fairly simple access description to the trailheads, giving directions from nearest mileposts. Every effort will be made to keep this book up-to-date, but changes beyond our control can rapidly happen!

HOW TO USE THIS BOOK

It is very important to BRING MAPS listed in each hike description, and a COMPASS to help you find your way. The U.S. Forest Service has a very excellent leaflet entitled "MAP AND COMPASS." It contains work sheets with practice drills that are easy to understand. It takes the confusion out of using a compass and may save your life!

The U. S. Geological Survey publishes TOPOGRAPHIC MAPS (Topos) that are available from libraries, sporting goods stores, stationary or book stores, and some office suppliers. They can be ordered directly from U. S. Geological Survey, Distribution Section, Federal Center, Denver Colorado 80225. The maps cover every section of the United States in minute detail. An "Index To Topographic Maps of Oregon" is also available from the USGS.

U.S. Forest Service maps are often printed in TOPO form. For the area covered by this book, the Pacific Crest National Scenic Trail, Mountain Lakes Wilderness and Sky Lakes Area maps are all topographic. TOPO MAPS are also available from the Applegate, Ashland, Butte Falls, Prospect, Tiller and Diamond Lake RANGER DISTRICTS.

TOPO MAPS have contour lines that determine elevation and the altitude of peaks, valleys and other landmarks. They also indicate roads, trails, rivers, streams, railroad tracks and other details. MOST ELEVATION DATA IN THIS BOOK WAS ESTIMATED FROM TOPO MAPS AND SHOULD NOT BE CONSIDERED ACCURATE NOR OFFICIAL.

EQUIPMENT NEEDED: In addition to MAPS and COMPASS, the following items are important:

BOOTS OR STURDY SHOES: Waterproof, well fitted with warm socks.
CLOTHING that can be layered, preferably wool.
RAINGEAR. Rainsuits have more wind protection than do ponchos.
EMERGENCY SUPPLIES: First aid,matches,flashlight,bug repellant.
CANTEEN - WATER PURIFICATION: There is no guarantee that any water in the woods is free from Giardia, or other harmful bacteria. The only sure way to avoid sickness is to BRING WATER FROM HOME or to have absolute resolve not to drink any water in the woods unless it has been treated. Water purification tablets are not quite 100% effective. The safest way is to boil the water for at least 10 minutes, or to bring a water filter, available from suppliers of recreation equipment.

The wood tick is much smaller than this but they can be easily seen if they get on you. They are in area all year long.

RULES TO CONSIDER.

SAFETY: Before you leave home, let others know where you are going and stick with the plan! When in the woods, stay with your group, as you may need to rely on each other in case of emergencies! Do not run on the trails or take needless chances. Help may be far away! Drive safely on forest roads and be alert for logging vehicles or other traffic.

OBEY FIRE REGULATIONS. Build fires only where allowed, and make sure they are COMPLETELY OUT before leaving camp. No smoking while traveling, except in vehicles on roads.

OBTAIN PERMITS. Before hiking in the woods, check with the appropriate agencies for fire or wilderness entry permits. TRAILHEAD PARKING PERMITS REQUIRED ON DESIGNATED TRAILS-SEE PAGE 6.

PACK OUT ALL TRASH. Don't bury it. Leave campgrounds cleaner than you found them! Remove litter encountered on the trail.

DO NOT POLLUTE. Keep soaps and other pollutants out of rivers and streams. Bury human waste away from streams or lakes.

PRIVATE PROPERTY. Respect posted signs, stay on the trail.

DON'T CUT ACROSS SWITCHBACKS. This can cause erosion and severe damage to the trails.

LISTEN TO THE WILDERNESS! Leave radios and tape players at home.

ALWAYS BE PREPARED. Bring the equipment listed on the previous page. CARRY DRINKING WATER ON EVERY OUTING!

4

HAZARDS TO AVOID. Poison oak, deer ticks or an occasional rattlesnake may be encountered while hiking in southern Oregon. Using caution can help minimize these hazards.

POISON OAK is generally found in the lower elevation hills (below 6000 feet) in the Applegate and Rogue River Valleys. Learn to identify this noxious plant. Its shiny green leaves are in groups of threes turning to red in late summer. Oils from the plant can cause an itching rash or blisters. The treatment methods include scrubbing the skin with naptha or alkaline soap, or by cleansing with rubbing alcohol. Calamine or other skin lotion may be beneficial if the rash is mild. It may be necessary to seek medical advice in severe cases.

TICKS can carry Lyme disease,or recently reported cases of H.G.E. (Human granulocytic ehrlichiosis) and Babesiosis. THESE DISEASES CAN BE DISABLING OR FATAL IF NOT DIAGNOSED AND TREATED. SEEK THE LATEST MEDICAL ADVICE.

PREVENTING BITES: Wear long sleeves and pants tucked into boots. Avoid trail margins, brush and grassy areas when in tick country. Use tick repellant on clothes and shoes. White clothes help make ticks visible. Check yourself and pets carefully for ticks.
TREATMENT: Remove attatched tick at once with fine-jaw tweezers, grasping the tick's mouth-parts as close to the skin as possible, slowly and gently pulling straight out. AUTHORITIES ADVISE not to squeeze tick or spray it with oil as it may inject fluid into you. Wash bite area, hands and apply antiseptic. GET MEDICAL TREATMENT IF ANY PARTS ARE LEFT IN THE SKIN OR IF COMPLICATIONS DEVELOP.

RATTLESNAKES. This is not a common problem in southern Oregon, but an occasional snake may be spotted at lower elevations. During summer months, look for them in shaded areas especially during early morning or late afternoon. In case of snake bite, the best treatment is to get the victim to a doctor or a hospital as soon as possible. Apply cold compresses if available. Loose constricting bands may be placed above the bite, but not so tight as to stop blood circulation.

WHERE TO GET INFORMATION AND PERMITS.
PARKING PERMITS ARE REQUIRED AT CERTAIN DESIGNATED TRAILHEADS.
CHECK WITH USFS SUPERVISOR OFFICES OR RANGER DISTRICTS.

ROGUE RIVER NATIONAL FOREST.
-Forest Supervisor, P.O. Box 520, 333 W. 8th St., Medford, Or.
97501   Phone (541)858-2200
-District Ranger, Ashland Ranger Station, 645 Washington St.,
Ashland, Oregon 97520   Phone (541)482-3333
-District Ranger, Butte Falls Ranger Station, P.O. Box 227, Butte
Falls, Oregon 97522   Phone (541)865-2700
-District Ranger, Prospect Ranger Station, Prospect, Oregon,
97536   Phone (541)560-3400
-District Ranger, Star Ranger Station, 6941 Upper Applegate Road,
Jacksonville, Oregon 97530   Phone (541)899-1812

WINEMA NATIONAL FOREST.
-Forest Supervisor, 2819 Dahlia St., Klamath Falls, Oregon, 97601
Phone (541)883-6714
-Klamath District Ranger, 1936 California Ave., Klamath Falls,
Oregon 97601   Phone (541)885-3400
UMPQUA NATIONAL FOREST.
-Forest Supervisor, P.O. Box 1008, Roseburg, Or. 97470   Phone
(541)672-6601
-Diamond Lake Ranger District, Toketee Route Box 101, Idleyld
Park, Oregon 97447   Phone (541)498-2531
-Tiller Ranger District, Route 2 Box 1, Tiller, Oregon 97484
Phone (541)825-3201
SISKIYOU NATIONAL FOREST.-Supervisor, 200 N.E. Greenfield Road,
Grants Pass, Oregon 97526. Phone (541)471-6500
KLAMATH NATIONAL FOREST. -Supervisor, 1312 Fairlane Road, Yreka,
California,96097. Phone (530)842-6131

-BUREAU OF LAND MANAGEMENT
3040 Biddle Road, Medford, Or.. 97504.   Phone (541)618-2200
1465 N.E. 7th St., Grant Pass, Or. 97526.   Phone (541)479-7244
-MEDFORD PARKS AND RECREATION DEPT., Medford City Hall, Rm. 140,
Medford, Oregon 97501   Phone (541)774-2400
-THE NATURE CONSERVANCY, 33 N. Central Ave., Medford, Oregon,
97501   Phone (541)770-7933
-OREGON DEPT. OF FORESTRY, 5286 Table Rock Rd., Central Point,Or.
97502 Phone (541)664-3328

-OREGON DEPARTMENT OF FISH AND WILDLIFE, 1495 Gregory Road, White City Oregon.
-PORTLAND DISTRICT, U.S. ARMY CORPS OF ENGINEERS, Lost Creek Project, Trail, Oregon, 97541.
-GEOLOGICAL INFORMATION: BLM staff, 3040 Biddle Road, Medford. USFS Supervisor's Office, 333 West 8th St., Medford, Oregon. Southern Oregon State College, Ashland, Oregon.
-BOTANICAL, BIOLOGICAL INFORMATION: BLM staff, Medford office. USFS Supervisor's Office, 333 West 8th St., Medford, Oregon.

TRAIL PARK PASSES are required when parking at certain trailheads on the Rogue River National Forest and most trailheads on the Siskiyou National Forest, to generate funds for trail and trailhead maintenance. They are required when parking within 1/4 mile of trailheads designated by the Forest offices. The Rogue River Ntl. Forest has a listing of trailheads upon request.

Day passes and annual passes are available at the Forest Service offices and selected commercial outlets. Golden Age and Golden Access Passport holders receive a 50% discount. Trail maintenance volunteers may qualify for a free annual pass. The passes are honored at all designated trailheads in Oregon and in Washington.

Forest officers will place fee envelopes on vehicles that are in non-compliance and will allow trail users the opportunity to pay the day pass fee or purchase an annual pass through the mail to avoid a fine.

HELPFUL ORGANIZATIONS: Several Rogue Valley organizations have scheduled meetings and field trips. Up-to-date information can be obtained from their chapter newsletters or from the local news media. Chambers of Commerce of the area may also have some listings. The organizations include:

-FRIENDS OF THE GREENSPRINGS
-MOUNT MAZAMA MUSHROOM ASSOCIATION
-NATIVE PLANT SOCIETY OF OREGON
-ROGUE VALLEY AUDUBON SOCIETY
-ROGUE GROUP SIERRA CLUB
-SODA MOUNTAIN WILDERNESS COUNCIL

BIKES ARE PERMITTED ON THE FOLLOWING TRAILS:

NOTE: Bikes are not permitted on: Pacific Crest Trail,
Wilderness area trails, National Recreation Trails,

*NOTE MOTOR BIKES ALSO ALLOWED WHEN INDICATED BY *

CONTACT LOCAL AGENCIES FOR UPDATED INFORMATION!

CHAPTER 1 - ASHLAND AREA

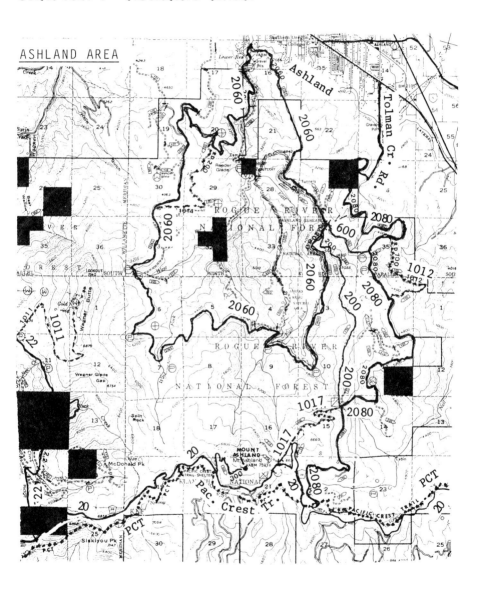

ASHLAND AREA

ASHLAND'S LITHIA PARK HIKING TRAILS.

PARK ENTRANCE: Adjacent to downtown Ashland Plaza, just below the Oregon Shakespeare Festival Theaters.
SEASON: All year, EASY TRAILS for hikers or joggers. Bicycles, animals and overnight sleeping prohibited. The park is closed from 11:30 pm to 5:30 am.

FEATURES: Hiking in Ashland's Lithia Park is a very relaxing and educational experience! From the park entrance, the trails extend about one mi. to the far end of the park along both sides of Ashland Creek. Foot-bridges inter-connect, allowing the visitor to create an individualized experience. Picnic and restroom facilities are located throughout the park.

From the upper park boundary, hikers often extend their outing by going 0.2 mi. further south on Granite St. to a newly constructed "Reservoir Trail" leading about 1/4 mile to a park setting along Ashland Creek. This area is used by picnickers and swimmers, and is located at the junction of Granite St. and Glenview Dr....that are often used for more hiking/jogging adventures!

The one mile LITHIA PARK WOODLAND TRAIL also begins from the park entrance and extends past 99 numbered interpretive posts located at various trees and shrubs that have been imported from all over the world. An excellent guide-booklet is available at a very minimal cost from Ashland Parks and Recreation Dept. (located in the park), or from Ashland Chamber of Commerce. A companion booklet entitled "Lithia Park", by Marjorie O'Harra, provides information on the history of Lithia Park and is available from the above locations.

Lithia Park is a very special place that provides various recreational activities for many visitors. Because of its professional landscaping design and maintenance,Lithia Park is included in the National Register of Historic Places.

ENJOY!

BEAR CREEK GREENWAY   (Please refer to map on page 27)

CENTRAL ASHLAND TO SUNCREST ROAD IN TALENT- 5.7 miles.

Access to Nevada Street trailhead: From downtown Ashland, travel
north on Helman Street, 1.0 mile to the intersection with Nevada
Street. The path is located just north of this intersection near
the Ashland Dog Park. From this trailhead, the path leads 2.0 mi.
northwest to a point where it uses the underpass of South Valley-
View Road at its intersection with Highway 99. The path then continues 0.7 mile along Highway 99 to a parking area on the RIGHT.
The path continues 3.0 miles, passing Lynn Newbry Park where parking, telephone and restroom are available and just beyond to
Suncrest Road where there are no parking facilities.

Access to Highway 99 parking area: From Interstate 5 North Ashland Exit 19 South Valley View Road, travel west toward Ashland,
0.4 mile to the junction with Highway 99.   Turn RIGHT and go 0.7
mile to the parking area on the RIGHT.

Access to Talent-Lynn Newbry Park. Lynn Newbry Park is immediately west of Interstate Highway 5 Exit 21 off-ramps.

IN MEDFORD, a 5.75 mi. section is paved from Barnett Road to Pine
St. in Central Point. Fundraising is underway to extend the path
from Barnett Road to Suncrest Road in Talent.

"The Bear Creek Greenway is a corridor stretching 30 miles from
Emigrant Lake to the Rogue River. When completed, this project
will provide a natural greenbelt through the heart of the most
populated land in Jackson County and will link the cities of
Ashland, Talent, Phoenix, Medford and Central Point by a trail
system.   Eventually, the Greenway will include land along the
Rogue River and Little Butte Crk. to connect with Eagle Point.The
Greenway will provide a wide range of close-to-home recreation
opportunities including bicycling, horseback riding, hiking, jog-
ging and picnicking.   The Greenway will protect wildlife habitat
throughout the Bear Creek Basin."   (Quote: Jackson County Parks)

11

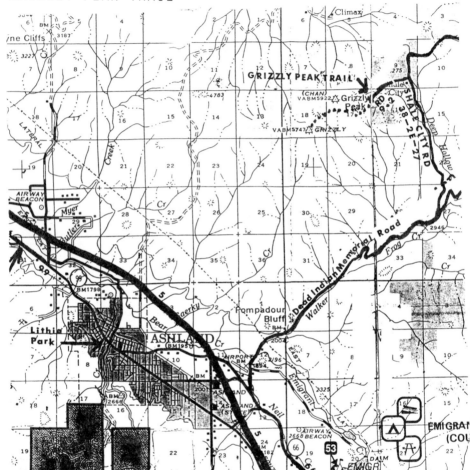

GRIZZLY PEAK. The peak northeast of Ashland that looms over the city. (See maps 21 and 22)

TRAIL BEGINS:	-BLM Road 38-2E-9.2	ELEV. 5200'
TRAIL ENDS:	-Scenic overlook. Moderate grades.	ELEV. 5747'
DISTANCE:	-2 mi. one way, 3.5 mi.when loop ready.	
USE:	-Hikers, horses, mountain bikes.	
SEASON:	-Spring to fall, trail can be muddy during winter.	
BRING MAPS:	-Local BLM information. Carry water!	
ACCESS:	From Interstate Hwy. 5, Ashland-Klamath Falls Exit	

14, travel 0.6 miles east on State Hwy. 66 to the junction with Dead Indian Memorial Road. Turn left (northeast) onto this road and follow mileposts to mile 6.6 at the junction with Shale City Road (BLM Road 38-2E-27). Turn left onto 38-2E-27 and go 2.9 mi. to the junction with BLM Road 38-2E-9.2 Turn left onto 38-2E-9.2 and go 3/4 mile to a 3-way road junction. Road 38-2E-9.2 continues straight ahead uphill 0.9 miles to a parking area on the left.

FEATURES: The trail begins through the woods and some meadows and reaches a trail junction after 1.5 mile. Keep straight ahead, a short distance to an overlook that gives views of Mt. Shasta, Black Butte, Mount Ashland, and of the I-5 freeway making its way over Siskiyou Pass.

Backing up to the above trail junction,turn left (south) and follow Grizzly Trail along the rim-top to another viewpoint at elevation 5747' that affords good views of Ashland and of the mountains to the south. A loop trail back to the trailhead is in the works. It is best to wait for trail signs, maps, and BLM Info.

The BLM advises that "fire danger is high during late summer, refrain from building fires or smoking"

This is one of the more outstanding trails in southern Oregon. It has been reported that because of the altitude, poison oak, ticks or snakes are not in the area. The trail was envisioned by John Ifft, a retired BLM trail planner. With BLM approval,the work was completed in stages by a group of many volunteers.

13

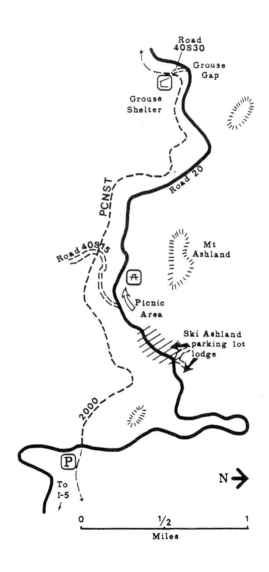

PACIFIC CREST NATIONAL SCENIC TRAIL–GROUSE GAP TO FOREST BOUNDARY.
(See map 28)

TRAIL BEGINS: –Forest Route 20–Grouse Gap.   ELEV. 6400'
TRAIL ENDS: –Forest Route 20–Forest Boundary.   ELEV. 6200'
DISTANCE: –3.5 miles (one way), USE: Easy for hikers, moderate for horses.
SEASON: –June through October.
BRING MAPS: –USFS Pacific Crest Trail–Oregon Southern Portion.
        –USFS Ashland Ranger Dist.–Rogue River Ntl.Forest.
        –USFS Recreation Opportunity Guide.

ACCESS   From Ashland Exit 14, drive south on Interstate 5
              9.0 miles to Mt. Ashland Exit 6.   Turn right and
go 1/4 mi.to Mt. Ashland Access Road (later becoming Forest Route
20). Follow this road 7.2 miles to the NATIONAL FOREST BOUNDARY
SIGN. The Pacific Crest Tr. crosses the road at this point. Look
along the left side of the road for the trail leading to Grouse
Gap. If making a car shuttle, leave one car here and drive to Access #2.

ACCESS # 2
Continue 4 mi. on the same road (from this point posted as Forest
Route 20) to Grouse Gap near milepost 11, at the junction of Road
40S30. The Pacific Crest Trail crosses Road 40S30 at this point,
proceed east along the trail to Access #1.

FEATURES: Beginning at Access #2, the Pacific Crest Trail
              follows along the southern flanks of Mount Ashland through a mixed conifer forest, granite rock formations and
small mountain meadows. Mid summer wildflowers include columbine,
scarlet gilia, Indian paintbrush, mountain gentians and lupine. A
selection of views would include Mt. Shasta, Marble Mountains and
the Trinity Alps. Water from several springs along the trail has
not been tested and may be unsafe to drink.

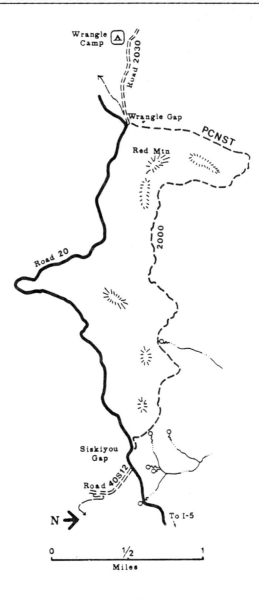

16

PACIFIC CREST NATIONAL SCENIC TRAIL -WRANGLE GAP TO SISKIYOU GAP.
(See maps 27 and 28)

TRAIL BEGINS:	-Forest Road 20 at Wrangle Gap.	ELEV. 6496'
TRAIL ENDS:	-Forest Road 20 at Siskiyou Gap.	ELEV. 5879'
DISTANCE:	-3.8 miles (one-way)-MODERATE.	
SEASON:	-June through October. USE: hikers/horses.	
BRING MAPS:	-USFS Pacific Crest Trail-Oregon Southern Portion.	
	-USFS Ashland Ranger Dist.-Rogue River Ntl. Forest.	
	-USFS Recreation Opportunity Guide.	

ACCESS #1   From Ashland Exit 14,drive south on Interstate 5,
9.0 miles to Mt. Ashland Exit 6.   Turn right and
go 1/4 mile to Mt. Ashland Access Road(later becoming Forest Road
20). Follow this road 17 miles (1.0 mile beyond the junction with
Road 22),to where the Pacific Crest Trail crosses Road 20 at Siskiyou Gap. If making a car shuttle, leave one car here and drive
to Access #2.

ACCESS #2   Continue 3.0 miles further on Road 20 to the junction
with Road 2030 at Wrangle Gap.   Park along Road 20 and hike 150'
down Road 2030.   The Pacific Crest Trail leads right (northeast)
to return to Siskiyou Gap (Access #1).

FEATURES: Beginning at Wrangle Gap,the trail contours along
the flanks of Red Mtn. through a forest of Shasta
red fir and mountain hemlock, and continues to contour the ridge-
line with vistas of Mt. McLoughlin, the Crater Lake Rim, Dutchman
Peak Lookout, Brown Mountain and the rim of Mountain Lakes Wilderness.   The trail contours above Monogram Lakes before beginning its moderate descent to Siskiyou Gap. CARRY WATER,there are
no water sources along the trail.

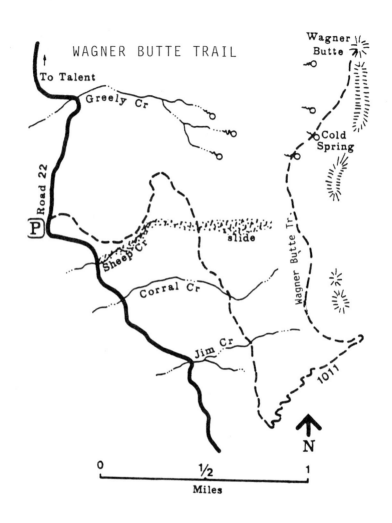

WAGNER BUTTE TRAIL

To Talent

Greely Cr

Wagner Butte

Cold Spring

Road 22

P

Sheep Cr

slide

Corral Cr

Jim Cr

Wagner Butte Tr.

1011

N

| 0 | ½ | 1 |

Miles

WAGNER BUTTE TRAIL #1011. (Old #972) (Maps 20 and 21)

TRAIL BEGINS: –Forest Route 22 beyond milepost 10.   ELEV. 4960'
TRAIL ENDS: –Wagner Butte Lookout (former site).   ELEV. 7140'
DISTANCE: –5.2 miles, time up 4 to 5 hours. USE: hiker only.
DIFFICULTY: –Difficult, steep 15% grade in first .65 mile.
SEASON: –June through October, wildflowers all summer.
BRING MAPS: –USFS Ashland Ranger Dist.–Rogue River Ntl. Forest.
–USFS Recreation Opportunity Guide–Wagner Butte Tr.

ACCESS: From Talent, Oregon, at the intersection of Talent Ave. and Main St., travel south on Main Street for 0.4 mile after which Main Street becomes Wagner Creek Road. Continue south on Wagner Creek Road, which veers left at a junction beyond milepost 7, and continues 2 miles to a three-way junction. Keep left onto Forest Road 22 and go 2.0 miles to a large parking area on the right. The Wagner Butte Trailhead is on the opposite (east) side of the road, look for a sign nailed to a tree. WATCH CAREFULLY FOR TRAFFIC–ROADS ARE NARROW, STEEP WITH MANY CURVES.

Hike the trail 0.3 mi. to an old road. Turn right and go about 0.6 mile to the northern edge of a meadow. Look for a "Trail" sign. It is about 2.3 mi. further to Wagner Glade Gap. Portions of the trail were hard to follow through hillside meadows or at a large landslide, but conditions improved after a 1987 trail reconstruction project. From Wagner Glade Gap, turn left at a sign indicating Wagner Butte 2 miles. The trail skirts the western slopes of Wagner Butte and ends at the base of the former Wagner Butte Lookout site. Find your way to the top by following old blazes or cairns.

TREES/PLANTS: Noble, white and Douglas-firs, mountain mahogany, quaking aspen, golden chinquapin, sage, serviceberry, ceanothus, manzanita and snowbrush. Wildflowers are abundant.

HISTORY: "WAGNER BUTTE: Named for Jacob Wagner, settler in the present area of Talent, Oregon, who later operated the flour mill near the Ashland Plaza." (USFS quote)

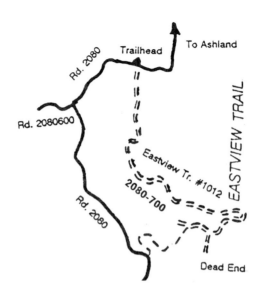

Rd. 2080

Trailhead

To Ashland

Rd. 2080600

Eastview Tr. #1012

2080-700

Rd. 2080

Dead End

EASTVIEW TRAIL

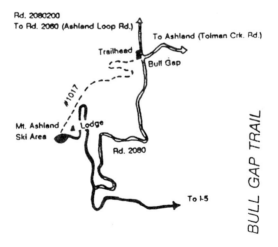

Rd. 2080200
To Rd. 2060 (Ashland Loop Rd.)

To Ashland (Tolman Crk. Rd.)

Trailhead

Bull Gap

#1017

Mt. Ashland
Ski Area

Lodge

Rd. 2080

To I-5

BULL GAP TRAIL

EASTVIEW MOUNTAIN BIKE TRAIL #1012.   (See map 21)

TRAIL BEGINS:	-Lower Trailhead Road 2080.	ELEV. 4320'
TRAIL ENDS:	-Upper Trailhead Road 2080.	ELEV. 4720'
DISTANCE:	-2.5 miles.	
USE:	-Mountain bikes, hikers.	
DIFFICULTY:	-Moderate.	
SEASON:	-June thru October.	
BRING MAPS:	-USFS Recreation Opportunity Guide (this trail).	
	-USFS Ashland Ranger Dist.-Rogue River Ntl.Forest.	

ACCESS: From Interstate Hwy 5, Ashland-Klamath Falls Exit 14, travel west on Hwy 66 (Ashland St.) one block to Tolman Creek Road traffic light. Turn left and follow Tolman Creek Road 1 mi. before crossing Siskiyou Blvd. Continue up Tolman Creek Road (later becoming Forest Road 2080), 6.5 mi. to the lower trailhead on the left. Ample parking is available in the landing located on the opposite side of Road 2080. Please do not park in front of the gate at the trailhead on Road 2080700. THE UPPER TRAILHEAD IS LOCATED 1.5 mile further up Road 2080.

FEATURES: From the lower trailhead on Forest Road 2080 the first 2.0 miles of Eastview Trail wind up Forest Road 2080700 (closed to motorized use), with panoramic views of the upper Bear Creek Valley and Emigrant Lake. At 2.0 miles the road forks and the route continues to the right another 0.1 mile before leaving the road. The singletrack trail heads uphill on the left and meanders another 0.4 miles to meet Road 2080 at the upper trail terminus.Along the way you'll pass beneath some huge old sugar pine sentinels.

ROAD 2080 receives a fair amount of vehicle traffic. Bikers should control their speed when descending this road and be watchful for oncoming cars or trucks. USFS advises to carry water and a snack for lunch.

-Excerpts USFS Recreation Opportunity Guide.

BULL GAP TRAIL #1017.   (See map 28)

TRAIL BEGINS:	-Mt. Ashland Ski Area.	ELEV. 6620'
TRAIL ENDS:	-Bull Gap, Forest Road 2080.	ELEV. 5520'
DISTANCE:	-2.5 miles.	
USE:	-Mountain bikes, hikers.	
DIFFICULTY:	-Moderate.	
SEASON:	-June thru October.	
BRING MAPS:	-USFS Recreation Opportunity Guide (this trail).	
	-USFS Ashland Ranger Dist.-Rogue River Ntl.Forest.	

ACCESS: From Ashland Exit 14, continue southeast on Inter-
              state Highway 5, nine miles to Mt. Ashland Exit 6.
This exit leads to the junction with Old Hwy.99 South. Keep right
at this junction and go 0.7 mile to Mt. Ashland Access Road. Turn
onto the Mt. Ashland Access Road and go 7.0 miles to the junction
with Forest Road 2080.

LOWER TRAILHEAD at Bull Gap: Turn right onto Road 2080 and go 3.2
miles to Bull Gap, trailhead parking with picnic table.
UPPER TRAILHEAD: located near the closed gate at the parking area
between the Mt. Ashland Ski Lodge and the rental Shop.

FEATURES: Follow the dirt road with blue diamond nordic ski
              trailblazers and traverse just below the lodge to
the north. Stay on the road: bikes are prohibited on the ski area
slopes! The blazers leave off when entering the forest just below
the ski area boundary, and the trail is easily followed to Bull
Gap.

CAUTION: The trail is located within the Ashland Watershed,
              which is the source of the city's water supply. It
is important to give special consideration to its protection. No
camping or campfires allowed. Bicycles must stay on the trail,and
their use is not recommended in rainy weather when soils are wet.
When fire danger is high, the Ashland Watershed may be closed to
all entry but the Bull Gap Trail will remain open.   However,Road
2080200 to the north will be closed; so if you are descending the
15.6 miles to town, use Tolman Creek (2080) Road to the east.(Excerpts USFS Recreation Opportunity Guide).

HOBART BLUFF-Via Pacific Crest National Scenic Trail. (Map 29)

TRAIL BEGINS:	-Soda Mountain Road.	ELEV. 5300'
TRAIL ENDS:	-Hobart Bluff Overlook.	ELEV. 5502'
DISTANCE:	-About 1.5 miles.	
SEASON:	-Usually snow-free late May through October. Wild-flowers abundant May to July.	
BRING MAPS:	-USFS Pacific Crest Trail-Oregon Southern Portion. -BLM Transportation Map -Medford District -Klamath Resource Area. -BLM Medford District-Pacific Crest Trail log.	
USE:	CLOSED TO MOTORIZED/MECHANICAL VEHICLES, INCLUDING BICYCLES.	

ACCESS: From Interstate Hwy. 5, Ashland Exit 14, follow the mileposts east on State Hwy. 66, 15.7 miles to the highway summit at Soda Mtn. Road. Turn right onto Soda Mountain Road and go 4.0 miles to a large meadow on the left, with a parking area and overhead power lines. Look just beyond, along the road, to where the Pacific Crest Trail leads left, uphill through the meadow on its 1.0 mile journey to the junction with Hobart Bluff Viewpoint Trail.

FEATURES: The trail begins with great views of the Greensprings area and of Mt. Shasta. Wildflowers are plentiful early in the season. After about 1.0 mile, look left for the junction of the Hobart Trail leading about 1/2 mile to the viewpoint, where there are outstanding views of Ashland, Medford and of the Rogue Valley.

To return to the parking area, it will be necessary to take the trails in the reverse direction.

HISTORY: "State Highway 66.......Known locally as the Green-springs Highway, this road parallels the 'Old Applegate Trail' which was used during the 1840's by pioneers who branched off the main Oregon Trail at Fort Hall Idaho and crossed the sagebrush desert of northern Nevada." (USFS quote)

SISKIYOU CREST MOUNTAIN BIKE ROUTE. (See maps 27 and 28)

ROUTE BEGINS: —Mt. Ashland Ski Area Parking Lot.   ELEV. 6600'
DISTANCE: —15 miles (one way).   HIGH POINT ELEV. 7418'
USE: —Mountain bikes.
DIFFICULTY: —Moderate (Rd.20) to More Difficult (Rd.800).
SEASON: —July thru October.
BRING MAPS: —USFS Recreation Opportunity Guide (this route).
              —USFS Ashland Ranger Dist.—Rogue River Ntl.Forest.

ACCESS: —From Ashland Exit 14, continue 9 mi. south on In-
              terstate Hwy.5 to Mt. Ashland Exit 6.   Follow the
signs 0.7 mile to the Mt. Ashland Access Road.   Turn right onto
Mt. Ashland Road and continue 9 mi. to Ski Ashland Parking Lot.

FEATURES: Beginning from the Mt. Ashland Ski Area Parking Lot,the
route follows Forest Road 20 for 14 miles along the crest of the
Siskiyou Mountains to Jackson Gap. From the Gap, Road 800 ascends
on the right 1.5 miles to the summit of Dutchman Peak. Road 20 is
a decomposed granite surface, is maintained each year but may be
rutted or rockfall in places.   Road 800 to Dutchman Peak is more
primitive, and requires some technical ability.

ALONG THE WAY: There is a picnic area and campground 1/2 mi. from
the ski area parking lot. Another 1/2 mi. further out is Road 300
to the right, affording a side trip to the summit of Mt. Ashland
(Elev. 7533'). Back on Road 20 again at about the 2 mi. point, a
short road to the left leads to Grouse Gap Shelter.   About 11 mi.
out is Wrangle Gap; here Road 2030 goes downhill to the right 1/2
mi. to Wrangle Camp,a good lunch spot with picnic tables, shelter
and vault toilet. At the top of Dutchman Peak is one of the very
few "cupola style"fire lookouts left in the Pacific Northwest.The
lookout was built in 1927.A brochure entitled "The Siskiyou Loop"
is available at the Ashland Ranger Station for $1.00. Designed as
as an auto tour guide, bikers will find it useful and very interesting.

Please note that the Pacific Crest Trail, which parallels Forest
Road 20 most of the route,is closed to bicycles. Bicycles are not
allowed on the ski slopes at Mt. Ashland. (Excerpts USFS Recreational Guide).

24

PILOT ROCK CLIMB -From Pacific Crest National Scenic Trail.
(See map 29)

SEASON: -Usually snow-free June through October.
BRING MAPS: -USFS Pacific Crest Trail-Oregon Southern Portion.
                  -BLM Transportation Map -Medford District, Klamath
                   Resource Area.
                  -BLM Medford District-Pacific Crest Trail Log.
CLIMB BEGINS: -Pacific Crest Trail below Pilot Rock. ELEV. 5120'
CLIMB ENDS: -Pilot Rock summit.   ELEV. 5910'
TIME UP: -Approx. 1 hour.
DIFFICULTY: -Easy route through west gully. Careful selection
                   of hand and footholds required in two places in
                   the middle of the route. Hard hats are suggested
                   in case of falling rock from above. CARRY WATER!

ACCESS: From Ashland Exit 14, travel southeast on Inter-
                  state Hwy. 5, 9 miles to Mt. Ashland Exit 6. The
off-ramp leads to a junction with Old Highway 99S. Keep right at
this junction, and continue under the freeway overpass, and go a
total of 1.9 miles to Pilot Rock Road 40-2E-33 (just beyond the
crest of Old Highway 99S). Turn left onto Pilot Rock Road and at:

Mile 2.0 -Turn right onto Road 41-2E-3.
Mile 2.7 -Keep right at an unsigned road junction.
Mile 2.9 -Ridge crest, the Pacific Crest Trail crosses the road,
         look for trail signs on trees. It is best to park here
and hike about 900' east on the Pacific Crest Trail, then follow
the uphill road track on the right that leads steeply to the base
of Pilot Rock. After reaching the end of the old road,follow the
route on the left leading to the mouth of an obvious gully rising
to the summit.

After climbing two 6 foot ledges, it is safest to stay along the
left wall of the gully for best footing. Several persons have
been seriously injured by slipping from the exposed slopes on the
right. Views from the summit include just about all of southern
Oregon and northern California!

25

CHAPTER 2 - MEDFORD AREA

BEAR CREEK GREENWAY. (See map on page 27)

MEDFORD TO CENTRAL POINT SECTION- 5.7 miles.
From Interstate Highway 5 Exit 27 Barnett Road in south Medford,
the path begins from the north side of Barnett Road,less than 0.1
mile east of the freeway exits and then continues through Bear
Creek, Hawthorne and Railroad Parks (all with restrooms), before
terminating at Pine St. in Central Point..immediately east of the
INTERSTATE Highway 5 Exit 32 off-ramps.

Fundraising is underway to extend the path from Barnett Road in
Medford to Suncrest Road in Talent that will connect with the 5.7
mi. section that now leads from Suncrest Road in Talent to Nevada
Street in central Ashland.

"The Bear Creek Greenway is a corridor stretching 30 miles from
Emigrant Lake to the Rogue River. When completed, this project
will provide a natural greenbelt through the heart of the most
populated land in Jackson County and will link the cities of
Ashland, Talent, Phoenix, Medford and Central Point by a trail
system.   Eventually, the Greenway will include land along the
Rogue River and Little Butte Creek to connect Eagle Point.   The
Greenway will provide a wide range of close-to-home recreation
opportunities including bicycling, horseback riding, hiking, jog-
ging and picnicking.   The Greenway will protect wildlife habitat
throughout the Bear Creek Basin."   (Quote: Jackson County Parks)

26

BEAR CREEK GREENWAY

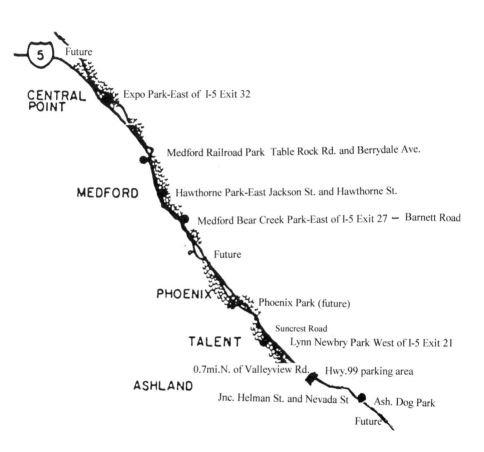

CENTRAL POINT — Future

Expo Park-East of I-5 Exit 32

Medford Railroad Park Table Rock Rd. and Berrydale Ave.

MEDFORD — Hawthorne Park-East Jackson St. and Hawthorne St.

Medford Bear Creek Park-East of I-5 Exit 27 — Barnett Road

Future

PHOENIX — Phoenix Park (future)

Suncrest Road

TALENT — Lynn Newbry Park West of I-5 Exit 21

0.7mi.N. of Valleyview Rd.   Hwy.99 parking area

ASHLAND

Jnc. Helman St. and Nevada St   Ash. Dog Park

Future

ROXY ANN TRAILS

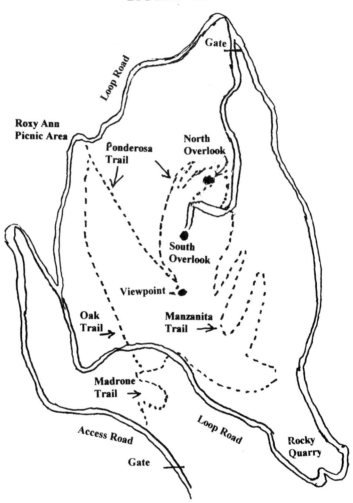

ROXY ANN PEAK HIKING TRAILS-Prescott Park. (Map 13)

SEASON: -All year for hikers, equestrians, and picnickers. Wildflowers late spring to early summer. Watch for poison oak, ticks, or an occasional rattlesnake.

INFORMATION: -Medford Parks and Recreation, Medford City Hall.

ACCESS: From Interstate Highway 5, South Medford Exit 27 (Barnett Road), travel east on Barnett Road 1.1 mi. to the junction with Black Oak Drive. Turn left onto Black Oak Drive and continue 1 mile to the intersection of Hillcrest Road. Turn right onto Hillcrest Road and go 3 1/4 miles to the junction with Roxy Ann Access Road. Turn left onto this road and go 0.4 mi. to a road gate (open from early morning till sunset when fire danger is low) and 1.0 mi. further to a seasonally closed gate. Park so as not to obstruct the gate, keep clear for emergency vehicles. The gate may be open during the summer months.

ROAD DISTANCE FROM SEASONALLY CLOSED GATE:

Mile 0.1   -MADRONE TRAIL to loop trail and lower trailheads of MANZANITA and OAK TRAILS.

Mile 0.9   -Junction with PRIMARY LOOP TRAIL. Mileage points LEFT (Clockwise) on the loop trail are:

Mile 0.5   -Roxy Ann Picnic Area. The lower PONDEROSA Trail-head is on the right, it leads to the upper ends of OAK & MANZANITA TRAILS & summit viewpoints.

Mile 0.9   -Private road on right.

Mile 1.9   -Keep right at a road junction.

Mile 2.4   -Upper end of MADRONE TRAIL and lower end of MANZANITA and OAK TRAILS.

Mile 2.6   -Back to access road leading down to Hillcrest Road.

Activities also include nature education, historic site restoration and wildlife protection. The area is closed to hunting, firearms, off-road vehicles, alcohol, narcotics, camping and building of fires. Trees include Oregon white oak, Calif. black oak, ponderosa pine, incense cedar and Douglas fir.

The picnic area and many of the trails were built by the Civilian Conservation Corps in the 1930s. More recent paths have been constructed by personnel from Medford Parks and Recreation and a dedicated crew of volunteers.

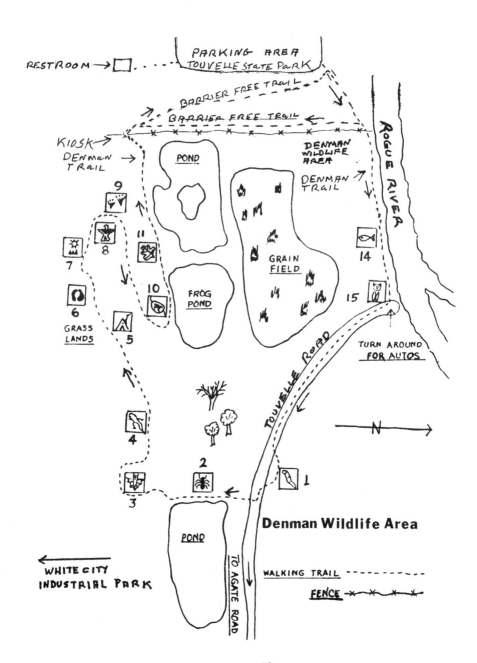

RESTROOM →

PARKING AREA
TOUVELLE STATE PARK

BARRIER FREE TRAIL

BARRIER FREE TRAIL

ROGUE RIVER

KIOSK →
DENMAN
TRAIL →

POND

DENMAN
WILDLIFE
AREA

DENMAN
TRAIL

9

11

8

7

10

GRAIN
FIELD

14

6

FROG
POND

15

GRASS
LANDS

5

TURN AROUND
FOR AUTOS

TOUVELLE ROAD

N →

4

2

1

Denman Wildlife Area

3

POND

WHITE CITY
INDUSTRIAL PARK

TO AGATE ROAD

WALKING TRAIL - - - - - -

FENCE ×—×—×—×—×

30

DENMAN WILDLIFE AREA AND TOUVELLE BARRIER FREE SEASONAL TRAIL.
(Day use fees apply at Touvelle State Park).

TRAILS BEGIN: -Touvelle State Park.   ELEV.1222'
SEASON: -Open all year. Hunting is conducted during the
                fall and early winter season in the Denman Wild-
                life Area, check schedules. RATED EASY.

ACCESS: From Interstate Highway 5, Central Point Exit 32,
                travel   east   one   mile   to   the traffic light   on
Table Rock Road. Turn left (north) onto Table Rock Road and follow mileposts to mile 6.5 at the entrance of TOUVELLE STATE PARK.
Turn right to enter the park and continue to the parking area at
the end of the road.

THE TOUVELLE BARRIER FREE SEASONAL TRAIL starts from the parking
area where a brochure is provided by Boy Scout Troop 7 of Medford
The trail has 10 interpretive stations with marker posts.At marker #1 you can observe and read about the value of a healthy riparian zone.   Cross the footbridge on the left to follow along the
Rogue River, and just beyond marker #4 the trail makes a turn to
the RIGHT. After marker #8 the trail turns RIGHT toward the point
of beginning.

After marker #10 you may wish to backtrack a short distance to a
KIOSK marking the entry point of the DENMAN INTERPRETIVE TRAIL.
Bark chips mark the route, passing two ponds, climbing a grassy
plateau before dropping to another pond at Touvelle Road. A left
turn leads to roads end at the pillar of a former military bridge
A left turn leads along the river to the parking area at Touvelle
State Park.

From the starting KIOSK carved symbols along the route resembling
Indian petrographs include:

"Oak Tree"   (Oak Trees)
"Frog Pond"   (The Pond)
"Rodent Track   (Ground Burrows)
"The Bird"   (Woodpecker Tree)
"Grasslands"   (Grassland Habitat)   continued....

"Deer Track"   (Rogue Valley Geology)
"Dwelling"   (Urban Valley Development)
"Lizard"   (Wedgeleaf Habitat)
"The Bat"   (Artificial Wildlife Nest Boxes)
"Spider"   (Woodrat Nest)
"Earthworm"   (The Agate Desert Soil)
"The Owl"   (Vandalism and Litter)
"The Fish"   (The Rogue River Habitat)

An edition of "Denman Interpretive Trail" guide printed by Oregon
Fish and Wildlife lists area specie names and numbers:

BIRDS, 129 species
MAMMALS 42 species
AMPHIBIANS AND REPTILES   21 species
TREES SHRUBS AND GRASSES   13 species
GRASSES AND INTRODUCED EXOTIC PLANTS   19 species

Although this trail is partially covered with bark chips, it may
be obscure in a few places. It is advisable to stay on the trail
to prevent contacting poison oak and destroying the vegetation.BE
AWARE THAT HUNTING IS CONDUCTED IN THE DENMAN WILDLIFE AREA DUR-
ING THE FALL AND EARLY WINTER MONTHS for deer, pheasant,quail and
water fowl. Otherwise, no firearms are permitted in the area.

HISTORY: The Denman Interpretive Trail, located on the Kenneth
            Denman Wildlife Management Area, is under the control
and management for enhancement of wildlife habitat by the Oregon
Department of Fish and Wildlife.   Except for 160 acres surrounding the management area's office and shop structure, the 1760
acres came under the General Services Administration control after Camp White Military Reservation was disbanded following World
War Two.

Credit has been given to John Ifft, U.S. Bureau of Land Management, for initial trail concept and station post materials. The
BLM's Young Adult Conservation Corps crew constructed the trail
with coordinating/planning by Oregon Dept. Fish and Wildlife.

Respect the rights of private property owners!

Table Rocks Location Map

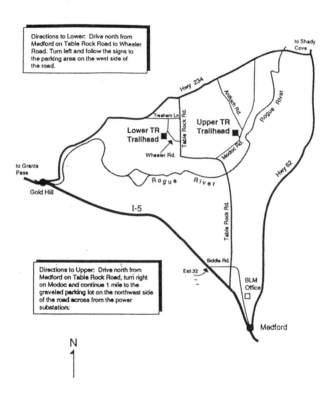

Directions to Lower: Drive north from Medford on Table Rock Road to Wheeler Road. Turn left and follow the signs to the parking area on the west side of the road.

to Shady Cove

Hwy 234

Antioch Rd.

Rogue River

Tresham Ln.

Upper TR Trailhead

Table Rock Rd.

Lower TR Trailhead

Modoc Rd.

Wheeler Rd.

to Grants Pass

Hwy 62

Gold Hill

Rogue River

I-5

Table Rock Rd.

Biddle Rd.

Directions to Upper: Drive north from Medford on Table Rock Road, turn right on Modoc and continue 1 mile to the graveled parking lot on the northwest side of the road across from the power substation.

Exit 32

BLM Office

Medford

N

UPPER TABLE ROCK.   (See map 13)

TRAIL BEGINS:	-Modoc Road between mileposts 1 and 2. ELEV.1294'
TRAIL ENDS:	-Top of Upper Table Rock. ELEV.2036'
DISTANCE:	-1.25 mi., moderate, hiker only, day use only.
SEASON:	-All year. High use in spring/limited parking. Low off-season use. Toilet facilities April and May only.
BROCHURE/MAP:	-U.S. Bureau of Land Management -Recreation Opportunity Guide. Brochure available.

ACCESS: From Interstate Highway 5, Central Point Exit 32, travel east one mile to the traffic light on Table Rock Road. Turn left (north) onto Table Rock Road and follow mileposts to mile 7.5 at the junction with Modoc Road. Turn right (northeast) onto Modoc Road and go 1.5 mile to the parking area on the left side of the road.

FEATURES: Scenic panorama of the Rogue Valley. Many species of flowers blooming Feb. through May. Unique geologic origin and features. Vernal pools with pacific tree frogs.
HAZARDS: Abundant poison oak, ticks, rattlesnakes, high cliffs.

BLM ADVICE: "No potable water. Please do not pick the wildflowers. Stay on the main trails and out of the sensitive vernal pools". DOGS NOT ALLOWED.

HISTORICAL: Long ago volcanic lava covered the Rogue Valley. Millions of years have eroded most of the lava and much of the underlying sandstone sediment leaving Upper and Lower Table Rocks......Table Rock was once a sanctuary and symbol for the Rogue River Indians; a site for many important meetings. In the early 1850's, settlers and gold prospectors invaded the valley. The Table Rocks afforded the Indians choice places for hiding, ambush, attack, and Indian councils during the years of resistance and war that followed. The trail was built in 1981 by the Young Adult Conservation Corps.

NOTE: UPPER TABLE ROCK is designated an Outstanding Natural Area. This designation is more oriented toward public use than is Lower Table Rock.

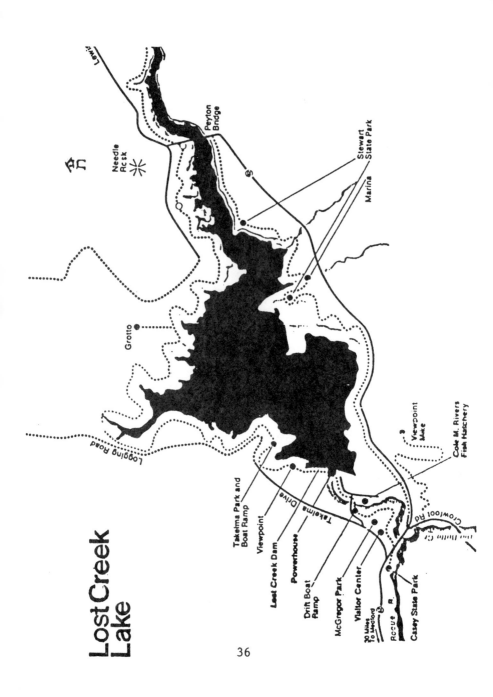

Lost Creek
Lake

Takelma Park and
Boat Ramp

Viewpoint

Lost Creek Dam

Powerhouse

Drift Boat
Ramp

McGregor Park

Visitor Center

30 Miles
To Medford

Rogue R.

Casey State Park

Crowfoot Rd.

Cole M. Rivers
Fish Hatchery

Viewpoint
Mile

Takelma Drive

Logging Road

Grotto

Lewis

Peyton
Bridge

Needle
Rock

Marina

Stewart
State Park

36

CHAPTER 3 - LOST CREEK LAKE AREA

LOST CREEK LAKE-NORTH SHORE TRAIL.   (See map 9)

TRAIL BEGINS: -Casey State Park, State Highway 62. ELEV. 1538'
TRAIL ENDS: -Boundary of U.S. Army Corps of Engineers land,
                 4.5 miles northeast of Peyton Bridge Trailhead.
DISTANCE: -16.5 miles with access points. Easy grades.
SEASON: -Open all year.
USE: -HIKERS on all trails. MOUNTAIN BIKES on all
                 trails except on Stewart Park hiker only trails.
BRING MAPS: -LOST CREEK LAKE HIKING TRAILS -U.S. Army Corps
                 of Engineers.
                -See also local road and forest maps.

ACCESS: From Medford, Oregon, travel north and east on
                Highway 62 to milepost 29 at Casey State Park.

DESCRIPTION: Condensed from "LOST CREEK LAKE HIKING TRAILS"
                brochure, U.S. Army Corps of Engineers.

From the east end of Casey State Park, follow the paved trail to
the first junction.   North shore hikers should take the right
fork and pass under McLeod Bridge. The trail follows the river
to McGregor Park and the Visitor Center. Hike through McGregor
Park on to the Hatchery/Powerhouse Road and follow painted "paw
prints" on the pavement, then cross the fish diversion dam for a
possible visit at Cole M. Rivers Fish Hatchery.

The trail begins again in an open field north of the hatchery and
then passes through River's Edge Park to the powerhouse.   Pass
between the two buildings and follow painted "paw prints" to the
trail at the base of the dam. The trail then climbs gradually
to the top of the dam.   Please stay on the developed trail, as
this area has restricted access. Follow the painted "paw prints"
to Takelma Park.   The trail continues 4.3 miles further to where
a long arm of the lake reaches the inlet of Lost Creek.   (There
are two "Lost Creeks" on the lake; the other one is on the south
shore.)

From Lost Creek, the trail leads south, then east 3.5 miles to a
short spur trail leading to the Grotto, where rock cliffs form
the walls of a small canyon.   Following heavy rains, a waterfall
may be spotted cascading down the far wall.   2.3 miles further
along the lakeshore, the trail comes out at the Lewis Road Trailhead and follows the road east for one mile to the Peyton Bridge
Trailhead.

Follow the trail under Peyton Bridge to where it enters the Rogue
River Gorge.   A rest area at the boundary of Corps of Engineers
land marks the end of Lost Creek Lake North Shore Trail.

FOR SHORTER HIKES: From Highway 62, the North Shore Trail can be
accessed by driving on TAKELMA DRIVE to the following points:

Mile 0.3   -McGregor Park and Visitor Center.
Mile 0.6   -Cole M. Rivers Fish Hatchery.
Mile 2.0   -Lost Creek Dam Viewpoint.
Mile 2.3   -Takelma Park, pavement ends, becoming Road 33-1E-27.
Mile 3.6   -Junction Road 33-1E-23, turn right for trail access.
Mile 5.0   -Rogue River Trail sign on right side of 33-1E-27.
Mile 5.8   -Lost Creek Trailhead, a parking area is on the right.

PEYTON BRIDGE TRAILHEAD is located on Highway 62 near milepost 36
at the north end of Peyton Bridge and the junction of Lewis Road.
LEWIS ROAD TRAILHEAD is 1 mile west of Peyton Bridge Trailhead.

NOTES: CARRY DRINKING WATER on long hikes or in warm weather.
Camping is permitted only at designated campsites.   Check local
fire conditions with the Oregon State Dept.of Forestry in Central
Point.   Phone (541) 664-3328.

LOST CREEK LAKE-SOUTH SHORE TRAIL. (See map 9)

TRAIL BEGINS:	—Casey State Park, State Hwy. 62.	ELEV. 1538'
TRAIL ENDS:	—Peyton Bridge.	ELEV. 2000'
DISTANCE:	—6.3 miles, gentle grades.	
SEASON:	—Open all year.	
USE:	—HIKERS on all trails. MOUNTAIN BIKES on all trails except Stewart Park hiker only trails.	
BRING MAPS:	—LOST CREEK LAKE HIKING TRAILS -U.S. Army Corps of Engineers. —See also local road or forest maps.	
ACCESS:	From Medford, Oregon, travel north and east on State Hwy. 62 to milepost 29 (Casey State Park).	
DESCRIPTION:	Condensed from "LOST CREEK LAKE HIKING TRAILS" brochure, U.S. Army Corps of Engineers.	

From Casey State Park, follow the paved trail to the first junction.   Take the LEFT fork, cross McLeod Bridge, then turn right
to where the trail drops down and passes back under the bridge.
Here the trail merges with a gravel road and follows the river.
The trail resumes from the end of the road, and after 0.5 mi. ascends to a point above the dam's spillway gates. Further on is a
junction with a trail cutting downhill to the left.   This trail
leads to the spillway gates and service road on top of the dam.
(You may hike the 0.8 mi. length of the dam to reach the intake
tower or North Shore Trail.)

The South Shore Trail drops down and remains near the lake's high
waterline, and around the bend is a small waterfall where Rumley
Creek tumbles to the lake.   In another 2.4 miles the trail enters Stewart State Park day use area. To stay on the South Shore
Trail, keep to the three-foot wide trail through the park. Pass
the swimming beach and picnic area, then cross the inlet of Lost
Creek. There are two "Lost Creeks" draining into the lake; the
other one is on the north shore.

Cross the pavement at the boat ramp. The trail parallels the lake shore and crosses Floras Creek. At the junction beyond the creek, the main trail bears to the left; a spur trail to the right leads to Stewart State Park Campground.

The trail passes between the lake shore and the edge of the campground. Where it joins the bike path, hikers should bear to the left and cross Taggarts Creek. The South Shore Trail ends at Peyton Bridge. Hiking across the bridge (0.3 mi.) brings you to the North Shore Trail at Peyton Bridge Trailhead.

For shorter hikes, the South Shore Trail can be accessed by driving to Stewart State Park, either at the picnic area or at the campground.Carry drinking water on long hikes or in warm weather.

VIEWPOINT MIKE-LOST CREEK LAKE (See map 9) LIMITED MAINTENANCE.
2.5 miles (1 Way), moderate grades, year-round for hikers, equestrians and mountain Bikes. Motor vehicles not allowed.

ACCESS: From Casey State Park Highway 62, travel east 0.2 mile to Crowfoot Road. Turn RIGHT onto Crowfoot Road for 0.2 mile to Big Butte Park. Viewpoint Mike Trailhead is directly across the road. (ELEVATION 1550')

The trail begins with switchbacks through an oak woodland, gaining elevation above Highway 62, providing views of the river and fish hatchery below. The trail ends at the viewpoint where you can rest and enjoy the view. (Elevation 2550') The panorama from this height includes views of the lake, the dam and intake tower. Massive Flounce Rock, weathered by the ages to a reddish color, rises above the north shore of the lake. Toward the northeast, you can see the rim of Crater Lake. CARRY DRINKING WATER as none is available along the trail. (Condensed from "LOST CREEK LAKE HIKING TRAILS" brochure, U.S. Army Corps of Engineers.)

CHAPTER 4 - JACKSONVILLE/RUCH AREA

Jacksonville Woodlands Historic Natural Park and Trail System has eight, great all weather hiking trails for hikers with different abilities. Trail maps are available at major trailheads. Jackson Creek Junction (behind the Post Office) is a great place to begin your hike, with free parking, a Visitor Center, public restrooms, water fountains and benches. The Britt Gardens Walking Path, located at the far end of the parking lot, crosses Highway 238 and leads to the Britt Gardens, the Sarah Zigler Interpretive Trailhead and the grounds of Britt Music Festivals.

Beekman Canyon Trail - One mile loop beginning behind the Beekman House at the corner of California and Laurelwood streets. Trailhead is located in the Beekman Native Plant Arboretum.
SARAH ZIGLER INTERPRETIVE TRAIL (National Recreation Trail) —One mi. beginning at the Britt Gardens. Follow Jackson Creek to where gold was discovered in 1852.

BRITT RIDGE TRAIL-3/4 mile -Begins behind the Britt Festivals Pavilion, West Fir Street.
JACKSON FORKS TRAIL- 1/2 mile-Begins at the west end of the Sarah Zigler Trail. A great trail to view the transitional forest as it changes from a riparian vegetation zone to a drier oak savanna.

RICH GULCH TRAIL- 2 miles- Stretching between West Fir Street and South Oregon Street, follows the old hydraulic mining gulches and glory holes of 1880.
CHINESE DIGGINGS TRAIL-1/2 mile- A spur route available from Rich Gulch. The best place to see old water ditches and mining tailings piled up by teams of Chinese workers.

PANORAMA POINT TRAIL-The Knoll-1/2 mile-A spur off the Rich Gulch Trail. View the town of Jacksonville, the Siskiyou and Cascade mountains, including the Rim of Crater Lake and Mt. Mcloughlin.
PETARD DITCH- 1/2 mile- The newest trail begins at Rich Gulch and follows the old Petard Water Ditch out toward Jackson Creek and Jacksonville Highway.When construction is complete the trail will eventually make a one mile loop back to Rich Gulch. Constructed about 1860, the Petard Ditch brought water from Jackson Creek into Rich Gulch where gold was blasted from the hillsides by hydraulic mining "giants".

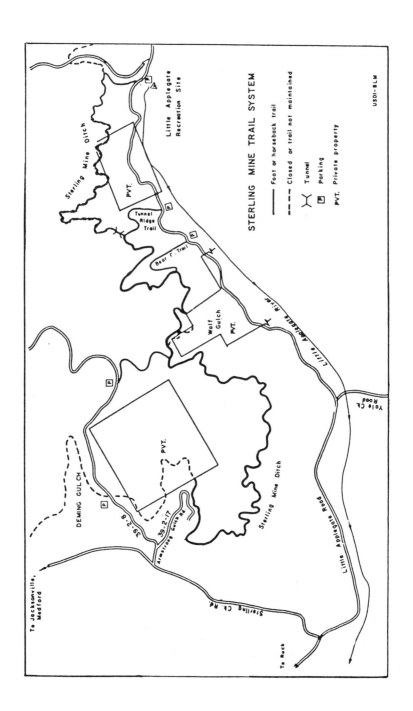

STERLING MINE TRAIL SYSTEM

——— Foot or horseback trail

– – – Closed or trail not maintained

⋉ Tunnel

▣ Parking

PVT. Private property

USDI-BLM

42

STERLING MINE TRAIL SYSTEM.

"The Sterling Mine Ditch, about 20.0 miles long and 3 feet deep, was started and completed in 1877 by nearly 400 workers, many of them being Chinese laborers. The ditch carried water from Little Applegate River to operate hydraulic jets for the Sterling Mine Company at the town of Sterlingville. The ditch continued to be used for gold mining through the 1930's." (BLM quote)

THE LITTLE APPLEGATE RIVER was once known by local settlers as Applegate Creek. The name was officially changed to the present form after the year 1900, in order to avoid confusion with the Applegate Creek of the South Umpqua River. (USFS information)

A trail system follows the route of the ditch, and the U.S. Bureau of Land Management advises to "Carry drinking water at all times of the year, please observe Oregon Department of Forestry fire regulations (telephone 664-3328) and respect property rights on adjoining private lands." The lower 2 mi. of trail below Deming Gulch are not open for public use.

See the text on the following pages for trailheads that provide access to the ditch:
1. Little Applegate Trailhead, Little Applegate Road.
2. Deming Gulch Trailhead, Deming Gulch Road.
3. Tunnel Ridge Trailhead, Little Applegate Road.
4. Bear Gulch Trailhead, Little Applegate Road.

SEASON: —All year. Ideal during late winter or early spring
           before poison oak leafs out. It is hard to avoid.
USE: —Hiker/horse, mountain bikes, no motorized vehicles.
           —Moderate grades.
BRING MAPS: —BLM brochure and map STERLING MINE TRAIL SYSTEM.
           —BLM Medford District Transportation Map, Jackson-
           ville Resource Area.
           —(This area is not on National Forest land, but is
           shown on USFS Rogue River National Forest maps.)

DEMING GULCH–STERLING MINE DITCH ACCESS. (See maps 19 & 20)

ROUTE BEGINS: –Road 39-2-8   (at Deming Gulch).
DISTANCE: –About 16 miles to Little Applegate Trail.
USE: –Hiker/horse/mountain bike. WATCH FOR POISON OAK.

ACCESS: From Jacksonville, travel southwest on Hwy. 238,
2.9 miles and turn left on Cady Road.   Continue
1/2 mile on Cady Road to the junction with Sterling Creek Road.
Turn right onto Sterling Creek Road and go 8.7 miles to Armstrong
Gulch Road 39-2-17.   Turn left onto Armstrong Gulch Road and go
0.3 mi. to the junction with Road 39-2-8 on the left. Take 39-2-8
0.6 miles, and look closely along the RIGHT side of the road for
the Sterling Mine Ditch.   There may be no signs.

FEATURES: Estimated distances along the ditch as it heads
southwest from Road 39-2-8 are:

Milepoint
  1.5   –Ditch crosses Armstrong Gulch Road. 39-2-17.

  9.0   BEAR GULCH TRAIL leads right 1 mile to Little
Applegate Road.

  11.0   TUNNEL RIDGE TRAIL leads right 1 mile to Little
Applegate Road.

  16.0   LITTLE APPLEGATE TRAIL leads right, one mile to
Little Applegate Road.

Poison oak is found along
trails up to about 5000
ft. altitude.

44

BEAR GULCH TRAIL, Sterling Mine Ditch.   (See map 19 and 20)

TRAIL BEGINS: -Little Applegate Road.
TRAIL ENDS: -Sterling Mine Ditch.
DISTANCE: -1 mile, moderately uphill.
                  USE: hiker/horse/mountain bikes. WATCH FOR
                  POISON OAK.

ACCESS: From the town of Ruch, Oregon, travel 2.8 miles
                  south on Upper Applegate Road to the junction of
Little Applegate Road. Turn left on Little Applegate Road and go
9.1 miles to a parking area on the left at Bear Gulch Trailhead.
It is about 1 mile from the trailhead to Sterling Mine Ditch.

FEATURES: After reaching the ditch, two options are avail-
                  able; (1). By TURNING RIGHT, a loop trip is pos-
sible by going about 2.0 miles to the Tunnel Ridge Trail leading
1.0 mile to Little Applegate Road. At the road, turn right (west)
and go 0.6 mile back to the starting point at Bear Gulch Trailhead. The total loop distance is 5 miles and requires 3 to 4 hrs.

(2). TURNING LEFT from the Bear Gulch Trail,it is about 9.0 miles
to the Deming Gulch Trailhead on Road 39-2-8.

TUNNEL RIDGE TRAILHEAD, Sterling Mine Ditch. (See map 19 and 20)

TRAIL BEGINS: -Little Applegate Road.
TRAIL ENDS: -Sterling Mine Ditch.
DISTANCE: -1 mile. Moderate uphill grades.
                 USE: hiker/horse/mountain bike.
                 WATCH FOR POISON OAK.

ACCESS: From Ruch, Oregon, take the Upper Applegate Road
                 2.8 miles to Little Applegate Road. Follow this
road 9.8 miles to a parking area on the right, at a former picnic
ground.   The Tunnel Ridge Trailhead is directly across the road.

FEATURES: The trail continues to the ridge, providing many
                 interesting views.   Where the trail reaches the
ditch, there is a tunnel dug by Chinese laborers to divert water
through the hillside. A loop trip is possible by turning left
(west) along the ditch, nearly 2.0 miles to the Bear Gulch Trail,
and following it about 1.0 mile to Little Applegate Road.   Turn
left (east) and follow the road 0.6 mile back to the Tunnel Ridge
parking area.

Another loop trip is possible by TURNING RIGHT at the tunnel and
traveling about 5 miles east to the Little Applegate Trailhead. A
portion of this trail climbs high above the ditch to avoid private property and later rejoins and follows the ditch to a signed
junction of a trail leading 1.0 mi.to the Little Applegate Trailhead on Little Applegate Road. Turn right (west) along the road
and go about 1.7 miles back to the Tunnel Ridge Trailhead.

                 Not very often do you see
                 these things but when you
                 do just give them room
                 and they will move out of
                 your way.

LITTLE APPLEGATE TRAILHEAD, Sterling Mine Ditch. (See map 19,20)

TRAIL BEGINS:	-Little Applegate Road.
TRAIL ENDS:	-Sterling Mine Ditch.
DISTANCE:	-1.0 mile, gentle uphill grade.
	USE: hiker/horse/mountain bike.

ACCESS: From the town of Ruch, Oregon, go 2.8 miles south
                 on the Upper Applegate Road to the junction with
Little Applegate Road.   Turn onto Little Applegate Road and follow the mileposts to mile 11.6, at the Little Applegate Trailhead
on the left side of the road. Parking is available at the Little
Applegate Picnic Ground, about 100 yards further.

FEATURES: This is the eastern-most BLM public access to the
                 Sterling Mine Ditch. It is about 1.0 mile to the
ditch. To reach Tunnel Ridge, TURN LEFT (WEST) at the ditch and
go about 5.0 miles. A portion of the trail rises above the ditch
to avoid private property.

A loop trip is possible by taking the Tunnel Ridge Trail one mile
down to Little Applegate Road. Turn left (east) on this road and
go 1.7 miles back to Little Applegate Trailhead.

A left-over from the old days.
A gold seeker's "SLUICE BOX".

47

GIN LIN TRAIL #917. (See map 19)

TRAIL BEGINS:	-Flumet Flat Campground.	ELEV. 1700'
TRAIL ENDS:	-Flumet Flat Campground.	
DISTANCE:	-3/4 mile interpretive loop trail. Easy, hikers only. Trail open all year.	

REFERENCES: USFS interpretive brochure "Gin Lin Trail."
                USFS "Rogue River National Forest" map. Both
publications available at Star Ranger Station or the USFS Supervisor's Office in Medford.

ACCESS: From the town of Ruch, Oregon, travel south on Up-
            per Applegate Road and follow mileposts to mile
8.6 at the junction with Palmer Creek Road. Turn right onto Palmer Creek Road and continue .8 mile just beyond the entrance to
Flumet Flat Campground. Turn right to the parking area and trailhead.

FEATURES   The Gin Lin Trail has 14 numbered "stations" that
             are keyed to the information and diagrams of the
brochure, available at the Star Ranger Station or the USFS Supervisor's Office in Medford.   You will see evidence of mining ditches, dug more than 100 years ago by Chinese laborers, to divert
water from Palmer Creek to a mining site where hydraulic pressure
was used to loosen gravel and cobbles from nearby slopes. Sluice
boxes were used to separate the materials washed down from the
hillside, with the resulting collection of gold dust and mine
tailings. WATCH FOR POISON OAK or an occasional rattlesnake.

HISTORICAL   Gin Lin was a Chinese mining boss who purchased mining claims along Palmer Creek in 1881 after being
successful in other local mining operations.   More than a million
dollars worth of gold dust were deposited by him in the Jacksonville Bank.   The actual fate of Gin Lin is uncertain.
(Condensed from USFS interpretive brochure)

GIN LIN TRAIL

49

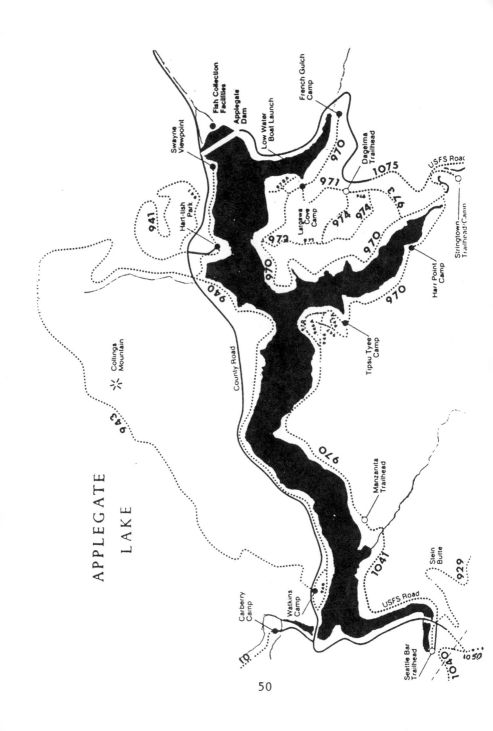

APPLEGATE LAKE

Collings Mountain

643

County Road

940

941

Hart-iish Park

Swayne Viewpoint

Fish Collection Facilities

Applegate Dam

Low Water Boat Launch

French Gulch Camp

970

Dagelma Trailhead

1075

971

973

Latgawa Cove Camp

974 974

972

970

970

Harr Point Camp

Stringtown Trailhead/Camp

USFS Road

Tipsu Tyee Camp

970

Manzanita Trailhead

Carberry Camp

Watkins Camp

1041

Stein Butte

929

1041

104

1050

USFS Road

Seattle Bar Trailhead

CHAPTER 5 - APPLEGATE AREA (see map 26)

APPLEGATE LAKE TRAILS

SEASON: -Open all year.

CAMPS: -ROAD ACCESS: Carberry, French Gulch, Stringtown, Watkins. HIKE-IN: Harr Point, Latgawa, Tipsu-Tyee. Schedule/facility info at Star Ranger Sta.

MAPS: -AVAILABLE AT STAR RANGER STATION, 6941 Upper Applegate Road.
-U.S. Army Corps of Engineers brochure "APPLEGATE LAKE."
-Applegate Ranger Dist. -Rogue River Ntl. Forest.
-USFS Recreation Opportunity Guides.

TRAIL USAGE: -HIKERS on all trails. HORSES on Stein Butte Trail but not recommended on Collings Mountain or Dakubetede Trails. MOUNTAIN BIKES on all trails. MOTOR BIKES on Stein Butte Trail.

TRAILHEADS:

SWAYNE VIEWPOINT. Near milepost 15, Upper Applegate Road. Drinking water, restrooms, interpretive viewpoint. DAKUBETEDE TRAIL 940 begins here.

HART-TISH PARK. Near milepost 16 on Upper Applegate Road. Check with Star Ranger Sta. for park schedules/facilities. DAKUBETEDE TRAIL 940, GROUSE LOOP TRAIL 941, and the north end of COLLINGS MOUNTAIN TRAIL 943 can be accessed from this park.

WATKINS PICNIC GROUND. Just beyond milepost 18 on Upper Applegate Road. Check with Star Ranger Station for park schedules and facilities. DAKUBETEDE TRAIL 940, and the south end of COLLINGS MTN. TRAIL 941 begin here.

SEATTLE BAR. Beyond milepost 18 on Upper Applegate Road, turn left at the junction with Carberry Creek Road and continue to milepost 20 at Seattle Bar. Check with Star Ranger Station for schedules/facilities. STEIN BUTTE TRAIL 929 begins here.

MANZANITA: From Seattle Bar Trailhead drive 2 miles north on Manzanita Creek Road. No facilities. PAYETTE TRAIL 970 begins here.

FRENCH GULCH: From Swayne Viewpoint, cross over Applegate Dam on Squaw Creek Road 1075 to the trailhead just beyond milepost 1. Check with the Star Ranger Station for camp schedules/facilities. PAYETTE TRAIL 970 begins here.

DAGELMA: From Swayne Viewpoint, cross over Applegate Dam and continue on Squaw Cr. Road 1075, 2.2 miles to the trailhead parking area on the right. No facilities. CALSH TRAIL 971, SINNS BAR TRAIL 972, OSPREY TRAIL 973 and PROSPECTORS LOOP TRAIL 974 begin here.

SQUAW CREEK ARM: From French Gulch Campground continue southeast on Road 1075 For 2 miles to Forest Road 100. Turn right onto Road 100 and go 0.5 mile to the large parking area and stock driveway on the left. This is an access to the Payette Trail. There are no facilities.

HIKING TRAIL DESCRIPTIONS.
Detailed "USFS Recreation Opportunity Guides" are available from Star Ranger Station or from Forest Supervisor's Office in Medford.

DAKUBETEDE TRAIL 940.   4.8 miles, moderately easy. Hiker/mountain bike.Stock use November through April only-from Hart-tish Park to Watkins Campground,and is not permitted in Hart-tish Park. A connector trail bypasses Hart-tish Park to connect with the Collings Mountain Trail. From Swayne Viewpoint the trail begins behind the restrooms, continues southwest along the lakeshore to Hart-tish Copper Boat Ramp and ends at Watkins Picnic Ground. CARRY WATER. Poison Oak, ticks, and snakes are hazards to be aware of.To avoid damaging the trail in winter, use only when the trail is dry or frozen.

An 18 mile mountain bike loop can be made: starting at the Swayne Viewpoint and using the Dakubetede and Payette Trails.

GROUSE LOOP TRAIL 941.

2.8 miles, moderate for hikers and mountain bikes ELEV.GAIN 700'.
At HART-TISH-PARK, the trailhead is at the upper end of the picnic area. Cross the highway to the trail beginning. The clockwise direction is suggested for ease of travel. There are good
views of Applegate Lake, Elliott Creek Ridge and the Red Buttes
to the south. CARRY WATER. High point 2700'.

COLLINGS MOUNTAIN TRAIL 943.

7 miles, moderate for hikers, difficult for horses/mountain bikes.
The northern end of the trail begins from the upper end of the
Hart-tish Park picnic area. The trail crosses the highway to the
edge of a guardrail then continues 1/2 mile to a miner's cabin,
an inactive "Bigfoot trap", a mine adit and then climbs to the
crest of a ridge. About 2 miles south along the ridge, the trail
passes along the west slopes of Collings Mtn. and then drops down
to Watkins Picnic Ground (the southern end of the trail), passing
through a wildlife foraging area and the site of a 1981 forest
fire burn. A 3 mile hike back to Hart-tish Park can be made via
the Dakubetede Trail 940. ELEV.GAIN 1040'. You may wish to start
at Watkins Picnic Ground for ease of travel.

The "Bigfoot" trap was installed by a Eugene-based wildlife research organization in 1974 for the unsuccessful efforts in cap-
turing the elusive "Bigfoot." The use of the trap was discontin-
ued in 1976.

STEIN BUTTE TRAIL 929. 4.9 Miles plus 2.6 mile on the New London

Trail to Road 1050 if you are doing a shuttle arrangement. Moderate for hiker/horses, difficult for Mtn./motor bikes.EL.GAIN 2331'
From SEATTLE BAR, the trail climbs up the west end of Elliot Ridge
passing a 19th Century water diversion ditch that was used by the
Seattle Mining Company. It then follows an old haul road past a
marble deposit before reaching the top of Elliot Ridge. The trail
then follows the ridge to a point just north of Stein Butte Summit, look for cairns and a faint trail on the right for a side-
trip to the summit. A lookout tower existed at this location between the years 1936 and 1968. ELEVATION 4400'

After returning to the main trail, proceed 0.5 mile to a saddle just east of Stein Butte at the junction with New London Tr. 928 and Elliott Ridge Tr. 969.

The New London Trail, formerly a continuation of the Stein Butte Trail, leads 2.5 miles downhill (south), passing two 20th Century mine adits before reaching Elliott Creek Road.

PAYETTE TRAIL 970. Moderate for hikers/mountain bikes.
9.2 MILES.....From FRENCH GULCH TRAILHEAD TO MANZANITA TRAILHEAD. The distance can be shortened by using the Squaw Creek Arm Trailhead. Hiker campgrounds are located at Latgawa Cove, Harr Point and at Tipsu Tyee.

Latgawa Cove Camp is 0.7 mile from French Gulch Trailhead. Just beyond, Calsh Trail 971 leads left to the Dagelma Trailhead, and Viewpoint Trail 970A Leads RIGHT to a viewpoint. Payette Trail 970 follows the lakeshore to the Squaw Creek Arm of the lake and on beyond Tipsu Tyee Campground. Near the mouth of the lake's Squaw Arm, CUTOFF TRAIL 946 is a short cut to the Payette Trail that ends at Manzanita Trailhead. Midway along the Cutoff Trail, SQUAW POINT TRAIL 946A leads to a viewpoint.

HARR RIDGE TRAIL 947 runs from Tipsu Tyee Campground to the mid-point of the Cutoff Trail. Culy Trail 947A branches off from the Harr Ridge Trail and leads to a viewpoint overlooking Tipsu Tyee Campground and the Squaw Creek Arm of the lake.

OUTDOOR STUDY AREA TRAILS FROM DAGELMA TRAILHEAD. Hiker/mtn. bike
CALSH TRAIL 971: Leads 0.7 mi.to Payette Trail near Latgawa Camp.
SINNS BAR TRAIL 972: 0.8 mi. long, links the Prospectors Loop and
    Payette Trails. (RATED MODERATE)
OSPREY TRAIL 973: Leads 0.6 mi. to the Payette Trail. (MODERATE)
PROSPECTORS LOOP TRAIL 974: 1.6 miles long, begins and ends at
    Dagelma Trailhead. (MODERATE)

WHERE THE NAMES CAME FROM: Excerpts from USFS Applegate Ranger District Recreation Opportunity Guides.

HART-TISH: Chief Hart-tish was the leader of the Dakubetede Indians that inhabited the Applegate Valley and resisted the influx of miners into their territory following the discovery of gold in southern Oregon.

COPPER VISITOR CENTER: Commemorates the Copper Store built in the 1920's near the mouth of Carberry Creek before construction of the dam.   The site of the store is now under water.

COLLINGS MOUNTAIN: Named for two prospectors, the Collings brothers, who mined in the Applegate Dam vicinity.

WATKINS: The name of a prospector who mined near the mouth of Carberry Creek in the 1850's.   A small community post office and schoolhouse were named for Watkins.

SEATTLE BAR: Commmemorates the Seattle Mining Co. (of Washington) which conducted hydraulic mining operations above the confluence of Carberry Creek and Applegate River during the 1890's.

DAKUBETEDE: A band of Indians that lived in the Applegate Valley.

TIPSU TYEE: A bearded Shasta Indian Chief.

STEIN BUTTE: Believed to be named for a prospector who mined in this vicinity during the early gold rush years.

DAGELMA: Named for "Dagelma" or "River Takelma" Indians.

CULY: Named for the family of George and Pamelia Culy, settlers in the mining community of Steamboat in the 1880's.

SINNS BAR: Named for a Chinese prospector who mined the gravel bars along the Applegate River during the early gold rush years.

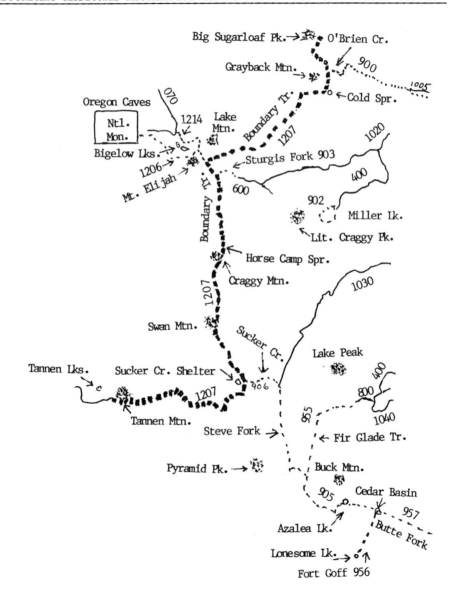

O'BRIEN CREEK TRAIL #900. (See map 18)

TRAIL BEGINS:	-Forest Road 1005,near mileposts 2 & 4	ELEV. 4080'
TRAIL ENDS:	-Boundary Trail 1207.	ELEV. 6240'
DISTANCE:	-About 2.3 miles each way.	
SEASON:	-Usually snow-free July through September.	
USE:	-Difficult for hikers and mountain bikes. PACK AND SADDLE STOCK NOT RECOMMENDED. TRAILERS NOT RECOMMENDED AT UPPER TRAILHEAD.	
CONNECTING TR.	-Boundary National Recreation Trail 1207.	
BRING MAPS:	-Applegate Ranger Dist.-Rogue River Ntl. Forest.	

ACCESS: From the town of Ruch, Oregon, travel west on Hwy.
238, 7 miles to the town of Applegate.   Cross the
bridge and   turn left onto Thompson Creek Road, which later becomes Forest Road 10.   Follow this road 12 miles to the junction
with Forest Roads 10 and 1005. Turn right onto 1005 and travel
2.1 miles to the junction with Forest Road 300 where a one mile
extension of trail 900 offers better parking facilities than what
is available at the upper milepost 4 trailhead.

FEATURES: About 1.5 mile from the lower trailhead at a junc-
                tion, keep right to bypass Grayback Snow Shelter
and Krause Cabin where Grayback Meadows is undergoing vegetation
repair for soil stabilization.   Keep right, it is approximately
0.8 mi. to BOUNDARY NATIONAL RECREATION TRAIL 1207 at the base of
Grayback Mountain.   The Boundary Trail is a popular route to the
Oregon Caves or for sidetrips to Windy Gap or Sugar Loaf Peak. It
is best to CARRY WATER!   Treatment of water is essential since
many cattle graze in the area.

HISTORY: "Grayback Snow Shelter was built for winter-time
               Forest Service snow surveyors who measured the wa-
ter content of snowpacks for irrigation supply projections (built
ca. 1944).   Krause Cabin was built by a local cattleman as a
round-up time 'line shack.' It was completed in August (V-J Day)
1945. 'Graybacks' were the lice that so plagued the early miners! They gave this name to a number of features." (USFS quote)

MILLER LAKE TRAIL #902. (See map 25)

TRAIL BEGINS: -End of Road 1020/400 ELEV. 4960'
TRAIL ENDS: -Miller Lake.   ELEV. 5300'
DISTANCE: -0.7 mile to the lake.
                  Moderate grades. USE: hiker/horse.
SEASON: -Usually snow-free June thru October.
BRING MAPS: -Applegate Ranger District-Rogue River Ntl. Forest.

ACCESS: From the town of Ruch, Oregon, travel west on Hwy.
                 238 for 7 miles to the town of Applegate.   Cross
the bridge and turn left onto Thompson Creek Road and go about 12
miles to the junction of Forest Road 1020. Follow Road 1020 3.0
miles to the junction with Road 1020/400. Keep left onto Road 400
and go about 2.5 miles to the trailhead at the end of the road.

FEATURES: From the parking area, the trail climbs, crossing
an old road (also leading to the lake).   For the more ambitious,
after reaching the lake hike left to a ridge above the lake for
spectacular views looking into both Sturgis Fork and Steves Fork
basins. Brewers spruce, Matthews sugar pine,white fir and Douglas
fir are among the tree species. Oracle and Saddlers oak are two
of the rare bush species. Rhododendrons usually are in bloom the
first part of June.   The lake was deepened and dammed to provide
irrigation water to the Thompson Creek ditch. It is stocked with
Brook trout every other year.

HISTORY: MILLER LAKE: Named for Walter Miller, a 19th Century
Applegate rancher who made his annual hunting camp at the Lake.

STURGIS FORK TRAIL #903. (See map 25)

TRAIL BEGINS:	–End of Forest Road 1020/600.	ELEV. 5040'
TRAIL ENDS:	–Boundary Trail 1207.	ELEV. 5600'
DISTANCE:	–0.8 miles (one way)	
USE:	–Moderate for hikers and horses, difficult for mountain bikes.	
SEASON:	–Usually snow-free July through September.	
CONNECTING TR.	–Boundary National Recreation Trail 1207. With a route to Oregon Caves.	
BRING MAPS:	–Applegate Ranger Dist.-Rogue River Ntl. Forest.	

ACCESS: From the town of Ruch, Oregon, travel west on Hwy. 238 for 7 miles to the town of Applegate.   Cross the bridge and turn left onto Thompson Creek Road which later becomes Forest Road 10. Continue southwest on Thompson Creek Road, 12 miles to the junction with Forest Road 1020.   Continue south and west on Rd. 1020, 8.1 mi. to the junction with Road 1020/600. Turn right onto Road 600 and go about 1/2 mile to the trailhead.

FEATURES: The trail criss-crosses streams of the Sturgis Fork thru a virgin stand of timber within Craggy Mountain Scenic Area and joins the Boundary National Recreation Trail #1207. Treatment of water is important due to cattle grazing.

FOR A SHORT ROUTE TO OREGON CAVES NATIONAL MONUMENT: "Turn Right (north) on the Boundary Trail for 0.2 miles to trail #1206 junction.   From this junction in a small meadow, go left and follow the trail grade that eventually begins an uphill climb through a series of switchbacks for about 1 mile.   At the trail junction on the ridge go left and follow the ridge line up to Mount Elijah for spectacular views of the Siskiyou Crest.   From Mount Elijah, continue west on a continual descent for approx. 2.0 miles to the Oregon Caves National Monument (O.C.N.M)Boundary. FROM THIS POINT THIS IS A HIKER ONLY TRAIL.   Within the O.C.N.M. the trail winds down to a junction with the Big Tree Loop Trail.   To go right at this junction will take you by a giant Douglas Fir tree and eventually comes out at Monument Headquarters.   The return trip follows the same route except you may want to try the other side of the Big Tree Loop Trail. TOTAL MILEAGE ONE WAY APPROX. 4 MILES." (USFS Quote)

STEVE FORK TRAIL #905   (See map 25)

TRAIL BEGINS:	–Forest Road 1030 near milepost 11.	ELEV. 4400'
TRAIL ENDS:	–Fir Glade Trail 955.	ELEV. 5200'
DISTANCE:	–3.0 miles. Moderate, hiker/horse.	
SEASON:	–Usually snow-free July to October.	
CONNECTING TR.	–Fir Glade Trail 955.	
BRING MAPS:	–USFS Applegate Ranger Dist. –Rogue River N.F.	
	–USFS Red Buttes Wilderness brochure.	

ACCESS: From the town of Ruch, Oregon, travel south on Up-
                 per Applegate Road, and go 18.8 miles to Carberry
Creek Road (County Road 777). Turn right onto Road 777 and follow
mileposts to mile 6.9 at the junction with Steve Fork Road 1030.
Go left onto Road 1030 and continue 11.1 miles to a parking area
and trailhead on the right. From the trailhead, it is about 1 mi.
to the Steve Fork and Sucker Creek Gap Trail junction. The Steve
Fork Trail bears left at this location. THE STEVE CREEK CROSSING
SUSTAINED 1997 FLOOD DAMAGE–CHECK WITH USFS APPLEGATE RANGER DIST.
FOR REPAIR STATUS.

FEATURES: The trail traverses the upper Steve Fork Valley,
                  swings to the east, crosses a ridge and joins the
Fir Glade Trail 955, about one mile southwest of Fir Glade. Turn
right (south) onto 955 if continuing to Azalea Lake. MOTOR VEHI-
CLES ARE NOT ALLOWED.

HISTORY: "STEVE PEAK, FORK: Named for Stephen Oster, a sol-
                  itary prospector of the area during the 1860s and
1870s.   Sometimes mapped as Steve's Fork, and shown on some ca.
1900 maps as Steamboat Creek." (USFS quote)

SUCKER CREEK GAP TRAIL #906. (See map 25)

TRAIL BEGINS:	-Near milepost 11, Road 1030.	ELEV. 4400'
TRAIL ENDS:	-Boundary Ntl. Recreation Trail 1207.	ELEV. 5200'
DISTANCE:	-2.0 miles. Moderate.	
USE:	-Hiker, horse. MOTORIZED VEHICLES NOT ALLOWED.	
SEASON:	-Usually snow-free July to October.	
CONNECTING TR:	-Boundary National Recreation Trail 1207.	
BRING MAPS:	-USFS Applegate Ranger District-Rogue River N.F.	
	-USFS Red Buttes Wilderness brochure.	

ACCESS: From the town of Ruch, Oregon, travel south on Upper Applegate Road and go 18.8 miles to Carberry
Creek Road (County Road 777). Turn right and follow mileposts on
777 to mile 6.9 at the junction with Steve Fork Road 1030.   Turn
left onto 1030 and continue 11.1 mi. to the Steve Fork Trailhead.
Follow the Steve Fork Trail about 1 mile upstream to the signed
junction with the Sucker Creek Gap Trail. Keep to the right for
the beginning of the Sucker Creek Gap Trail.

FEATURES: This Rogue River National Forest trail ends at the
Boundary/National Recreation Trail 1207 at Sucker
Creek Gap. Directly across the Boundary Trail, what appears to
be a continuation of Sucker Creek Gap Trail 906, is Sucker Creek
Trail 1237 dropping about 3 miles through the Siskiyou National
Forest to Road 4612/098.

From Sucker Creek Gap, the Boundary Trail leads south about 5 mi.
to Tannen Lakes, or north about 12 mi. to Sugarloaf Mtn.

HISTORY: "SUCKER CREEK GAP: The name 'Sucker Creek' resulted when large numbers of inexperienced men flocked
to the placer deposits of that stream, a tributary of the Illin-
ois River.   Actually, Sucker Creek proved to pay quite well during the 1860s and 1870s." (USFS quote)

WHISKEY PEAK LOOKOUT TRAIL #910. (See map 25)

TRAIL BEGINS:	-Forest Road 1035/350.	ELEV. 6000'
TRAIL ENDS:	-Whiskey Peak Lookout.	ELEV. 6497'
DISTANCE:	-1/2 mile. Moderate, hiker only.	
SEASON:	-Usually snow-free July to October.	
BRING MAPS:	-USFS Applegate Ranger Dist. Rogue Riv. Ntl. For.	

ACCESS: From the town of Ruch, Oregon, travel south on Up-
                per Applegate Road and go 18.8 miles to Carberry
Creek Road (County Road 777). Turn right onto Road 777 and follow
the mileposts 4.5 miles to Forest Road 1035. Turn left onto 1035
and travel 10.8 miles to the junction with Forest Road 1035/350.
Turn right onto 350 and continue 2.3 miles to the trailhead near
Whiskey Springs. The trail begins on a blocked Road 1035/356.

FEATURES: The trail to the lookout is maintained for hikers
                only.   Views of the surrounding mountain tops are
terrific! The lookout building is no longer being used.

HISTORY: "WHISKEY PEAK, CREEK: Named in the 19th Century
                when a group of inebriated hunters camped at the
base of the steep-walled peak and one extremely drunk member of
the party began running away, screaming that the mountain 'was
falling over on them.'"   (USFS quote)

BALDY PEAK TRAIL SYSTEM   (See map on following page)
Mule Mtn./Mule Creek/Charlie Buck-Baldy Peak Trails.

USE: -Hiker/horse (Difficult),Mtn.bike(Most Difficult).
                  Motor Bikes not recommended.
SEASON: -Year round except for occasional winter snows.
BRING MAPS: -USFS Applegate Ranger District-Rogue River N.F.

ACCESS TO LOWER END, MULE MTN./MULE CREEK TRAILS ELEV. 1800'
From the town of Ruch, go south on Upper Applegate Road to milepost 12. MULE MTN. TRAIL 919 climbs about 1/4 mile to a junction
where MULE CREEK TRAIL 920 leads right, or Mule Mtn.Trail continues uphill left, 4.0 miles to Baldy Peak-Charlie Buck Trail.

ACCESS TO LOWER END, CHARLIE BUCK/BALDY PEAK TRAIL 918.
From Ruch,follow Upper Applegate Road just beyond milepost 9, and
turn left onto Forest Route 20. Go 1.3 miles on 20 and turn onto
Road 940, then go about 1.25 miles to a parking place near a rock
quarry just before Road 940 makes a sharp uphill bend. ELEV.2560.
From here it is best to hike 3/4 Mi. up to the trailhead as Road
940 is steep, narrow, rockfall and limited turn-around.ELEV.3000'

ACCESS TO UPPER END, MULE MTN, MULE CREEK, CHARLIE BUCK/BALDY
PEAK TRAILS.
From the junction of Upper Applegate Road and Forest Route 20, go
3.6 miles on Route 20 to Forest Road 2010. Follow Road 2010 and
go 4.8 miles to Road 2010-300. Turn onto Road 300 to a road gate
that seasonly is locked (do not block gate).Beyond the gate it is
1.0 mi.to a road triangle from where Road 329 leads downhill left
(west) about 1/4 mile to the UPPER TRAILHEAD of Mule Creek Trail
920 ELEV. 4000'.

From the above triangle, Road 300 continues north, about 200 feet
to Road 330. Just before a gate on 330,BALDY PK.TRAIL 918 begins
left as a Jeep trail, soon becoming a hiking trail. From here it
is 2.0 miles to the junction with MULE MOUNTAIN TRAIL #919.
ELEV. 4300' (at the base of Baldy Peak). Look on the left (west)
for Mule Mountain Trail sloping 4.0 miles down to Upper Applegate
Road. From the above junction,Charlie Buck/Baldy Peak Trail continues 2.0 miles to Road 940.

FEATURES: Trails can be combined for making LOOP or SHUTTLE trips. For example, a loop starting from Upper Applegate Road, up on MULE CREEK TRAIL 920 and down MULE MTN. TRAIL 919 would be almost 12.0 miles, rated strenuous for hikers. Shuttle trips starting from the upper elevations would be considerably easier.

From the upper elevations, there are wide-open views of the Mule Creek or Rock Gulch canyons, and of the surrounding area. The remoteness of the trails lead to a very memorable experience!

Mule Mountain, Mule Tie, Mule Creek and Charlie Buck/Baldy Peak Trails are maintained by "Lutheran Evergreens".

Middle Fork Trail 950, A beautiful trail but a little difficult in places in the upper portion of the trail.

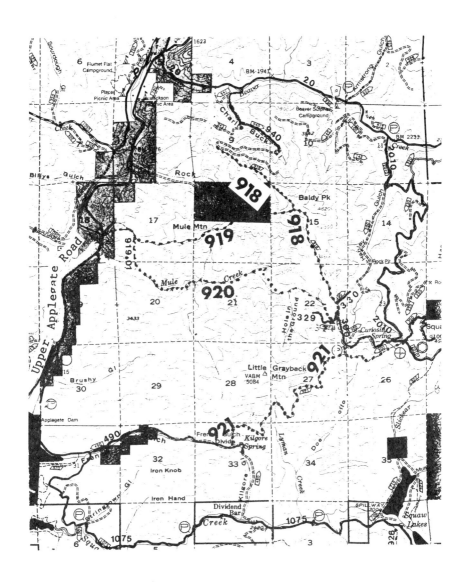

LITTLE GRAYBACK TRAIL #921. (See map 26)

TRAIL BEGINS:	-French Gulch Road.	ELEV.	3220'
TRAIL ENDS:	-Forest Road 2010 near milepost 5.	ELEV.	4440'
DISTANCE:	-4.0 mi. Moderate for hikers,horses		
USE:	and motor bikes. Difficult for mountain bikes.		
SEASON:	-Snow-free most of year, access roads may be haz-ardous during winter. Look for poison oak.		
BRING MAPS:	-USFS Applegate Ranger District -Rogue River N.F.		

LOWER ACCESS: From the town of Ruch, Oregon, follow mileposts on
Upper Applegate Road to mile 14.9 and turn east
across Applegate Dam onto Squaw Creek Road. Follow this road 1.5
miles then turn left onto French Gulch Road, past a row of mail-
boxes. Continue 2.1 miles to where the road reaches its crest at
a logging road junction. The trailhead is on the left.

UPPER ACCESS: From the town of Ruch, travel 9.2 miles on Upper
Applegate Road to the junction with Forest Rd. 20.
(Beaver Creek Road). Follow Road 20 for 3.6 miles and turn right
onto Forest Road 2010.   Continue on Road 2010 for 5.1 miles and
look on the right for Forest Road 2010-340.Take Road 340, 0.3 mi.
west to a parking area and trailhead.

FEATURES: This trail climbs along the south slopes of Little
Grayback Mountain, with open views of Squaw Lakes
directly below, Elliott Ridge and of the Siskiyou Mtns.   The one
mile route to Squaw Peak Lookout begins near the upper trailhead.

LITTLE SQUAW TRAIL #923.   (See map 26)

TRAIL BEGINS:	-Squaw Lakes parking area.	ELEV.3100'
TRAIL ENDS:	-Mulligan Bay on Big Squaw Lake.	
DISTANCE:	-1.0 mile.	
DIFFICULTY:	-Easy for hikers, moderate for mountain bikes.	
SEASON:	-All year.	
BRING MAPS:	-USFS Applegate Ranger Dist.Rogue River Ntl.Forest.	

ACCESS: From the town of Ruch, Oregon, follow mileposts on
                 Upper Applegate Road to mile 14.9 then turn left
across the dam. Keep right at a junction 1.5 miles further.Squaw
Creek Road becomes Forest Road 1075, and the Squaw Lakes parking
area is just beyond milepost 8, uphill to the right.

From the parking area, the trail follows a maintenance road for
1/8 mile to Big Squaw Lake. Immediately after reaching the lake,
continue east 100 yards further to a road junction. Turn right
and follow this road for another 1/4 mi. to Little Squaw Lake.The
trail crosses a foot bridge below the outlet of the lake,and then
climbs a short distance before entering a mixed conifer and hard-
wood forest.   Interpretative signs identify trees and vegetation
along the trail.

The trail ends at Mulligan Bay on Big Squaw Lake. For those wish-
ing to extend the hike, continue north on the lakeshore road that
circles Big Squaw Lake.   Visitors ending their hike at Mulligan
Bay can return to the parking area by following the maintenance
road west for 1/2 mile. CARRY WATER.

This outing provides the visitor with opportunities for picnicking, swimming, and fishing for rainbow and cutthroat trout.

67

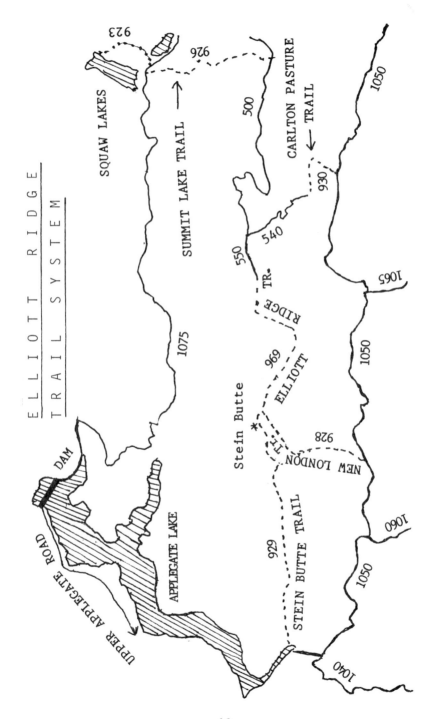

ELLIOTT RIDGE

TRAIL SYSTEM

SQUAW LAKES

923

926

500

CARLTON PASTURE

TRAIL

930

SUMMIT LAKE TRAIL

540

550

1050

1065

TR.

RIDGE

969

ELLIOTT

1050

1075

Stein Butte

*

TR.

928

NEW LONDON

DAM

929

STEIN BUTTE TRAIL

1060

1050

UPPER APPLEGATE ROAD

APPLEGATE LAKE

1040

SUMMIT LAKE TRAIL #926.   (See map 26)

TRAIL BEGINS:	-Squaw Lakes parking area.	ELEV.	3040'
TRAIL ENDS:	-Elliott Creek Ridge.	ELEV.	4720'
DISTANCE:	-2.0 miles. Difficult.		
USE:	-Hiker, horse, mountain and motor bike.		
	Check with Star Ranger Station for updates.		
SEASON:	-All year except for occasional winter snows.		
BRING MAPS:	-USFS Applegate Ranger Dist.-Rogue River N.F.		

ACCESS: Follow directions to Little Squaw Lake Trail. The
               Summit Lake Trail begins as an old logging track
from the Squaw Lakes parking area and leads uphill to the south.

FEATURES: The trail travels through a mixed conifer forest
               with small water crossings along the way. Look for
various aquatic plants within these areas.   The trail traverses
along black schist soils creating unique flora habitats.   It is a
steep climb before reaching Road 1075-580. Do not cross the road,
keep right and drop a short distance to Summit Lake.   Paths lead
up to the ridge for some good views of the surrounding area.

"The lake is surrounded by old growth ponderosa pines, and due to
the thick multi canopy forest, it is home to various wildlife including spotted owls, black bear and deer.   Do remember to tread
lightly within their domain."

"Summit lake is a small pond located on the summit of Elliott
Ridge.It was located along the early 20th Century Penn Sled Trail
between Squaw Creek and Elliott Creek and was probably named because of its location on the summit of a very steep ridge, and a
welcome landmark along the trail."   (USFS Quotes)

Summit Lake, Carlton Pasture, Elliott Ridge, New London and Stein
Butte Trails comprise a trail system maintained by "Motorcycle
Riders Association."

NEW LONDON TRAIL #928.
(Map 26)
(Formerly the eastern portion of Stein Butte Trail #929)

TRAIL BEGINS:	-Forest Road 1050.	**ELEV.** 2160'
TRAIL ENDS:	-Jnc. Stein Butte and Elliot Ridge Tr.	**ELEV.** 4000'
DISTANCE:	-2.57 miles plus 5.0 miles on Stein Butte Trail if using a shuttle arrangement to Seattle Bar.	
DIFFICULTY:	-Difficult for hikers and horses, most difficult for mountain and motor bikes.	
SEASON:	-All year except for occasional winter snows.	
CONNECTING TR.	-Stein Butte Trail 929, Elliott Ridge Trail 969.	
BRING MAPS:	-USFS Applegate Ranger Dist.- Rogue River N.F.	

ACCESS: From the town of Ruch, Oregon, follow mileposts on Upper Applegate Road 18.8 miles to Carberry Creek Road. Turn left (southeast) to the California-Oregon border near milepost 20 at the signed junction of Forest Roads 1040 and 1050. Turn left on 1050 and travel 2.7 mi.to the trailhead on the left. Parking is available directly across the road.

The 2.7 mile New London Trail meanders steeply, passing two mine adits and ends at a saddle just east of Stein Butte at the junction with the Stein Butte and Elliott Ridge Trails. Stein Butte Trail is on the left (west) leading 0.5 mi. to a ridge from where a side trail leads uphill left to Stein Butte. The Stein Butte Trail continues about 4.5 miles to its Seattle Bar Trailhead at Applegate Lake.

Elliott Ridge Tr. #969 leads right (east) from the above saddle, 1.7 mi. to Road 550. A road system from this point makes connections with Carlton Pasture Trail 930, and Summit Lake Trail 926. CARRY WATER ON ALL OF THE ABOVE TRAILS!

For a car shuttle using the above trails, cars could be placed at the appropriate lower trailheads.

New London, Stein Butte, Elliot Ridge, Summit Lake and Carlton Pasture Trails are maintained by Motorcycle Riders Association.

CARLTON PASTURE TRAIL #930.   (See map 26)

TRAIL BEGINS:	-Forest Road 1050.	ELEV. 2640'
TRAIL ENDS:	-Forest Road 1075/540	ELEV. 3680'
DISTANCE:	-1.6 miles. DIFFICULT.	
SEASON:	-All year except for occasional winter snows.	
USE:	-Hiker, horse, mountain and motor bikes.	
BRING MAPS:	-USFS Applegate Ranger Dist.- Rogue River N.F.	

ACCESS: From the town of Ruch, Oregon, follow mileposts on
                 Upper Applegate Road 18.8 miles to Carberry Creek
Road. Turn left (southeast) to the California-Oregon border near
milepost 20 at the signed junction of Forest Roads 1040 and 1050.
Turn left on 1050 and travel 6.6 mi.to the Carlton Pasture Trailhead on the left.

The 1.6 mile Carlton Pasture Trail climbs steeply, about 1/2 mile
to the base of Carlton Pasture, and then heads west about 1.0 mi.
to Forest Road 1075/540. To reach Elliott Ridge, follow Road 540
0.5 mile to Road 550. TURNING LEFT(West) onto Road 550 leads 0.5
mi. to Elliott Ridge Trail that continues 1.7 mi. to the junction
with Stein Butte and New London Trails.

From the above junction of Roads 540 and 550,TURNING RIGHT (east)
onto Road 550 leads 0.5 mile to Road 500.   Keep RIGHT onto Road
500 and go about 2.5 miles. Look on the left (downhill north)for
Summit Lake and Summit Lake Trail 926.

For a car shuttle using the above trails, cars could be placed at
the appropriate lower trailheads.

New London, Stein Butte, Elliott Ridge, Summit Lake and Carlton
Pasture Trails are maintained by Motorcycle Riders Association.

MIDDLE FORK TRAIL #950.   (See map 25)

TRAIL BEGINS:	–Forest Road 1035, northern Calif. ELEV. 2860'
TRAIL ENDS:	–Forest Road 1040/600. ELEV. 4200'
DISTANCE:	–Lower section 3.4 mi., upper section 2.3 miles.
USE:	–Hiker/horse. Easy lower section, more difficult upper section. Horses not recommended on upper section due to narrow tread and rocky creek crossings, best access and turn-around for vehicles with trailers is at Road 1035 Trailhead.
SEASON:	–April through October.
CONNECTING TR:	–Frog Pond Trail 953.
BRING MAPS:	–USFS Applegate Ranger Dist.-Rogue River Ntl. For.
	–USFS "Red Buttes Wilderness" brochure.
	–USFS Recreation Opportunity Guide-Middle Fork Tr.

ACCESS: From the town of Ruch, Oregon, follow mileposts on Upper Applegate Road to mile 18.8 at Carberry Creek Road. Turn left and continue 1.3 miles to the junction with Forest Road 1040 and 1050. Turn right on 1040 and drive the following distances:

LOWER TRAILHEAD–5 miles to junction with Rd. 1035. Turn right onto Road 1035 and go 0.2 mile to the trailhead on the left.

MIDDLE TRAILHEAD: Continue 7.0 mi. on Road 1040 to where Middle Fork Trail crosses the road and continues upstream from the Frog Pond Trailhead.

UPPER TRAILHEAD: Continue 2.0 miles on Road 1040 to the junction with Road 1040/600. Turn left onto Road 600 and go 1/8 mi. to the Bean Gulch Trailhead on the left.

FEATURES: The lower end of the trail begins as a rough road that very soon breaks into a trail on the right. It follows the Middle Fork of the Applegate River and passes two old mining cabin sites along the way (ca.1930). The trail continues its climb then crosses Road 1040 at the Frog Pond Trailhead. Keep right on Middle Fork Trail, 2.3 miles to its upper trailhead There is an abundance of autumn color from the vine maples, alder yew,dogwood, huckleberry and other surrounding plants.

FROG POND TRAIL #953. (See map 25)

TRAIL BEGINS:	-LOWER END: Forest Road 1040.	ELEV. 3440'
TRAIL ENDS:	-UPPER END: Forest Road 1040.	ELEV. 3880'
DISTANCE:	-5.4 miles, steep grades.	HIGHPOINT ELEV. 5200'
DIFFICULTY:	-Moderate for hikers/difficult for horses and they are not recommended.	
SEASON:	-Early July through October.	
CONNECTING TR:	-Middle Fork Trail 950. NO MOTORIZED VEHICLES.	
BRING MAPS:	-USFS Applegate Ranger Dist.-Rogue River N.F.	
	-USFS "Red Buttes Wilderness" brochure.	

ACCESS: From the town of Ruch, Oregon, follow mileposts on
               Upper Applegate Road 18.8 miles to Carberry Creek
Road. Turn left and continue 1.3 miles to the junction with Forest Roads 1050 and 1040. Keep right onto 1040 and go 9.7 miles to
the lower trailhead or 2 miles more to the upper trailhead.

FEATURES: From the lower end, the trail begins along a faint
               track soon becoming a good trail.   Near the top
end of the loop the trail may become obscure. Follow the blazes,
stakes, and green "X" trail signs. At one point the trail passes
a small pond into a larger meadow and becomes difficult to follow. Follow cairns in the center of the meadow and head for the
uprooted tree on the far side. The trail becomes easy to follow
then climbs steadily to the north with views of the Red Buttes.
After reaching a crest, the trail descends sharply to the southwest shore of Frog Pond and then passes an old cabin that uses a
cluster of cedar trees as its mainstay.   The cabin was built by
John Knox McCloy in about 1900. The trail drops sharply 1.0 mile
to the upper trailhead on Road 1040.

FIR GLADE TRAIL #955. (A ROUTE TO AZALEA LAKE (See map 25)

TRAIL BEGINS: -Forest Road 1040/800.   ELEV. 5200'
TRAIL ENDS: -Azalea Lake.   ELEV. 5400'
DISTANCE: -5.8 miles.   HIGH POINT ELEV. 6000'
SEASON: -Usually open late June through October.
USE: -Hiker/horse MODERATE GRADE, NO ORV'S.
BRING MAPS: -USFS Applegate Ranger Dist.-Rogue River N.F.
              -USFS "Red Buttes Wilderness" brochure.
CONNECTING TR.-Steve Fork Trail 905, Phantom Meadows Trail 955A,
               Butte Fork Trail 957.

ACCESS: ROUTE 1:   From Ruch, Go 18.8 miles south on Upper
              Applegate Road to the junction with Carberry Creek
              Road. Turn LEFT and go 1.3 miles to the junction
of Forest Roads 1040/1050. Turn right onto Road 1040 for 17 miles
to Road 800 on the left.   Follow Road 800 0.4 mile and turn left
0.1 mile to Fir Glade Trailhead.

ROUTE 2:   18.8 miles south Of Ruch on Upper Applegate Road, turn
RIGHT onto Carberry Road (777) and go 6.9 miles to Road 1030. Go
4.8 miles on 1030 to Road 400 THAT HAD SEVERE STORM DAMAGE. TRAF-
FIC MAY BE ONE-WAY, WORK SCHEDULED AROUND 2001. CHECK WITH USFS).
Follow Road 400, 4.2 mile to the Road 1040/700 junction then keep
RIGHT onto 1040, 0.1 mi.to Road 800 leading 0.5 mi. to trailhead.

FEATURES: This trail affords open views of the Middle Fork
              drainage, Buck Peak, Figurehead Mountain and Klam-
ath Mountains. Not far from the trailhead, the route follows an
old road for a short distance. Look left to where the trail continues to Fir Glade, a large open meadow with a collapsed shelter.   On the near edge of the meadow, look left for the continuation of the trail. 1 mile further, pass the junction with the
Steve Fork and Phantom Meadows Trails then continue to the crest
of the divide between Rogue River and Klamath Ntl. Forests.   The
trail switchbacks to a saddle N.W. of Figurehead Mountain before
dropping down to Azalea Lake. At Azalea Lake,hikers camp is north
of the lake and stock camp east of the lake. "No camping in the
day-use area between the perimeter trail and the lake. LIMIT PER
GROUP 8 persons,12 stock. Bring pellets/grain for stock" (USFS)

(THE BUTTE FORK TRAIL ALSO LEADS TO AZALEA LAKE, SEE PAGE 75).

BUTTE FORK TRAIL #957.   (See map 25)

TRAIL BEGINS: -From Horse Camp Trail 958,or from SHOO FLY TRAIL-
                 HEAD on Forest Road 1040.
TRAIL ENDS: -Azalea Lake.
DISTANCE: -10 miles to Azalea Lake via the Horse Camp
                 Trail, or 8 miles from the Shoo Fly Trailhead.
SEASON: -June through October. Moderate HIKER,HORSE ONLY.
CONNECTING TR.   -Horse Camp Trail #958, Shoo Fly Trail #954, Fort
                 Goff Trail #956, Fir Glade Trail #955.
BRING MAPS: -USFS "Red Buttes Wilderness" brochure.
                 -USFS Applegate Ranger Dist. -Rogue River N.F.

ACCESS: From the town of Ruch, Oregon, follow mileposts
                 on Upper Applegate Road, 18.8 miles to Carberry
Creek Road. Turn left and go 1.3 mile to the signed junction of
Forest Roads 1040 and 1050. Turn right onto Road 1040 and go 3.6
miles to the Horse Camp Trailhead on the left (At the former Cook
and Green Campground).Take the Horse Camp Trail about 3/4 mile to
where the Butte Fork Trail leads RIGHT.

SHOO FLY TRAILHEAD is 4 mi. further on Road 1040 near milepost 9.
The trail drops 0.7 mile to the Butte Fork Trail. Turn right and
continue about 7.5 miles upstream to Azalea Lake.

FEATURES: From its junction with Horse Camp Trail,the Butte
                 Fork Trail passes below the Butte Fork Slide be-
fore dropping to Echo Canyon and the Butte Fork of the Applegate
River. In another 0.5 miles,you reach a bridge taking you to the
north bank of the river with a good view of Hello Canyon. Follow
the trail about 0.5 mile to the lower end of the Shoo Fly Trail.

Butte Fork Trail continues upstream,passing an old Forest Service
toolhouse and a marked grave of persons killed in a 1945 airplane
crash, before reaching Cedar Basin and the junction of Fort Goff
Trail 956. Azalea Lake is one mile west of Cedar Basin.

HORSE CAMP TRAIL #958. (See map 26)

TRAIL BEGINS:	—Forest Road 1040.	ELEV. 2400'
TRAIL ENDS:	—Echo Lake.	ELEV. 5460'
DISTANCE:	—3.9 miles, very steep grades. CARRY WATER.	
SEASON:	—June through October. USE: hikers/horses.	
CONNECTING TR:	—Butte Fork Trail 957.	
	—Pacific Crest National Scenic Trail.	
DIFFICULTY:	—Difficult for hikers, most difficult for horses.	
BRING MAPS:	—USFS Applegate Ranger Dist. —Rogue River N.F.	
	—USFS "Red Buttes Wilderness" brochure.	
	—USFS Recreation Opportunity Guide-Horse Camp Tr.	

ACCESS: From the town of Ruch, Oregon, follow mileposts
               on Upper Applegate Road, 18.8 miles to Carberry
Creek Road. Turn left and go 1.3 miles to the junction of Roads
1050 and 1040. Turn right onto Road 1040 and go 3.9 miles to the
former Cook and Green Campground on the left. Signs may be missing. Turning left onto the camp roads leads 1/4 mile to the Horse
Camp Trailhead.

FEATURES: Horse Camp Trail is popular with backpackers as
               an   access to the   Pacific Crest National Scenic
Trail. About 3500 ft. of elevation is gained in only four miles,
rating the trail one of the steepest in the Siskiyou Mountains.

In about 0.6 mi. KEEP LEFT at the new Butte Fork Trail junction.
It is 1.0 mile further to Horse Camp and a nearby spring. (WATER
TREATMENT IS RECOMMENDED). The trail continues another 1.5 miles
to a high mountain meadow before reaching the Echo Lake junction.
The trail to the right leads to Echo Lake nestled in a small cir-
que basin below Red Buttes. To reach the Pacific Crest National
Scenic Trail, keep left at the above junction and go 0.5 miles at
ELEV. 5900' A 15 mile loop is possible by using the Horse Camp,
Pacific Crest, and Cook and Green Trails. MOTORIZED VEHICLES ARE
NOT ALLOWED ON THE PACIFIC CREST TRAIL OR IN THE RED BUTTES WIL-
DERNESS.

HISTORY: "HORSE CAMP: Named by John Knox McCloy in the
               early 20th century." (USFS quote)

COOK AND GREEN TRAIL #959. (See map 26)

TRAIL BEGINS: -(Lower Trailhead) Forest Road 1040. ELEV. 2280'
TRAIL ENDS: -(Upper Trailhead) Cook and Green Pass ELEV. 4765'
Forest Road 1055 near milepost 10. Storm damage
temporarily repaired, CHECK USFS FOR UPDATES!
DISTANCE: -About 8.2 miles.
DIFFICULTY: -Moderate for hikers, horses; difficult for motor
and mountain bikes.
SEASON: -Usually snow-free June through October.
CONNECTING TR: -Pacific Crest National Scenic Trail.
BRING MAPS: -USFS Applegate Ranger Dist.-Rogue River Ntl. For.
-USFS Recreation Opportunity Guide-this trail.
-USFS Pacific Crest Trail-Oreg. Southern Portion.

ACCESS: (LOWER TRAILHEAD). From Ruch, Oregon, turn left
onto Upper Applegate Road and continue 18.8 miles
to the junction with Carberry Creek Road. Turn left and go 1.3
miles to the junction of Forest Roads 1050 and 1040. Turn right
onto Road 1040 and go 2.8 mi. to the trailhead on the left.

FEATURES: The trail passes through a sizable stand of the
rare Brewer spruce trees recognizable by its four
to eight foot long, string-like branchlets hanging down from its
limbs. Noble and white fir are also seen at higher elevations.
No-See-Em Camp is reached just before crossing Cook and Green Cr.
The trail then climbs along the west side of Bear Gulch and passes a small spring just before reaching Cook and Green Pass.

MOTORIZED VEHICLES NOT ALLOWED ON THE PCNST OR IN RED BUTTES WIL-
DERNESS.

HISTORY: "COOK AND GREEN CREEK, PASS, CAMPGROUND: Robert
Cook and the two Green brothers were partners in
several mining ventures in this vicinity during the 1870s and
1880s; the name undoubtedly resulted from their activities."

"NO-SEE-EM CAMP: Probably named by early day Forest Service
employees, for the clouds of small gnats (no-see-ums) which ha-
rass campers during the spring and summer months." (USFS quotes)

77

TIN CUP TRAIL #961.   (See map 26)

TRAIL BEGINS: -End of Forest Road 1060/600.   ELEV. 5240'
TRAIL ENDS: -Siskiyou crest.   ELEV. 6000'
DISTANCE: -1.6 miles, moderate grades. USE: hiker/horse.
SEASON: -Usually snow-free July through October.
CONNECTING TR. -Pacific Crest National Scenic Trail.
BRING MAPS: -USFS Applegate Ranger Dist.- Rogue River N.F.

ACCESS: From the town of Ruch, Oregon, follow mileposts on
                Upper Applegate Road 18.8 miles to Carberry Creek
Road.   Turn left (southeast) to the California-Oregon border near
milepost 20 at the signed junction of Forest Roads 1040 and 1050.
Turn left on 1050 and travel 1.6 miles to the junction with Forest Road 1060.   Turn right onto 1060 and continue 3.5 mi. to a
hairpin turn leading back to the north. (The old Blue Ledge Copper Mine is located on the right, southwest of this turn.)   Continue northeast on 1060, gaining Nabob Ridge in about 2 miles at
the junction with Forest Road 1060/600.

From this point it had been necessary to park and hike about one
mile on Road 600 to the trailhead due to storm damage.   Repairs
are scheduled, check with USFS Star Ranger Station for updates!

FEATURES: This short trail connects with the Pacific Crest
                National Scenic Trail near Lowdens' Cabin and
                Slaughterhouse Flat.   MOTORIZED VEHICLES ARE NOT
                ALLOWED ON THE PCNST OR IN RED BUTTES WILDERNESS.

HISTORY: "JOHN LOWDEN settled at the mouth of Seiad Creek in
                1860 and operated a ferry across the Klamath River
for several years.   He and his two sons mined, raised wheat and
began a small dairy.   Their beef cattle ranged on the high meadows of the Siskiyou crest during the summers."

"SLAUGHTERHOUSE FLAT may have been the site of an early hog butch-
ering operation   providing meat for the sudden influx of miners
during the 1850s."   (USFS quotes)

CHAPTER 6 - SKY LAKES WILDERNESS

Sky Lakes Wilderness is a land of lakes, rocky ridges and timbered slopes, and was designated by Congress in 1984. Its 113,590 acres straddles southern Oregon's Cascade Range from Crater Lake National Park southward to Highway 140. It is approx. six miles wide and twenty seven miles long, with elevations ranging from 3800 feet in the canyon of the Middle Fork of the Rogue River to a lofty 9495 feet at the top of Mt. McLoughlin.

More than 200 pools of water, from small ponds to lakes of 30-40 acres, dot the landscape. Fourmile Lake, near the southern end of the area, exceeds 900 acres. The lake basins can sometimes be crowded with other campers, but the wilderness has thousands of acres of forest and scenic ridges where the visitor can find solitude.

SPECIAL RULES are enforced to protect the Wilderness resource:

1) Campsites must be at least 100 ft. from lakeshores and 50 ft. from streams.

2) Graze and tether horses and pack animals at least 200 feet from lakes or ponds and 50 feet from streams. Avoid tying animals directly to trees and do not picket. Use a "high-line" stretched between two trees.

3) Stay out of specially marked areas being revegetated.

4) Visitors should travel in groups no larger than 8 people and twelve animals throughout Sky Lakes Wilderness.

5) Bicycles, motorbikes, hang gliders, carts, wagons and other forms of mechanized transport are not allowed (disabled persons in wheelchairs permitted).

6) Bring adequate food (pellets or grain, not hay) for your animals because feed is scarce in the Wilderness, use nosebag.

(continued on next page)

SPECIAL RULES CONTINUED:

7. Refrain from operating loud radios or other audio devices. Discharging of firearms within or near occupied areas or across lakes is prohibited.

8. Grazing is not allowed before August 1, unless otherwise posted at trailhead bulletin boards.

THE WILDERNESS CONTAINS TWO LAKE BASINS WHERE FURTHER RESTRICTIONS APPLY (SEVEN LAKES BASIN and BLUE CANYON BASIN).

A. In sensitive areas of these two basins, groups with pack/saddle animals must camp only within designated "horse camp" sites. These sites are marked with signs; sensitive areas and horse camp locations are shown on maps posted at trailheads.

B. In the two basins, grazing is permitted only in designated meadows and only after August 1 (unless otherwise posted at trailhead bulletin boards).

Be sure to check the trailhead bulletin board for current rules and other information pertaining to the Sky Lakes Wilderness. The complete management regulations enforced in the area may be reviewed in the Forest Supervisor or District Ranger offices.

A SKY LAKES WILDERNESS MAP, and other very detailed information, can be obtained from:

Forest Supervisor, Rogue River National Forest, 333 W. 8th St., Medford, OR 97501.
-District Ranger, P.O. Box 227, Butte Falls, OR 97522.

Forest Supervisor, Winema National Forest, 2819 Dahlia St., Klamath Falls, OR 97601.
-Klamath District Ranger, 1936 California Ave., Klamath Falls, OR 97601.

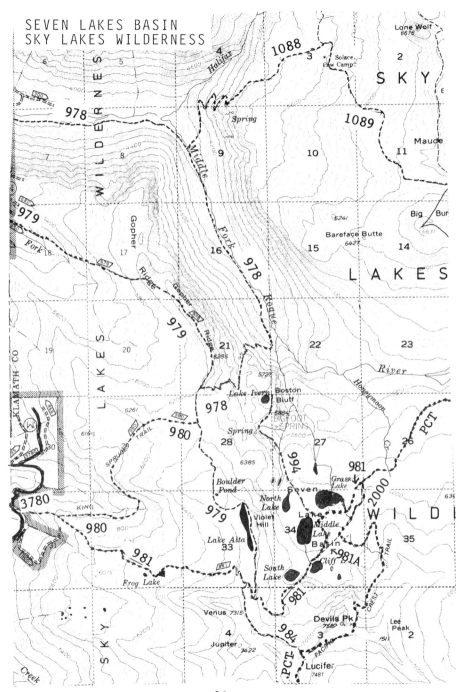

SEVEN LAKES BASIN
SKY LAKES WILDERNESS

MIDDLE FORK TRAIL #978.   (See map 11)

TRAIL BEGINS:	–Middle Fork Trailhead Road 3790. ELEV. 3500'
TRAIL ENDS:	–Alta Lake Trail junction. ELEV. 6200'
DISTANCE:	–8.5 miles, moderate/difficult. Hiker/horse.
SEASON:	–Lower segment of trail usually open by May 15.
	–Upper segment of trail, July–October.
CONNECTING TR.	–Halifax Tr. 1088 AFTER DIFFICULT RIVER CROSSING.
	–Alta Lake Trail 979.
BRING MAPS:	–Butte Falls Ranger Dist.–Rogue River Ntl.Forest.
	USFS Sky Lakes Area–Rogue River/Winema Ntl. For.
	USFS Rec. Opportunity Guide, Middle Fork Trail.

ACCESS: From the town of Butte Falls, Oreg., travel east out of town 1.0 mile to County Route 992,leading north to the town of Prospect. Turn onto this route and follow it 8.7 miles to Forest Route 34. Turn east and continue 8.2 miles to Forest Route 37. Turn left on 37 and continue 5.2 miles to Forest Road 3790. Travel 3 miles east on 3790 to the trailhead.

FEATURES: For the first six miles, the trail follows along the south bank of the river. There are a number of camp spots, though not obvious from the trail. (The junction with Halifax Tr. is reached after the first 3.5 miles).The Middle Fork Trail then climbs steeply out of the canyon to the junction with Alta Lake Trail on Gopher Ridge. A 30 mile loop is possible by linking the Alta Lake, Devils Peak, Pacific Crest, McKie Camp and Halifax Trails.   There is no bridge crossing the Rogue River connecting Halifax and Middle Fork Trails.   Hikers can cross on downed logs. Horses may ford the river.

The USFS advises that there is no horse feed in the canyon, and that water is available not far from the trail along most of its length.   Visitors should recognize that water in wilderness and backcountry areas may not be safe to drink. Water is not tested. (Excerpts USFS Recreation Opportunity Guide)

See beginning of Chapter 6 for historical notes and regulations.

ALTA LAKE TRAIL #979. (See map 11)

TRAIL BEGINS:	-Forest Road 3785.	**ELEV.** 4800'
TRAIL ENDS:	-Seven Lakes Trail junction.	**ELEV.** 6800'
DISTANCE:	-6.2 miles, moderate to difficult.	
SEASON:	-Usually snow-free July to October. Preferred use: Hikers. No horse feed at Alta Lake.	
CONNECTING TR.	-Middle Fork Trail 978, King Spruce Trail 980 and Seven Lakes Trail 981.	
BRING MAPS:	-Butte Falls Ranger Dist.-Rogue River Ntl. Forest. -USFS Rec. Opportunity Guide-Alta Lake Trail. -USFS Sky Lakes Area-Rogue River/Winema Ntl. For.	

ACCESS: From the town of Butte Falls, Oreg., travel east one mile to County Route 992 leading north to the town of Prospect. Turn onto this route and follow it 8.7 miles to Forest Route 34. Turn right onto 34 and go 8.2 miles to the junction with Forest Route 37. Keep left onto 37 and travel 2.2 miles to the junction with Forest Road 3785. Turn onto Road 3785 and go 3.5 miles to the Alta Lake Trailhead. Parking is limited to roadside turnouts with space for horse trailer turn-around.

FEATURES: This trail gets little use. It begins at Wallowa Creek and climbs to the open parklands on the south slope of Gopher Ridge. The trail junctions with the Middle Fork and King Spruce Trails, then ends at Seven Lakes Trail 981. Camp sites are on high ground both east and west of Alta Lake. A 9.1 mile loop uses the upper section of the Alta Lake Trail, the Seven Lakes Trail 981 and King Spruce 980 Trail. Water is available at Alta Lake and seasonally at Boulder Pond, but should be treated. Alta Lake has no horsefeed. See beginning of Chapter 6 for Sky Lakes Wilderness regulations and historical notes.

HISTORY: "ALTA LAKE: One of the lakes in the Seven Lakes Basin, probably named by early Forest Svc. personnel because of its location on the slopes of a bluff, several hundred feet higher than the other six lakes." (USFS quote)

KING SPRUCE TRAIL #980. (See map 11)

TRAIL BEGINS: -Near Seven Lakes Trailhead, Road 3780. ELEV. 5600'
TRAIL ENDS: -Junction with Alta Lake Trail. ELEV. 6350'
DISTANCE: -2.8 miles, moderate, preferred use: Hikers.
SEASON: -Usually snow-free July to October.
CONNECTING TR.-Alta Lake Trail 979, Seven Lakes Trail 981.
BRING MAPS: -Butte Falls Ranger Dist.-Rogue River Ntl. Forest.
-USFS Sky Lakes Area-Rogue River/Winema Ntl. For.

ACCESS: From the town of Butte Falls, travel east one mile
            to County Route 992, leading north to the town of
Prospect. Turn onto this route and follow it 8.7 miles to Forest
Route 34. Turn onto 34 and go 8.2 miles to Forest Route 37. Keep
left onto 37, and travel 0.4 miles to Forest Road 3780. Turn onto
3780 and go 3.6 miles to the Seven Lakes Trailhead. There is
ample parking/turnaround space at the trailhead. Water not available. The lower end of the KING SPRUCE TRAIL is reached by hiking
along the Seven Lakes Trail, 0.5 mile from its trailhead.

FEATURES: The 2.8 mi. King Spruce Tr. passes the site of the
            old King Spruce Camp before climbing to the junc-
tion with the Alta Lake Trail 979. TURNING LEFT at this junction
leads to the Middle Fork Trail in less than 1 mile, or 3.6 miles
to the Alta Lake lower trailhead.

TURNING RIGHT from King Spruce Trail leads 2.5 miles, past Alta
Lake, to the Seven Lakes Trail. See beginning of Chapter 6 for
Sky Lakes Wilderness regulations and history.

It is a good idea to keep
Raingear in your pack

SEVEN LAKES TRAIL #981. (See map 11 and 12)

TRAIL BEGINS:	-Forest Road 3780. ELEV. 5000'
TRAIL ENDS:	-Pacific Crest National Scenic Trail, ELEV. 6200'
DISTANCE:	-6.1 miles, moderate to difficult. Hiker/horse.
SEASON:	-Usually snow-free July to October.
CONNECTING TR.	-King Spruce Trail 980, Alta Lake Trail 979, Devils Peak Trail 984, Lake Ivern Trail 994, Pacific Crest National Scenic Trail.
BRING MAPS:	-USFS Butte Falls Ranger Dist., Rogue River N.F. -USFS Rec. Opportunity Guide, Seven Lakes Trail. -USFS Sky Lakes Area-Rogue River/Winema Ntl. For.

ACCESS: From the town of Butte Falls, travel east 1 mile
                   to County Route 992,leading north to the town of
                   Prospect.Turn onto this route and travel 8.7 mi.
to Forest Route 34. Turn east on 34 and travel 8.2 miles to the
junction with Forest Route 37 and keep left for .4 mile to Forest
Road 3780. Follow 3780, 3.6 miles to the trailhead. Parking and
turnaround space is ample. Water is not available.

FEATURES: The Seven Lakes Trail gains 1700 feet in elev-
                   ation to a saddle, junctioning with the Alta Lake
and Devils Peak Trails, before dropping to South Lake and Cliff
Lake in Seven Lakes Basin.   The trail continues to the junctions
of Lake Ivern and Pacific Crest Trails.   For a cross-wilderness
experience, continue on the Pacific Crest Trail 2.5 miles to the
junction with Sevenmile Trail 3703 that travels northeast to its
Sevenmile Marsh Trailhead in Winema National Forest.

A 9.1 mile loop uses Seven Lakes Trail,the upper end of Alta Lake
Trail, and King Spruce Trail. Seven Lakes Trail may be very dusty
due to overuse, and Cliff Lake may be overcrowded. Carry water as
lake water in the area is not recommended for drinking unless it
is treated.

Please see beginning of Chapter 6 for Sky Lakes Wilderness regulations and historical information.

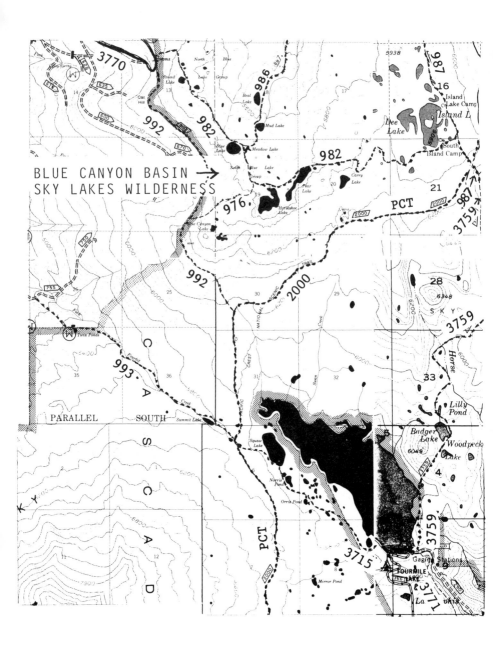

BLUE CANYON BASIN →
SKY LAKES WILDERNESS

BLUE CANYON TRAIL #982 (See maps 11 and 16)

<u>TRAIL BEGINS:</u>	-Road 3770 at Saddle Camp. <u>ELEV.</u> 6200'
<u>TRAIL ENDS:</u>	-Junction with Red Lake Trail 987. <u>ELEV.</u> 6000'
<u>DISTANCE:</u>	-5.1 miles, easy to moderate. <u>USE:</u> hiker/horse.
<u>SEASON:</u>	-Usually snow-free June to October, trailhead often not accessible by car until the end of June or the first of July. Mosquitos are numerous until about August 15.
<u>CONNECTING TR.</u>	-Cat Hill Way Tr.992, Meadow Lake Tr. 976, South Fork Tr. 986, Red Lake Tr. 987.
<u>BRING MAPS:</u>	-USFS Butte Falls Ranger Dist., Rogue River N.F.
	-USFS Sky Lakes Area, Rogue Riv.-Winema Ntl. For.
	-USFS Rec. Opportunity Guide-Blue Canyon Trail.

<u>ACCESS:</u>   From White City, OR., follow mileposts on State Hwy. 140, 28.6 miles to the junction with County Route 821.Continue north on 821,8.8 mi. just beyond milepost 26 to a junction where Route 37 leads right(east). Follow mileposts on 37, 10.9 miles to the junction with Road 3770 on the right. Follow 3770, 6 miles to the trailhead. Parking and turn-around space is adequate.

<u>FEATURES:</u>   Trail 982 passes Blue, Meadow, Horseshoe, Pear and Island Lakes. The trail may be dusty from overuse, and the surrounding lakes may be overcrowded. There is no horsefeed in the Blue Canyon Area. A 5.6 mile day loop hike is possible by using the Cat Hill Way Trail 992 (trailhead just a few hundred feet down from the Blue Canyon Trailhead), Meadow Lake Trail 976 and the Blue Canyon Trail. A longer 12.5 mile loop uses the Cat Hill Way, the Pacific Crest and Blue Canyon Trail.

Please see beginning of Chapter 6 for Sky Lakes Wilderness regulations and history notes.

SOUTH FORK TRAIL #986   (See maps 11 and 16)

TRAIL BEGINS: -Forest Road 37/720.   ELEV. 4000'
TRAIL ENDS: ¬Junction with Blue Canyon Trail. ELEV. 5700'
DISTANCE: -5.1 miles, moderate to difficult.
               Primitive Trail, little to no maintenance.
SEASON: -Usually snow-free June to October. Mosquitos bad
               until mid-August. USE: Recommended, hiker only.
CONNECTING TR: -Blue Canyon Trail 982.
BRING MAPS: -Rogue River Ntl. Forest-Butte Falls Ranger Dist.
               -USFS Sky Lakes Area-Rogue River/Winema Ntl. For.
               -USFS Rec. Opportunity Guide-South Fork Trail.

ACCESS: From White City OR.,   follow mileposts on State
               Hwy. 140, 28.6 miles to the junction with County
Route 821.Turn north on 821 and go 8.8 miles(just beyond Milepost
26) to where Forest Route 37 leads right (east). Follow mileposts on 37, 13.3 miles to the junction with Forest Road 37/720
on the right. Turn and continue on 720, 1 mile to the end of the
road at the South Fork LOWER TRAILHEAD.

ALTERNATE ALL PAVEMENT ROUTE: From Butte Falls, travel east one
mi.to County Route 821, that leads north to the town of Prospect.
Turn onto this route and go 8.7 miles to the junction with Forest
Route 34.   Turn right onto 34 and go 8.2 miles to the junction
with Forest Route 37. Turn right onto 37 and go 5.7 miles to the
junction with Road 720. Turn left and follow 720 one mile to the
LOWER TRAILHEAD at the end of the road.

FEATURES: This trail is recommended for hiker use only. It
               passes Beal, Mud and Meadow Lakes before termina-
ting at Blue Lake and Blue Canyon Trail 982. If using a car shuttle, the hike could be made easier by hiking from the Blue Canyon
Trailhead to Blue Lake, and taking the South Fork Trail down to
Forest Road 37/720. Water is plentiful along the trail, but like
all wilderness water, should be treated before drinking. (See the
beginning of Chapter 6 for historical notes and a mention of Wilderness regulations).

<u>CAT HILL WAY TRAIL #992.</u> (See maps 11 and 16)

<u>TRAIL BEGINS:</u>	-Road 3770 at Saddle Camp.	<u>ELEV.</u> 6200'
<u>TRAIL ENDS:</u>	-Junction with Pacific Crest Trail.	<u>ELEV.</u> 6160'
<u>DISTANCE:</u>	-3.4 miles, moderate. Preferred use: hikers.	
<u>SEASON:</u>	-Usually snow-free June to October, trailhead of-ten not accessible by car until the end of June or first of July. Mosquitos are numerous until mid August.	
<u>CONNECTING TR.</u>	-Blue Canyon 982, Meadow Lake 976 and Pacific Crest Trails.	
<u>BRING MAPS:</u>	-USFS Butte Falls Ranger Dist., Rogue River N.F. -USFS Sky Lakes Area-Rogue River/Winema Ntl. For.	

<u>ACCESS:</u>   From White City, OR., follow mileposts on State Hwy. 140, 28.6 miles to the junction with County Route 821. Continue north on 821, 8.8 miles just beyond milepost 26, to where Forest Route 37 leads right (east). Follow mileposts on 37, 10.9 miles to the junction with Road 3770 on the right. Follow 3770, 6 miles to the trailhead. Parking and turn-around space is adequate.

<u>FEATURES:</u>   To reach the Cat Hill Way Trail, hike a few hun-dred feet down from the Blue Canyon Trailhead. Look for a trailhead sign on the right.

A 5.6 mile day loop hike is possible by using the Cat Hill Way Trail 992, Meadow Lake Trail 976, and Blue Canyon Trail 982.   A longer 12.5 mile loop uses the Cat Hill way, Pacific Crest and Blue Canyon Trails.

Please see beginning of Chapter 6 for Sky Lakes Wilderness regu-lations and historical notes.

TOM AND JERRY TRAIL #1084. (See map 6)

TRAIL BEGINS: -Forest Road 3795/600.   ELEV. 5000'
TRAIL ENDS: -McKie Shelter.   ELEV. 5500'
DISTANCE: -5 miles, moderate, hiker/horse, June to October.
CONNECTING TR: -Mudjekeewis Trail 1085 and McKie Camp Tr. 1089.
BRING MAPS: -USFS Butte Falls Ranger Dist., Rogue River N.F.
              -USFS Sky Lakes Area-Rogue River/Winema Ntl. For.
              -USFS Rec. Opportunity Guide, Tom and Jerry Trail.

ACCESS: From the town of Prospect, Oregon, travel east on
                County Route 992,leading toward Butte Falls, for
2.5 miles to Forest Route 37. Turn onto 37 and continue east, 2.8
miles to Road 3795. Turn left onto 3795 and continue 5.7 miles to
the junction with Forest Road 3795/600.   Turn right onto 600 and
go 0.6 mile to the trailhead. Parking and turn-around space is
adequate.

FEATURES: After 1.5 miles, you reach the junction with the
                5.1 mile Mudjekeewis Trail 1085 (that skirts the
south edge of Kerby Peak with views of the Middle Fork Canyon before re-joining the Tom and Jerry Trail at Mckie Shelter.)   KEEP
LEFT AT THE 1.5 MILE JUNCTION to reach McKie Shelter via the Tom
and Jerry Trail. Water is usually available on the first portion
of the trail and at McKie Camp.   Horse feed is plentiful in the
McKie vicinity. Returning (westbound) on the Tom and Jerry Trail,
a saddle is reached in about 1.5 miles.   Just west of the saddle
look for the trail as it leads southwest. BEWARE OF A TREE BLAZE
ON AN OLD ABANDONED TRAIL THAT LEADS NORTHWEST.

If making a 11.5 mile loop with the Tom and Jerry and the Mudje-
keewis Trails, stay along the west edge of the meadow at McKie
Camp. See beginning of Chapter 6 for Sky Lakes Wilderness information and regulations.

HISTORY: "McKIE SHELTER: (now collapsed), is an old trail camp
          location. The shelter was built between 1934 and 1936
and was named after a sheepherder, Tom McKie." (USFS quote)

RED BLANKET TRAIL #1090. (See map 6 and 7)

TRAIL BEGINS:	-End of Road 6205.	ELEV. 3800'
TRAIL ENDS:	-Stuart Falls Trail 1078.	ELEV. 5000'
DISTANCE:	-3.9 miles, moderate grades.	USE: hiker/horse.
SEASON:	-Usually snow-free June to October. Closed to all use from the end of elk hunting season until April 1 for protection of winter range.	
CONNECTING TR:	-Lucky Camp Tr. 1083, and Stuart Falls Tr. 1078.	
BRING MAPS:	-USFS Butte Falls Ranger Dist., Rogue River N.F.	
	-USFS Sky Lakes Area-Rogue River/Winema Ntl. For.	

ACCESS: From the town of Prospect, Oregon, drive east on
                   County Route 992,leading toward Butte Falls, 1.1
mile   to the junction with Red Blanket Road.   Follow Red Blanket
Road 0.3 mile and turn left onto Forest Road 6205.   Continue on
6205, about 12 miles to the trailhead at the end of the road.

FEATURES: The Red Blanket Trail begins near the southwest
                   corner of Crater Lake National Park.   After 1/4
mile,   look for the large concrete corner post on the left.   The
trail follows along Red Blanket Creek and reaches the Lucky Camp
Trail 1083 in approx. three miles.   Keeping to the left at this
junction brings you to Stuart Falls Trail 1078 in about one mile.
To reach Stuart Falls, keep left for about 1/2 mile.   This is a
popular access route to Sky Lakes Wilderness and Crater Lake National Park.   See beginning of Chapter 6 for Sky Lakes Wilderness
information and regulations.

HISTORY: "RED BLANKET CREEK, MOUNTAIN: Said to have been
                    named in about 1865 after a white man purchased
a large parcel of land from a group of Indians for one red blanket." (USFS quote)

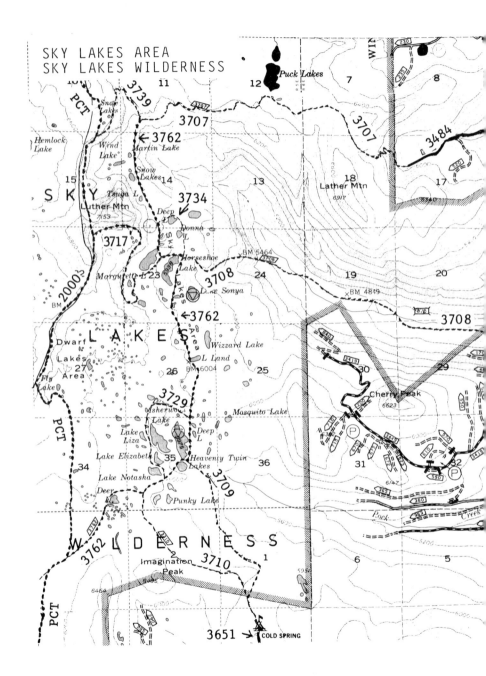

SKY LAKES AREA
SKY LAKES WILDERNESS

92

SKY LAKES TRAIL #3762 and connecting trails. (See map 12)

TRAIL BEGINS: -PCNST South of Deer Lake.   ELEV. 5900'
TRAIL ENDS: -Snow Lakes Trail #3739, Nannie Creek Tr. #3707.
DISTANCE: -6.0 miles, moderate grades. USE: hiker/horse.
SEASON: -June through October.
BRING MAPS: -USFS Sky Lakes Wilderness.
            -USFS Pacific Crest National Scenic Trail-Oregon
             Central Portion.
            -USFS Recreation Opportunity Guide (this trail).
            -USFS Winema National Forest.

ACCESS: The Sky Lakes Trail,once called the Skyline Trail,
            parallels the Pacific Crest through the Sky Lakes
Basin. This intra-wilderness trail departs from the Pacific Crest
Trail south of Deer Lake, and passes the trailhead access trails
of Cold Springs, South Rock Creek, Cherry Creek and Nannie Creek.
This route ends at the junction with Snow Lakes Tr. on the north,
which is not maintained for stock users.

TRAIL LOG-MILEAGE READINGS ARE APPROXIMATE.
Mile 0.6 Deer Lake.
Mile 0.9 Junction (Right) COLD SPRINGS TRAIL #3710.
Mile 1.3 Junction (Left)   South end of ISHERWOOD LOOP TR. #3729.
Mile 1.5 Junction (Right) SOUTH ROCK CREEK TRAIL #3709,
          just past Heavenly Twin Lakes.
Mile 2.0 Junction (Left)   North end of ISHERWOOD LOOP TR. #3729.
Mile 4.0 Junction (Right) CHERRY CREEK TRAIL #3708.
Mile 4.1 Junction (Right) (North end of Trapper Lake), South end
          DONNA LAKE LOOP TR. #3734-NOT MAINTAINED FOR STOCK USE.
Mile 4.4 Junction (Left)   Between Lakes Margurette and Trapper.
          DIVIDE TRAIL #3717, 2.9 miles,elevation gain 600',main-
          tained for stock users,connects to Pacific Crest Trail.
Mile 4.7 Junction (Right) North end-DONNA LAKE LOOP TRAIL #3734.
Mile 5.6 Martin Lake.
Mile 6.0 Junction (Right) NANNIE CREEK TRAIL #3707.
          SNOW LAKES TRAIL #3739 begins from this junction,a 2.3
          mile steep climb to re-join the Pacific Crest Trail.Not
          maintained for stock users. Elevation gain 800'.

Please see beginning of Chapter 6 for Sky Lakes Wilderness information and regulations.

SEVENMILE TRAIL #3703.   (See map 12)

TRAIL BEGINS: -Sevenmile Trailhead Forest Road 3334,ELEV. 5480'
TRAIL ENDS: -Pacific Crest Trail.   ELEV. 5800'
DISTANCE: -1.9 miles, moderate.   USE: hiker/horse.
SEASON: -June through October.
CONNECTING TR. -Pacific Crest National Scenic Trail (PCNST).
BRING MAPS: -USFS Sky Lakes Area-Rogue River/Winema Ntl. For.
                -USFS Winema National Forest.
                -USFS Pacific Crest Trail-Oregon Southern Portion.

ACCESS: This description begins from State Hwy. 140 just
                 east of milepost 43 (43.6 miles east of White
City).   Turn north onto Westside Road (County Route 531), and go
16.9 miles to the junction with Forest Route 33. Follow Route 33,
2.8 miles to a 3-way junction,then go northwest on Road 3334, 5.7
miles to the trailhead at the end of the road.

FEATURES: This 2 mile trail provides a quick and easy ac-
                 cess to the Pacific Crest National Scenic Trail.
From the PCNST, options exist for a side-trip to Ranger Springs,
an entry into Seven Lakes Basin near Devils Peak and Cliff Lake,
or numerous other possibilities.

Ranger Springs is one of the headwater springs that feed the Middle Fork of the Rogue River.   To get there, take Sevenmile Trail
3703 to the junction with the Pacific Crest Trail. Turn right and
go 1/4 mile north to a junction on the left leading another mile
to the springs.

See beginning of Chapter 6 for Sky Lakes Wilderness information
and regulations.

NANNIE CREEK TRAIL #3707. (See map 12)

TRAIL BEGINS:	–End of Forest Road 3484.	ELEV. 6000'
TRAIL ENDS:	–Jnc. Snow Lakes & Sky Lakes Trails.	ELEV. 6000'
DISTANCE:	–4.3 miles.	HIGH POINT 6520'
USE:	–Hikers/horses.	
DIFFICULTY:	–Strenuous, moderate 2.4 miles to Puck Lakes.	
SEASON:	–June through October, mosquitos till mid–August.	
BRING MAPS:	–USFS Winema National Forest.	
	–USFS Sky Lakes Area–Winema/Rogue River Ntl. For.	

ACCESS: This description begins from State Hwy. 140 just
                      east of milepost 43 (43.6 mi. from White City).
Turn north onto Westside Road (County Road 531), and go 12.1 mi.
to the junction with Forest Road 3484 on the left.   Travel north
and west on 3484, about 5.5 miles to the trailhead at the end of
the road.

FEATURES: From the trailhead, the trail climbs up a steep
                      slope and follows the rocky contours through the
heavily forested slopes of Lather Mtn.(Elev. 6917') to the southwest. After coursing across a relatively level basin, the trail
passes the southern shore of Puck Lakes and up through towering
mixed conifer groves. The trail reaches the junction of the Snow
Lakes and Sky Lakes Trails about 0.3 mile south of the Snow Lakes
group.

See the page describing SKY LAKES TRAIL 3762, and the map showing
how it connects with other lakes in Sky Lakes Basin.

Sky Lakes Wilderness information and regulations are noted at the
beginning of Chapter 6.

SNOW LAKES TRAIL #3739.   (See map 12)

TRAIL BEGINS: ⌐Junction of Sky Lakes Trail #3762
                  and Nannie Creek Trail #3707.   ELEV. 5800'
TRAIL ENDS: -Pacific Crest National Scenic Trail ELEV. 6600'
DISTANCE: -2.3 miles, moderate.   USE: hiker/horse.
SEASON: -Summer season: July-Oct.
BRING MAPS: -USFS Sky Lakes Wilderness.
                  -USFS Pacific Crest National Scenic Trail-Oregon
                   Central Portion.
                  -USFS Recreation Opportunity Guide (this trail).
                  -USFS Winema National Forest.

ACCESS: The Snow Lakes trail is an intra-wilderness trail
                  connecting Sky Lakes Trail and Pacific Crest Tr.
It has a rather steep section that is not maintained for stock
use. This trail departs from the northern end of Sky Lakes Trail
at the junction with the Nannie Creek Trail #3707.

FEATURES: The Snow Lakes Tr. begins at an elevation of 5800'
                  as it departs from Sky Lakes Trail.The route ini-
tially climbs gradually along the northern slopes of Sky Lakes
Basin, crossing flower-splashed meadows.   The trail then climbs
steeply up the rock outcrops and windswept ridges offering breath-
taking vistas to the south and east. Gaining nearly 1000 feet in
elevation in just under 1 mile, the trail joins the Pacific Crest
Trail on the backbone of the Cascade Mountain range.   The rugged
scenery and magnificent views along this trail are a vivid reminder of our responsibility to practice minimum impact visitation so
the primitive wilderness environment may remain.   (USFS INFO)

See the page describing SKY LAKES TRAIL 3762, and the map showing
how it connects to other lakes in Sky Lakes Basin.

Please see beginning of Chapter 6 for Sky Lakes Wilderness information and regulations.

CHERRY CREEK NATIONAL RECREATION TRAIL #3708. (See map 12)

TRAIL BEGINS:	–Forest Road 3450.	ELEV. 4600'
TRAIL ENDS:	–Sky Lakes Trail 3762.	ELEV. 6000'
DISTANCE:	–5.3 miles, strenuous.	USE: hiker/horse.
SEASON:	–Usually snow-free June to October. Mosquitos bad until mid-August.	
BRING MAPS:	–USFS Winema National Forest. –Sky Lakes Area-Winema/Rogue River Ntl. Forests.	

ACCESS: FROM WHITE CITY, Oregon, follow mileposts east on State Hwy. 140, 43.6 miles to the junction of Westside Road (County Road 531).. FROM ASHLAND, take Dead Indian Memorial Road (Jackson County 722, Klamath County 533), 36 miles to the junction with State Highway 140. Turn right (east) on 140 and go 6 miles to Westside Road.

Follow Westside Road 11 miles (near milepost 6) to the junction with Road 3450 (on the left). Turn west onto Road 3450 and go 1.6 mile to the trailhead at the end of the road. Trailhead parking and turn-around space is limited.

FEATURES: Although strenuous, this trail is a good access route to the Sky Lakes Wilderness. The Cherry Creek drainage, a U-shaped canyon formed by glaciation, is being proposed as a Research Natural Area. The USFS encourages "horse-back riders to dismount and walk their horses through the (creek) crossings and wet boggy areas."

See the page describing SKY LAKES TRAIL 3762, and the map showing how it connects to other lakes in Sky Lakes Basin.

Cherry Creek Trail became a part of the National Recreation Trail System in 1979. Sky Lakes Wilderness information and regulations are noted at the beginning of Chapter 6.

DIVIDE TRAIL 3717. (See map 12)

TRAIL BEGINS:	-Sky Lakes Trail #3762.	ELEV. 6000'
TRAIL ENDS:	-Pacific Crest National Scenic Trail.	ELEV. 7000'
DISTANCE:	-2.9 miles, moderate grades.	USE: hiker/horse.
SEASON:	-June through October.	
BRING MAPS:	-USFS Sky Lakes Wilderness.	

-USFS Pacific Crest National Scenic Trail-Oregon
  Central Portion.
-USFS Recreation Opportunity Guide (this trail).
-USFS Winema National Forest.

ACCESS: The Divide Trail is an intra wilderness trail con-
               necting Sky Lakes Trail and the Pacific Crest Tr.
Although the trail is steep, it is maintained for stock use.   It
departs from Sky Lakes Trail between Margurette Lake and Trapper
Lake, and climbs to the west to join the Pacific Crest Trail.

FEATURES: The Divide Trail begins at an elevation of 6000'
               as it departs from the Sky Lakes Trail. The route
climbs gradually along the southwestern shores of Lake Margurette
crossing flower-splashed meadows,then climbs steeply up the rock
outcrops and wind swept ridges of Luther Mountain.The trail gains
1000 feet in elevation in just under 3 miles. The rugged scenery
and magnificent vistas along this trail are a vivid reminder of
our responsibility to practice minimum impact visitation so the
primitive wilderness environment may remain. (USFS info)

See the page describing SKY LAKES TRAIL 3762, and the map showing
how it connects to other lakes in Sky Lakes Basin.

Please see beginning of Chapter 6 for Sky Lakes Wilderness information and regulations.

SOUTH ROCK CREEK TRAIL #3709. (See map 12)

TRAIL BEGINS:	–Cold Springs Trail, Forest Road 3651, ELEV. 5600'
TRAIL ENDS:	–Sky Lakes Trail 3762. ELEV. 6000'
	(At Heavenly Twin Lakes).
DISTANCE:	–1.6 mile·
USE:	–Hiker/horse. EASY.
SEASON:	–Usually snow-free June to October.
CONNECTING TR:	–Cold Springs Trail 3710, Sky Lakes Trail 3762.
BRING MAPS:	–USFS Winema National Forest.
	–USFS Rec. Opportunity Guides, Winema Ntl. For.
	–Sky Lakes Area-Rogue River/Winema Ntl. Forests.

ACCESS: FROM WHITE CITY, Oregon, follow mileposts east on State Hwy. 140, 40.9 miles to the junction of Lost Creek Road 3651. If driving FROM ASHLAND, take Dead Indian Memorial Road (Jackson County 722, Klamath County 533) to State Highway 140, and turn right 3.1 miles to Road 3651.

Turn onto Road 3651 and go 10.5 miles to the COLD SPRINGS TRAIL-HEAD at the end of the road.

After about 0.7 mile along the Cold Springs Trail, the SOUTH ROCK CREEK Trail begins on the right and continues about 1.6 mile to the Sky Lakes Trail near Heavenly Twin Lakes. From here, a loop trip back to Cold Springs Campground is possible by taking a left turn (southwest) on the Sky Lakes Trail and going 1.0 mile to the junction with Cold Springs Trail 3710 on the left. Follow Cold Springs Trail, 2.7 miles southeast to the campground on Road 3651.

See the page describing SKY LAKES TRAIL 3762, and the map showing how it connects to other trails in Sky Lakes Basin.

Mosquitos are bad, especially at Cold Springs Campground, usually until mid-August. Sky Lakes Wilderness information and regulations are noted at the beginning of Chapter 6.

COLD SPRINGS TRAIL #3710.   (See map 12)

TRAIL BEGINS:	-Cold Springs Camp, Forest Road 3651. ELEV. 5600'
TRAIL ENDS:	-Sky Lakes Trail 3762. ELEV. 6000'
	(Near Lake Notasha).
DISTANCE:	-2.7 mile. EASY
USE:	-Hiker/horse.
SEASON:	-Usually snow-free June to October.
	Mosquitos bad till about mid-August.
CONNECTING TR.	-South Rock Creek Trail 3709 and Sky Lakes Trail 3762.
BRING MAPS:	-USFS Winema National Forest.
	-USFS Rec. Opportunity Guides, Winema Ntl. For.
	-Sky Lakes Area-Rogue River/Winema Ntl. Forests.

ACCESS: FROM WHITE CITY, Oregon, follow mileposts east
               on State Hwy. 140, 40.9 miles to the junction of
Lost Creek Road 3651.   If driving FROM ASHLAND, take Dead Indian
Memorial Road (Jackson County 722, Klamath County 533) to State
Highway 140 and turn right for 3.1 miles to Road 3651.

Turn onto Road 3651 and go 10.5 miles to COLD SPRINGS TRAILHEAD
at the end of the road.

After about 0.7 mile on the Cold Springs Trail, keep left at the
junction with the South Rock Creek Trail and continue on the Cold
Springs Trail to the Sky Lakes Trail near Lake Notasha.

FEATURES: This is a short and easy access to Dwarf Lakes-
                 Sky Lakes Basin.   A loop trip back to Cold Spr.
Campground is possible by turning right (northeast) onto the Sky
Lakes Trail and go one mile to the junction with South Rock Creek
Trail 3709 on the right just beyond Heavenly Twin Lakes.   Follow
3709 southeast 1.6 miles to its junction with Cold Springs Trail,
and turn left and go 0.7 miles back to Cold Springs Camp.

See the page describing SKY LAKES TRAIL 3762, and the map showing
how it connects to other lakes in Sky Lakes Basin.

Sky Lakes Wilderness information and regulations are noted at the
beginning of Chapter 6.

TWIN PONDS TRAIL #3715, Winema National Forest.   (See map 16)

TRAIL BEGINS: -Fourmile Lake Campground.   ELEV. 5700'
TRAIL ENDS: -Pacific Crest National Scenic Trail. ELEV. 5900'
DISTANCE: -2.5 miles. EASY
SEASON: -June to October. USE: hiker/horse.
CONNECTING TR. -Pacific Crest Trail, Twin Ponds Trail #993.
BRING MAPS: -Sky Lakes Area-Rogue River/Winema Ntl. Forests.
                -USFS Recreation Opportunity Guides.

ACCESS: FOURMILE LAKE.   From White City, follow mile-
                posts on Hwy. 140, 35.7 miles to the junction of
Road 3661. Go 5.6 miles north on 3661 to a road junction at Fourmile Lake. Turn left and go 0.1 mi. to a spur leading left to the
trailhead at a PARKING FACILITY FOR ALL TRAILS.

Beyond the trailhead, pass the link leading left to the Rye Spur
and Badger Lake Trails. KEEP RIGHT toward the Pacific Crest Trail

FEATURES: In the vicinity of Fourmile Lake, Trail #3715 is
                 often swampy or partly submerged.   After pass-
ing Squaw Lake, it joins the Pacific Crest Trail about 2.5 miles
northwest of the trailhead.

TWIN PONDS TRAIL #993,managed by the Rogue River National Forest,
continues northwestward for 3.5 miles down Fourbit Creek. Summit
Lake is reached within the first 0.5 mi., Twin Ponds 2.0 mile beyond, and 1.0 mile further to the lower trailhead on Road 3760.
These waters sometimes dry-up in late summer.

Trail 993 has a very rocky surface in places but is much easier
to follow than in previous years.   In a couple of places, it is
still suggested to look carefully for rock cairns and tree blazes

ACCESS TO LOWER TRAILHEAD, TRAIL #993.   From White City OR,
follow mileposts on Hwy. 140, 28.6 miles to County Road 821. Turn
north onto 821 and go 8.8 mi. to where Forest Route 37 turns east
Follow Route 37, 1.5 mi. to Road 3760 on the right. Go 4.4 miles
on 3760 to the trailhead at the end of the road. ELEV. 4800'

Trails #3715 and 993 follow the route of the 1864 Fort Klamath-
Jacksonville Military Wagon Road.

MT. McLOUGHLIN

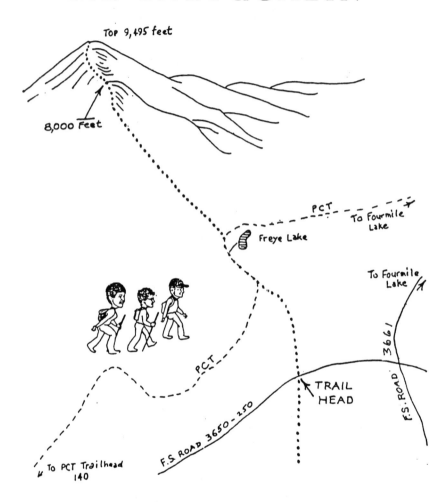

Top 9,495 feet

8,000 Feet

PCT
To Fourmile Lake

Freye Lake

To Fourmile Lake

PCT

3661

TRAIL HEAD

F.S. ROAD

F.S. ROAD 3650-250

To PCT Trailhead 140

Mt. McLOUGHLIN TRAIL #3716. (See Map 16)

TRAIL BEGINS:	-Trailhead, Forest Road 3650.	ELEV. 5580'
TRAIL ENDS:	-Mt. McLoughlin summit.	ELEV. 9495'
DISTANCE:	-About 5.5 miles, strenuous-time up 4 to 5 hours.	
SEASON:	-July thru September. Hiker only	
CONNECTING TR.	-Pacific Crest National Scenic Trail.	
BRING MAPS:	-USFS Sky Lakes Area-Rogue River/Winema Ntl. For.	
	-USFS Winema National Forest.	
	-USFS "Mt. McLoughlin" information leaflets.	
	-USGS Mount McLoughlin, 7.5 minute series.	

ACCESS: From White City, Oregon, follow mileposts east on State Hwy. 140, 35.7 miles to the junction of Forest Road 3661. Turn left and follow mileposts on 3661, 2.9 miles to the junction with Road 3650. Turn left on 3650 and continue 0.3 mile to the trailhead and parking area.

ROUTE: The Mt. McLoughlin Trail meets the Pacific Crest (PCNST) Trail in about 1 mile. Turn right (N.W.) and follow the PCNST, 1/2 mile to where the Mt. McLoughlin Trail continues its northwesterly ascent to the summit. The trail is not maintained beyond the tree line. ON THE WAY UP, NOTICE THAT THE ROUTE PARALLELS A RIDGE THAT SLOPES IN AN EAST TO WEST DIRECTION.

ON THE RETURN TRIP.....KEEP THE SAME RELATIONSHIP WITH THE RIDGE! INFORMAL PATHS CAN BE MISLEADING! NOTE THAT THE RIDGE RUNS MORE EAST THAN IT DOES SOUTH. THERE IS NO TRAIL OUT FROM THE SOUTH SLOPES OF THE MOUNTAIN OTHER THAN THE PACIFIC CREST TRAIL! WATCH ALSO FOR THE JUNCTIONS WITH THE PACIFIC CREST TRAIL. The Mcloughlin Trail follows the Pacific Crest Trail southeast for 1/2 mile and turns southeast to the Road 3650 Trailhead.

From the summit; Mt. Shasta, the Klamath Basin, Rogue River Valley, Crater Lake Rim and points into Central Oregon come into view. A fire lookout building was once located at the summit.

103

PRECAUTIONS: (Quotes from USFS -HIKING THE McLOUGHLIN TRAIL)
"Remember.....Every year someone gets lost hiking Mt. McLoughlin.
This could be prevented by following three basic rules: 1). Never
travel alone. 2). Stay with your group.   3). Stay on the trail.
Allow plenty of time for your climb (average 8 hours round trip).
Travel only during the daylight hours and don't attempt to travel
during unsettled weather or when storms are forecast. Wilderness
areas challenge your skills in traversing using map and compass."

"BE AWARE OF THE SYMPTOMS OF HYPOTHERMIA. Hypothermia is a rapid
and progressive mental and physical collapse, resulting from low-
ering the inner temperature of the body.   Left untreated, hypothermia can result in death.   Briefly, the symptoms to watch for
are: uncontrollable shivering; vague, slow speech; memory lapses;
immobile or fumbling hands; frequent stumbling; drowsiness and
apparent exhaustion. The best treatment is to eliminate exposure.
Get the victim out of the wind and rain. Strip off all wet clothing and put him in a sleeping bag with another person........also
stripped.   Keep the victim awake and give warm drinks.   If possible, build a warming fire."

BRING DRINKING WATER: THERE IS NO WATER ALONG THE SUMMIT TRAIL.
FOOD: "High energy foods such as nuts, raisins, hard candy,
fruit, fruit juices and grain products are excellent choices."
CLOTHING AND EQUIPMENT: "Vibram-soled hiking boots, extra wool
socks, light/warm clothing (preferably wool) that can be layered,
raingear, gloves, and hat. EQUIPMENT: MAP AND COMPASS, FIRST AID
KIT with matches, moleskin or tape for blisters, goggles or sun-
glasses, suntan cream and a flashlight for emergencies."

NOTE: The Mt. McLoughlin trail can also be accessed by hiking
the Pacific Crest Tr. about 4 mi. north from its Hwy. 140 Trailhead, located between mileposts 32 and 33 on State Highway 140.
Sky Lakes Wilderness information and regulations are noted at the
beginning of Chapter 6.

<u>BADGER LAKE TRAIL #3759</u>   (See Maps 16,17)

<u>TRAIL BEGINS:</u>	-Fourmile Lake Campground. <u>ELEV.</u> 5700'
<u>TRAIL ENDS:</u>	-Pacific Crest National Scenic Trail. <u>ELEV.</u> 5950'
<u>DISTANCE:</u>	-Woodpecker Lake 1.3 mile, Badger Lake 1.7 mile, Long Lake 3.7 mile. Easy grades. Hiker/horse.
<u>SEASON:</u>	-June to October, mosquitos until mid-August.
<u>CONNECTING TR.</u>	-Rye Spur 3771, Red Lake 987, unmaintained Lost Creek 3712.
<u>BRING MAPS:</u>	-USFS Sky Lakes Area-Rogue River/Winema Ntl. For.
	-USFS Winema National Forest.

<u>ACCESS:</u>   From White City, follow mileposts on State Highway 140, 35.7 miles to the junction with Forest Road 3661. Turn north onto 3661 and go 5.6 miles to the junction at Fourmile Lake.

<u>A PARKING AREA FOR ALL TRAILS</u> can be reached by turning left for 0.1 mile, then left again to the parking area and trailhead.   NO FEE IS REQUIRED TO PARK AT THE TRAILHEAD.

Beyond the trailhead, at a trail junction, turn left onto a link trail leading to the Rye Spur Trail. Turn left along the Rye Spur Trail and in a short distance cross the Cascade Canal to the BADGER LAKE TRAILHEAD.

<u>FEATURES:</u>   This is an easy access route into Sky Lakes Wilderness leading north to Woodpecker,Badger,Lilly Pond, and Long Lakes before ending at the junction with the Pacific Crest National Scenic Trail. Total 1-way distance 5.2 miles from Fourmile Lake Campground.

Turning southward on the Pacific Crest Trail to the Twin Ponds Trail and back to Four Mile Lake Campground makes for an adventurous day trip, total loop distance about 13 miles.

Sky Lakes Wilderness information and regulations are noted at the beginning of Chapter 6.

CHAPTER 7 - MOUNTAIN LAKES WILDERNESS

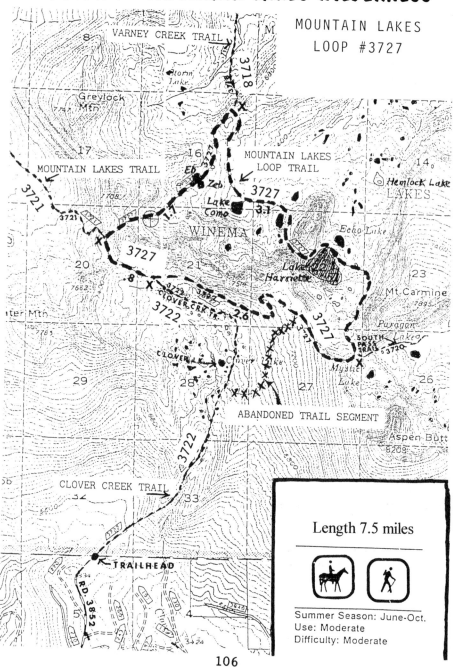

MOUNTAIN LAKES
LOOP #3727

VARNEY CREEK TRAIL

Storm Lake

Greylock Mtn

MOUNTAIN LAKES TRAIL

MOUNTAIN LAKES LOOP TRAIL

3727

Hemlock Lake

LAKES

3721

3721

1.7

Eb

Zeb

Lake Como

3.1

WINEMA

Echo Lake

3727

Lake Harriette

Mt. Carmine

.8

CLOVER CRK TR

3722

3727

2.6

3727

Paragon

3722

SOUTH PASS TRAIL

3720

CLOVER L.

Clover Lake

Mystic Lake

ABANDONED TRAIL SEGMENT

Aspen Butt

3722

CLOVER CREEK TRAIL

33

TRAILHEAD

RD. 3852

Length 7.5 miles

Summer Season: June-Oct.
Use: Moderate
Difficulty: Moderate

106

MOUNTAIN LAKES WILDERNESS AREA.   (See map 17)

<u>HISTORY:</u>   "In 1930 Mountain Lakes was established as one of the
first three primitive areas in the Pacific Northwest
Region.   In 1940 the original 13,444 acres was increased to
23,071 acres and the name was changed to the Mountain Lakes Wild
Area.   The Mountain Lakes became a part of the National Wilderness System in 1964." (Quote: USFS Winema National Forest)

<u>FEATURES:</u>   Most of the area is above 6000 ft. elevation. The
"hub" of the maintained trail system is the Mountain
Lakes Loop Trail that circles the old volcanic caldera rim in the
heart of the wilderness. It is accessed by the Varney Creek Trail
3718 from the north, Mountain Lakes Trail 3721 from the west and
Clover Creek Trail 3722 from the south.   Eb and Zeb Lakes, Lake
Como, Lake Harriette and Clover Lake are just a few of the high-
lights on the loop trail.   Aspen Butte (elevation 8208') is the
highest point in the wilderness.

<u>REGULATIONS.</u>   "To protect the wilderness resource, the follow-
ing regulations are enforced: .

1. Hiking and camping group size is limited to 10 people and/or
   stock in any combination.
2. Hikers must camp at least 100 feet from lakeshores, streams
   and springs.
3. Pack and saddle stock should stay at least 200 feet away from
   all water sources,except when traveling on established trails.
4. Campers with pack and saddle stock must camp at least 200 feet
   from lakeshores, streams and springs.
5. Bicycles, motorbikes, and other mechanized equipment are not
   allowed within the wilderness area. Please contact the Klamath Ranger District Office for information on areas designated
   for these and other recreation opportunities."
   (Quote: Winema National Forest-Klamath Ranger District)

VARNEY CREEK TRAIL #3718.   (See map 17)

TRAIL BEGINS:	–End of Forest Road 3664.	ELEV. 5600'
TRAIL ENDS:	–Mountain Lakes Loop Trail 3727.	ELEV. 6630'
DISTANCE:	–4.4 miles, moderate. USE: hikers/horses.	
SEASON:	–Usually snow-free June through October, carry insect repellant during early summer months.	
BRING MAPS:	–USFS Recreation Opportunity Guide, Varney Cr. Tr.	
	–USFS Mountain Lakes Wilderness.	
	–USFS Winema National Forest.	

ACCESS: From White City, Oregon, follow mileposts on State Highway 140 to the following:
NEAR MILEPOST 48.   Turn south onto Forest Road 3637 and continue 1.8 miles to Forest Road 3664.   Turn left and continue 2 miles to the trailhead at the end of the road.

FEATURES: Trail 3718 maintains a steady uphill grade as it follows Varney Creek into the wilderness area. The "hub" of the maintained trail system is the Mountain Lakes Loop Trail 3727, forming a 7.5 mile loop around the old caldera rim in the heart of the wilderness.   This loop trail can also be accessed by Mountain Lakes Trail 3721 from the west and Clover Cr. Trail 3722 from the south.   THE SOUTH END OF THE LOOP TRAIL HAS BEEN REROUTED   THROUGH MAP SECTIONS 21 and 22 AT THE   7000' LEVEL AND NO LONGER DROPS DOWN TO CLOVER LAKE.   THE CLOVER CREEK TRAIL HAS BEEN EXTENDED NORTHWEST OF CLOVER LAKE TO JOIN THE LOOP TRAIL REROUTE.   (THE SECTION OF THE OLD LOOP TRAIL LEADING EAST   FROM CLOVER LAKE TO THE LOOP TRAIL HAS BEEN ABANDONED.)   See beginning of Chapter 7 for information and wilderness regulations.

MOUNTAIN LAKES TRAIL #3721.   (See map 17)

TRAIL BEGINS:	-Forest Road 3660.	ELEV. 5200'
TRAIL ENDS:	-Mountain Lakes Loop Trail 3727,	ELEV. 7400'
DISTANCE:	-5.1 miles. USE: hiker/horse. Moderate. HIKERS can also access the trail from Rainbow Bay Picnic Area, across from the restrooms.	
SEASON:	-Usually snow-free June through October.	
BRING MAPS:	-USFS Winema National Forest Recreation Map/Guide. -USFS Mountain Lakes Wilderness map.	

ACCESS: Follow mileposts (numbering from WHITE CITY) on State Hwy. 140 to mile 37.7 at the junction with Dead Indian Memorial Road (Klamath County Rte. 533). If using the UPPER ACCESS where parking is limited and there is no turn-around facility, turn right onto Dead Indian Memorial Road and go 0.1 mi to Road 3610. Turn left onto Road 3610, and go 0.8 mile to Road 3660. The trailhead is 0.8 mile up Road 3660.

Using the LOWER, Lake of the Woods facility where horses are not allowed: across from the restrooms at the Rainbow Bay Picnic Area, follow the Family Loop(Mtn.Lake) Trail a short distance, crossing the Sunset Trail and Road 3704. A junction is soon reached at the beginning of the Family Trail Loops, and where MOUNTAIN LAKES TR. turns right to cross Dead Indian Memorial Rd. and on to the upper Mountain Lakes Trail access on Road 3660.

FEATURES: The trail climbs up Seldom Creek through tranquil meadows and along volcanic outcrops. The scenery gradually changes to higher elevation mountain hemlock/subalpine fir communities before ending at Mountain Lakes Loop Trail #3727.

Mountain Lakes Loop Trail makes an 7.5 mile loop around the old caldera rim in the heart of the wilderness.The loop trail is also accessed by Varney Creek Trail 3718 from the north and Clover Cr. Trail 3722 from the south.   THE SOUTH END OF THE LOOP TRAIL HAS BEEN REROUTED THROUGH MAP SECTIONS 21 and 22 AT THE 7000' LEVEL, AND NO LONGER DROPS TO CLOVER CREEK TRAIL SOUTH OF CLOVER LAKE. THE CLOVER CREEK TRAIL HAS BEEN EXTENDED NORTHWEST OF CLOVER LAKE TO JOIN THE LOOP TRAIL REROUTE.   See beginning of Chapter 7 for Mountain Lakes historical notes and regulations.

CLOVER CREEK TRAIL #3722. (See map 17)

TRAIL BEGINS:	-End of Forest Road 3852.	ELEV.	5600'
TRAIL ENDS:	-Mountain Lakes Loop Trail 3727.	ELEV.	7000'
DISTANCE:	-About 3.6 miles. Moderate grades.		
SEASON:	-Usually snow-free June-Oct. Hiker/horse.		
BRING MAPS:	-USFS Mountain Lakes Wilderness.		
	-USFS Winema National Forest.		
	-USFS Recreation Opportunity Guide, Clover Creek Trail 3722.		

ACCESS: From Interstate Hwy. 5, Ashland-Klamath Falls Exit 14, travel 0.6 mi. east on State Highway 66 to the junction with Dead Indian Memorial Road(Jackson County Route 722, Klamath County 533). Turn left and follow this road 28.3 miles to the junction with Clover Creek Road (Klamath County Route 603). Travel southeast on Clover Creek Road, 5.8 miles to the junction with Forest Road 3852 on the left. Turn onto Road 3852 and go 3.3 miles to the trailhead at the end of the road.

FEATURES: It is 2.3 miles up the trail to an older,abandoned section of the Mountain Lakes Loop Trail heading east.   The Clover Creek Trail has been extended from this point, passing Clover Lake and junctions WITH A RELOCATED SECTION OF THE MOUNTAIN LAKES LOOP TRAIL 1.1 MILE FURTHER   THROUGH MAP SECTIONS 20 and 21, elevation 7000'

Mountain Lakes Loop Trail 3727 is a 7.5 mile loop around an old caldera rim in the heart of the wilderness and can also be accessed via Mountain Lakes Trail 3721 from the west, and Varney Creek Trail 3718 from the north.

See beginning of Chapter 7 for Mountain Lakes historical notes and regulations.

MOUNTAIN LAKES LOOP TRAIL #3727. (See map 17)

DISTANCE: -7.5 miles,moderate grade. USE: hiker/horse.
SEASON: -June to October. ELEV. 6900-7400'
CONNECTING TR. -Mountain Lakes #3721; Varney Creek #3718, South
                   Pass Trail #3720 and Clover Creek Trail #3722.
BRING MAPS: -USFS Recreation Opportunity Guide-Trail #3727.
                   -USFS Mountain Lakes Wilderness.
                   -USFS Winema National Forest.

ACCESS: This trail can be accessed by entering the wil-
                   derness from any of the 3 Mountain Lakes Trail-
heads; Varney Creek, Clover Creek, and Mountain Lakes(See text).

FEATURES: "Following this trail clockwise from the junction
                   of the Loop Trail with Mountain Lakes trail, the
Loop Trail climbs gently through a pass north of Whiteface Peak
and descends into the caldera between crystal blue Lake Eb & Lake
Zeb.   Past the junction with Varney Creek Trail, the Loop Trail
passes along gentle slopes north of Lake Como and many small wilderness lakes. The trail then climbs a short steep pass to skirt
the windblown waters of Lake Harriette, the largest lake in the
Mountain Lakes Wilderness." The loop passes the junction with the
SOUTH PASS TRAIL, that leads 1.9 mile to South Pass Lake after it
passes Mystic Lake and Paragon Lake.

The Mountain Lakes Loop Trail continues "meandering up the lower
slopes of Mt. Carmine before steeply climbing the southern Caldera rim. The views of the wilderness lakes and peaks, as well as
vast southern vistas, are spectacular from this vantage point.
The route then switchbacks down a rugged rock scree,past the junction with the Clover Creek Trail, then continues west to the junction with the Mountain Lakes Trail at an elevation of about 7200'
From here you have a perfect view of Mt. McLoughlin.The wet meadows and lakeshores along this route require the practice of minimum trace visitation to endure." (USFS quote)

See beginning of Chapter 7 for Mountain Lakes historical notes &
regulations.

CHAPTER 8 - FISH LAKE - LAKE OF THE WOODS

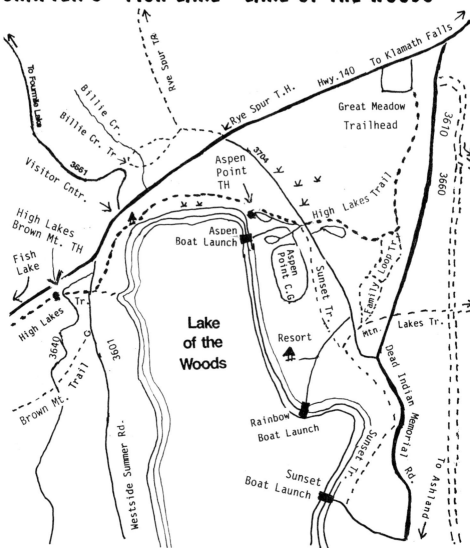

SEE FISH LAKE TRAIL MAP ON PAGE 116

TRAILS FROM RAINBOW BAY PICNIC AREA, LAKE OF THE WOODS.

Usually snow-free June through October, for hikers and bikers.

The FAMILY LOOP TRAIL begins just after the entrance to Rainbow Bay Picnic Area, on the LEFT across from the restroom. Follow the trail a short distance to the junction with the SUNSET TRAIL that leads RIGHT about 1.5 mi. to Sunset Campground OR leads LEFT to Aspen Point Campground in about 0.5 mile.

Family loop trail continues, crosses Road 3704 and soon meets the junction on the RIGHT with Mountain Lakes Trail #3727 that leads into Mountain Lakes Wilderness. Keep LEFT a short distance to the beginning of the FAMILY LOOP TRAIL where both ends of the loop reach the HIGH LAKES TRAIL in less than 1.0 mile.

From here the High Lakes Trail leads RIGHT about 1.0 mi. to Great Meadow Trailhead on Highway 140, OR leads left to the Aspen Point Campground in about 0.5 mile. You may wish to return to Rainbow Bay Picnic Area, leaving Aspen Point Campground along the Sunset Trail, back to the Family Loop Trail.

Please refer to the map on the previous page for the above trails and others in the area.

<u>HIGH LAKES TRAIL.</u>   (See map on Page 112)

<u>TRAIL BEGINS:</u> -WEST TRAILHEAD-Fish Lake,Hwy 140 near milepost 30.
<u>TRAIL ENDS:</u>   -EAST TRAILHEAD-Great Meadow-140 near milepost 37.
<u>DIFFICULTY:</u>   -Easy for hikers/bikers between Great Meadow and
                Brown Mountain Trailheads. Moderate for hikers
                and bikers between Brown Mountain and Fish lake
                Trailheads. Bikes are not allowed on the PCNST.
<u>SEASON:</u>   -May through October.
<u>CONNECTING TR.</u>-Family Loop,Sunset, Pacific Crest,Fish Lake Trails.
<u>MAPS, INFO:</u>   -Rogue River and Winema National Forest Offices.

<u>DISTANCES:</u>   Mileages from Fish Lake Trailhead ..with numbers in
parenthesis = the distance from Great Meadow.

FISH LAKE BOAT RAMP PARKING AREA...........0 (9.3)   <u>ELEV. 4634'</u>
JUNCTION FISH LAKE TRAIL...................1 (8.0)
JUNCTION PACIFIC CREST TRAIL...............2 (7.0)
BROWN MTN. TRAILHEAD, ROAD 3640............6 (3.0)
ASPEN POINT CAMPGROUND-TRAILHEAD...........7 (1.5)
GREAT MEADOW REST AREA-TRAILHEAD...........9 (0.0)   <u>ELEV. 4949'</u>

<u>FEATURES:</u> The High Lakes Trail travels through 2.5 miles of lava
flows and groves of aspen and fir. You can also experience views
of Mt. McLoughlin and Pelican Butte. Interpretive signs indicate
geological, wildlife and botanical features. A map at the beginning of Chapter 8 shows loops and connection opportunities with
other trails.

Pack and saddle stock are not allowed on the High Lakes Trail ex-
cept for 1.0 mi. between the Pacific Crest Trail junction and the
Fish Lake Trail junction.   Stock users should take the <u>FISH LAKE
TRAIL</u> to the tethering area provided on the east side of the lake.
Pack and saddle stock are not allowed elsewhere in the Fish Lake
Resort area.

<u>CONSIDERATIONS:</u>
If you choose to do the route one way with a car shuttle, it is
easier to begin at an east trailhead,as Lake of the Woods is more
than 300 feet higher than Fish Lake. CARRY WATER.

RYE SPUR TRAIL #3771. (See maps 16 and 17)

TRAIL BEGINS:	-Fourmile Lake Campground.	ELEV. 5750'
TRAIL ENDS:	-State Hwy. 140, near milepost 36.	ELEV. 5000'
DISTANCE:	-6.1 miles, Season: July-October.	
USE:	-Hikers, horses. Motor bikes allowed, but beginning riders may find lower 1.5 mi. too steep.	
BRING MAPS:	-USFS Winema Ntl. Forest/Rec. Opportunity Guide.	

ACCESS: From White City,OR,follow mileposts on State Highway 140, 35.7 mile to the jnc. with Road 3661. UPPER TRAILHEAD: Turn left (north) onto 3661 and go 5.6 miles to the signed PARKING AREA FOR ALL TRAILS, at Fourmile Lake Campground. South of a trail sign, a trail leads east, crossing Road 3661, to the jnc. with Rye Spur Trail,just south of the dam at the southeast end of the lake.Turn right (south) to continue toward the lower trailhead.

LOWER TRAILHEAD: From the above junction of Highway 140 and Road 3661, continue east on Hwy.140, 0.4 mile,just beyond milepost 36, and turn left (north) onto a road track paralleling Hwy.140. Make an immediate right turn leading toward RYE SPUR TRAILHEAD.The one mile BILLIE CREEK NATURE TRAIL, for hikers and horses only,is located 1000ft. up the trail and loops through stands of ponderosa pine, white fir and other coniferous trees. It crosses Billie Cr. in two locations. Decayed logs from past logging activities provide food and cover for wildlife. After passing Billie Cr.Trail, Rye Spur Trail continues about 6 mi. to Fourmile Lake Campground.

HIKERS would benefit mostly by hiking 3.4 mi.from the upper trailhead to the viewpoint and return. From the viewpoint, there are views of Pelican Butte,Mountain Lakes Wilderness and of the fault systems below, leading north into Sky Lakes Wilderness and south into California.You could also return to the campground by hiking beyond the viewpoint to the Cascade Canal and turning left(northeast) along the canal road. Total loop distance 9.0 miles.

South of the Cascade Canal, Rye Spur Trail continues,crossing Rd. 3633, and 0.9 more miles to the junction with BILLIE CREEK NATURE TRAIL, for hikers and horses only. Keep left and go about 1000ft. to Rye Spur lower trailhead. Rye Spur Trail,a portion of the former Oregon Skyline Trail, is maintained by "Desert Trail Riders" of Klamath Falls.

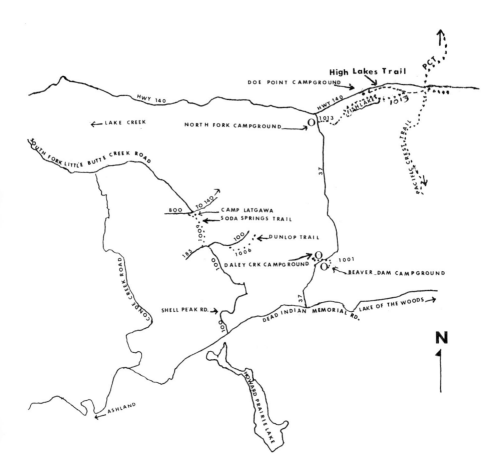

<u>FISH LAKE TRAIL #1013.</u>   (See map on page 116)

TRAIL BEGINS: -North Fork Campground,Forest Route 37-ELEV. 4560'
TRAIL ENDS: -High Lakes Trail #6200   ELEV. 4950'
DISTANCE: -4.0 miles (one way) moderate,May-October.
USE: -Hikers/mountain bikes. Bikes not allowed on PCT!
BRING MAPS: -USFS Ashland Ranger Dist.-Rogue River Ntl. Forest.
    -USFS Pacific Crest Trail-Oregon Southern Portion.
    -USFS Recreation Opportunity Guide-(this trail).

ACCESS: LOWER TRAILHEAD: From the junction of Highways 62 and 140 in White City, drive about 28 miles on Hwy. 140 to the Junction with Forest Route 37 on the right. Turn right onto Route 37 and go 1.0 mile to NORTH FORK CAMPGROUND. The trail head is on the left (east side) of Route 37.

FEATURES: From the trailhead at North Fork Campground, the trail follows the North Fork of Little Butte Creek and after 0.5 mi., a side trail leads right to Fish Lake Dam. The main trail turns left and follows the north shore of Fish Lake. The picnic areas at DOE POINT and FISH LAKE campgrounds are good midpoints to begin a hike either direction on the trail. Continuing through these campgrounds, the trail leads past Fish Lake Resort, skirts the end of the lake and heads east through a forest with large openings of basalt lava. After 4.0 mi. the trail ends at the junction with High Lakes Trail 2600. If you continue EAST on the High Lakes Trail, at 0.6 miles you can see where water from the Cascade Canal disappears into a lava tube and enters Fish Lk. one mile away.The PCNST is 0.4 miles further(Bicycles prohibited).

TO BEGIN AT THE PCNST SUMMIT TRAILHEAD: Drive EAST on Highway 140 just beyond milepost 32 to Summit Parking Area on the left. Hike the PCNST south crossing Highway 140 and go 0.5 mile to the junction with HIGH LAKE TRAIL. Go WEST on High Lakes Trail ONLY 1.0 mile and look for the Fish Lake Trail on the left (South), leading 4.0 miles to the lower trailhead on Forest Route 37.

Pack and Saddle stock are not permitted in the recreation area at Fish Lake or on Fish Lake and High Lakes Trails except between the PCNST and a tethering area/campsite at the east end of Fish Lake. Stock can be led via the posted path to the lakeshore.

117

PACIFIC CREST NATIONAL SCENIC TRAIL-HWY. 140 TO FOREST ROAD 700.
(See maps 16 and 23)

TRAIL BEGINS: -PCNST Summit Trailhead MP 32 Hwy. 140   ELEV. 5100'
TRAIL ENDS   -Forest Road 700.   ELEV. 5200'
DISTANCE: -10.6 miles (one way) MODERATE.
SEASON: -June through October. USE: Hiker/horse.
CONNECTING TR:-High Lakes and Brown Mountain Trails.
BRING MAPS: -USFS Pacific Crest Trail-Oregon Southern Portion.
              -USFS Ashland Ranger Dist.-Rogue River Ntl. Forest.
              -USFS Recreation Opportunity Guide.

FEATURES: CARRY WATER- There are no sources along the way!
              Beginning from the Pacific Crest Trailhead on Hwy.
              140,a 0.2 mile access trail leads to the PCNST. At
this junction, turn left (SOUTH) and follow the trail along the
Cascade Canal for 0.5 mile to Hwy. 140. The trail crosses the Hwy.
and continues 0.5 miles to the junction with High Lakes Trail. It
is about 1.6 miles to the Fish Lake Resort area to the west.

Continuing south, the trail begins a 5.0 mile traverse over Brown
Mountain lava flows (on a cinder trail surface), gaining 800 ft.
in elevation. Once leaving the lava flows, the trail enters a
dense conifer forest. Solomon's seal, prince's pine, and huckle-
berries blanket the forest floor. A small campsite is reached
just prior to the junction with the Brown Mountain Trail. (8.6
mile point). From this junction, the trail continues south another 2 miles to Forest Road 700. This is the ending point for
this hike.

Along this section of trail, there are good views of Brown Mtn.,
Robinson Butte and Mt. McLoughlin. (Excerpts USFS Recreation Opportunity Guide).

Some folks may wish to extend the trip to the trailhead on Dead
Indian Memorial Road, 1.9 trail miles further south. Just 800 ft.
south of Rd.700, a short side-trail leaves the PCNST to the SOUTH
BROWN MOUNTAIN SHELTER. A WATER PUMP HAS BEEN INSTALLED AT THIS
LOCATION.

-continued

HWY.140 ACCESS   From Ashland Interstate 5 Exit 14,   drive east on Highway 66, 0.6 mile to Dead Indian Memorial Road (Jackson County Route 722, Klamath County 533).   Turn onto this road and go 22 miles to the junction with Forest Route 37. Turn left onto Route 37 and proceed 8 miles to the junction with Highway 140. Turn right onto 140 and go 4.2 miles to Forest Rd. 3650. Turn left onto Rd. 3650 and an immediate left onto Road 010 leading to the Pacific Crest Summit Trailhead. A short 0.2 mi. access trail leads to the Pacific Crest Trail.

RD. 700 ACCESS   From Ashland Interstate 5 Exit 14,   drive east on Highway 66, 0.6 mile to Dead Indian Memorial Road (Jackson County Route 722, Klamath County 533).   Turn onto this road and go 26.5 miles to Forest Road 3720. Turn left onto 3720 and go 2 miles to Road 700. Turn right onto 700 and continue 0.4 mile to where the PCNST crosses the road.   Parking is available between the Road 500 spur and the trail.

DEAD INDIAN MEMORIAL ROAD ACCESS: From Ashland Interstate 5 Exit 14,drive east on Highway 66, 0.6 mile to Dead Indian Memorial Rd. (Jackson County Route 722, Klamath County 533). Travel left onto this road, 27.2 miles to the Pacific Crest Trail parking area, at Pederson Snow Park.

SHUTTLE ARRANGEMENTS:
Driving distance between Pederson Park-PCT Trailhead and the PCT Summit Trailhead on Hwy. 140 is 15.1 miles, (north on Dead Indian Memorial Rd. to Hwy. 140 and turning west 5.1 mi. to the PCT Summit Trailhead).

Driving distance from the Road 700 PCT crossing-to the PCT Summit Trailhead on Hwy. 140 is 12.8 miles,by returning 0.4 miles to Rd. 3720. Turn right and go 2 miles to Road 3705.   Turn right again and go 4 miles to Route 37. Turn right onto 37 and go 2.2 miles to Hwy. 140. Turn right and go 4.2 miles to Road 3650 (PCT Trailhead) on the left.

BROWN MTN. TRAIL #1005-ROGUE RIV. NTL. FOREST SECTION. (Map 16)

TRAIL BEGINS:	-Forest Road 3705.	ELEV. 4850'
TRAIL ENDS:	-Forest Road 3640.	ELEV. 5650'
DISTANCE:	-5.3 miles (one way), moderate.	
SEASON:	-Mid May to October.	
USE:	-Hikers, horses, mountain bikes when trail surfaces are dry.	
CONNECTING TR.	-Pacific Crest National Scenic Trail #2000.	
	-Brown Mtn. Trail 3724 (Winema Ntl. Forest).	
BRING MAPS:	-USFS Ashland Ranger Dist.-Rogue River Ntl. Forest.	
	-USFS Pacific Crest Trail-Oregon Southern Portion.	
	-USFS Rec. Opportunity Guide-Brown Mountain Trail.	

ACCESS: FOREST ROAD 3705 TRAILHEAD. From Interstate Hwy.
        5 Ashland-Klamath Falls Exit 14, go 0.6 mile east
on State Hwy. 66 to the junction with Dead Indian Memorial Road
(County Route 722). Turn left onto this road and travel 22 miles
to the junction with Forest Route 37 (Big Elk Road). Turn left
onto Route 37 and go 6.0 miles to Forest Road 3705. Turn right on
3705 and continue 3.0 miles to the trailhead.

FOREST ROAD 3640 TRAILHEAD. From the above Road 3705 Trailhead,
continue southeast on Road 3705 for 1.0 mile to the junction with
Forest Road 3720. Turn left onto Road 3720 and continue for 1.5
miles to the junction with Road 700. Turn left onto Road 700 and
travel 3 miles to Road 3640. Turn left onto Road 3640 and proceed
1.5 miles to the trailhead.(Alternate directions on next page).

FEATURES: From the Rd. 3705 Trailhead, the Brown Mtn. Trail
        crosses Road 500 in 1.5 miles. At 2.5 miles you
cross Road 560 and at 2.9 miles you cross the Pacific Crest National Scenic Trail. At 5.2 miles the trail forks; TAKE THE TRAIL
TO THE RIGHT 0.1 MI. TO THE RD. 3640 TRAILHEAD. (The trail to the
left is Brown Mtn. Trail 3724 (Winema Ntl. Forest section) that
continues 2.5 miles to Lake of the Woods.

BROWN MTN. TRAIL #3724 WINEMA NTL. FOREST SECTION. (Maps 16 & 17)
(See preceding page for continuation in Rogue River Ntl. Forest).

TRAIL BEGINS:	-Forest Road 3640 Trailhead.	ELEV. 5640'
TRAIL ENDS:	-Forest Road 3601 Trailhead.	ELEV. 4960'
DISTANCE:	-2.5 miles.	
SEASON:	-June-October.	
USE:	-Hiker/horse.	
CONNECTING TR.	-Brown Mtn. Trail 3705- Rogue River Ntl. Forest.	
BRING MAPS:	-USFS Winema National Forest.	

ACCESS: Take State Highway 140 to summer home Road 3601,
           located at the west end of Lake Of The Woods near
milepost 35. Turn south on Road 3601 and go 0.1 mile to the junction with Forest Road 3640 and:

Keep left on Road 3601 and go 0.4 mi. to the LOWER TRAILHEAD near
Camp McLoughlin, OR.....

Turn right onto Rd. 3640 and go 3 miles to the UPPER TRAILHEAD on
the right side of the road.

121

DUNLOP TRAIL #1006. Difficult May—Oct., hiker only beyond meadow.
SODA SPRINGS TRAIL #1009.Moderate, year-round from Soda Springs.
BRING MAPS: -USFS Recreation Opportunity Guides.
               -Rogue River Ntl. Forest- Ashland Ranger District.
               (See map on page 123)

ACCESS to UPPER TRAILHEADS-SHELL PEAK ROAD- Forest Road 2500-100.
From Interstate Hwy. 5 Ashland-Klamath Falls Exit 14, go 0.6 mile
east on State Hwy. 66 to the junction with Dead Indian Memorial
Road (County Route 722) and travel 18.5 miles to Shell Peak Road
on the left. Follow Shell Peak Road 5.6 miles to the junction of
Road 2500-185 and turn left 250 ft. to SODA SPRINGS TRAILHEAD.

SODA SPRINGS TRAIL #1009 begins at ELEVATION 4060'dropping steeply 2.5 miles to the lower trailhead on Forest Road 3730-800 ELEV-
ATION 2740'. The trail begins through heavy timber and soon comes
to a site of a clearcut that affords a wide view of the surrounding area before re-entering the forest. A grove of oak and maple
is reached at the lower elevations,soon to be followed by a rocky
ledge with more good views. Descending further, you come to the
junction with the trail leading right to Latgawa Church Camp. But
turn left to the soda springs, cross a foot bridge, and continue
to the temporary lower trailhead on Road 3730-800.

The DUNLOP TRAILHEAD is reached by going 0.9 mile further on ROAD
2500-100 at a road gate just before MILEPOST 7, ELEVATION 3700'.
Trail distance is 1.5 miles one way,that takes you past beautiful
meadows, an interesting old homestead site,and some of the grand-
est ponderosa pines that you will ever see. The trail ends in the
canyon of the South Fork of Little Butte Creek where fishing for
small cutthroat trout is usually very good. ELEVATION 3400'.

Sierra Club volunteers and Forest Service trail crews rebuilt the
Dunlop Trail in 1990, with further work in 1992 by Forest Service
crews and the Northwest Youth Corps.

"The Dunlop Ranch was said to have been settled by a bootlegger
referred to as 'ol' man Dunlop-in the 1920's.   During the 1930's
a family named Nickerson'got by' raising goats, whose hides were
used for car upholstery and convertible tops.   The site has been
abandoned since the late 1930's."

                        —Continued

FROM MEDFORD: Follow Hwy. 62, 6 mi. to the junction with Highway 140. Turn right onto 140 and go 12.6 miles to South Fork Little Butte Creek Road on the right. Go 13.7 miles on South Fork Little Butte Creek Road, to a small turnout on the right just before the entrance to Camp Latgawa. Follow signs to Soda Springs Trailhead.

FROM ASHLAND: Take Dead Indian Memorial Road and just before mile-post 14, turn left onto Conde Creek Road and go 11.3 miles to the junction with South Fork Little Butte Creek Road. Turn right and go about 3.8 mi. to a small turnout on the right, just before the entrance to Camp Latgawa. Follow signs to Soda Springs Trailhead.

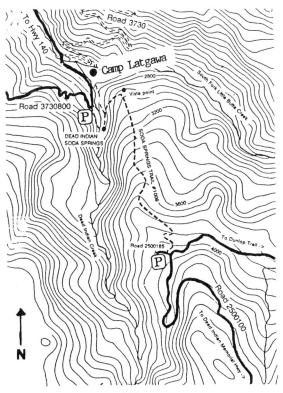

123

BEAVER DAM TRAIL #1001, hiker only.
2.1 mi.,easy, May–Oct. Elev. 4500'.

Beaver Dam Trail is between two different types of habitat; streamside
and forest. The setting is the confluence of three small creeks which
drain the southern Dead Indian Plateau. Beaver Dam Creek, Daley Creek
and Deadwood Creek flow through an
area of grassy banks, willows, false
hellbore and beaver ponds. The trail
connects Beaver Dam and Daley Creek
Campgrounds, forming a partial loop.

TREES: Douglas fir, white pine. Pacific yew is poisonous, eating fo-
liage or seeds contained in bright
red berries can result in death.

WILDFLOWERS: bleeding heart,calypso
orchid and trillium.

BIRDS: CAVITY NESTERS:pileated woodpecker, red-breasted nuthatch. ALSO,
watch and listen for the belted king-
fisher who makes his livlihood cap-
turing small fish.

BEAVERS may be spotted in early morning or evening. Gnawed branches and
several active dams are visible from
the trail.

ACCESS: From Ashland Interstate 5, Exit 14, drive east on Hwy.66,
0.6 mi. to Dead Indian Memorial Road (County 722). Turn left onto
this road and go 22 mi. to the junction of Forest Route 37. Turn
left onto Route 37 and go 1.5 miles to Beaver Dam and Daley Creek
Campgrounds. You can begin in either campground. (Excerpts: Rogue
River National Forest, Ashland Ranger District, Recreation Opportunity Guide)

CHAPTER 9 - BUTTE FALLS AREA

<u>WHISKEY SPRINGS INTERPRETIVE TRAIL.</u>   (See map 16)

<u>TRAIL BEGINS/ENDS: WHISKEY SPRINGS CAMPGROUND PICNIC AREA.</u>

<u>DISTANCE:</u>	-1.0 mile.	<u>ELEV.</u> 3200'
<u>DIFFICULTY:</u>	-Easy, wheelchair accessible.	
<u>SEASON:</u>	-June thru October. <u>USE:</u> hikers only.	
<u>BRING MAPS:</u>	-Butte Falls Ranger Dist.-Rogue River Ntl. Forest.	

<u>ACCESS:</u>   <u>From Butte Falls:</u> Go 10 miles east on the Butte Falls-Fish Lake Hwy.(County Route 821)to Whiskey Springs Campground.

<u>From Ashland:</u> Go 0.6 mile east on Hwy. 66, turn left onto Dead Indian Memorial Road (County Route 722), and continue 22 miles to the junction with Forest Route 37. Follow Route 37, 8 mi. to Hwy. 140. Turn right and go 1/4 mi. to County Route 821 that continues north 9.3 miles to Whiskey Springs Campground.

<u>FROM WHITE CITY:</u> Follow mileposts on Highway 140, 28.6 miles and turn north onto County Route 821. Follow 821, 9.3 mi. to Whiskey Springs Campground.

<u>FEATURES:</u> The one mile loop trail starts at the picnic area and leads through a forested area before arriving at a viewing platform that overlooks a marshland created by beavers. Wood Ducks, frogs,and other wildlife habitats may be seen along the way. Interpretive signs are frequently located throughout the area.

SOUTH FORK ROGUE RIVER TRAILS

SOUTH FORK TRAILS

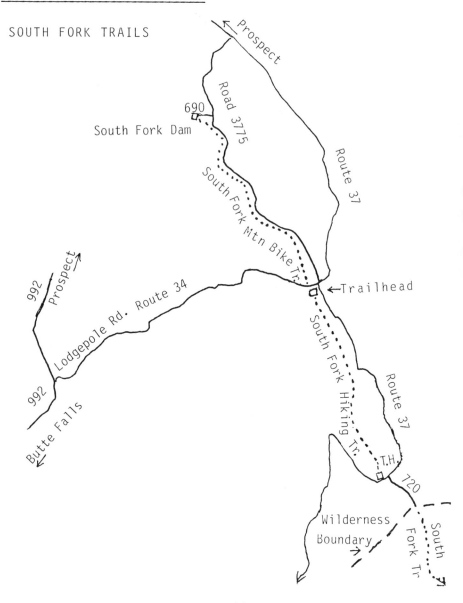

LOWER SOUTH FORK ROGUE RIVER TRAIL #988. (See map 11)

TRAIL BEGINS: -Upper Trailhead-Forest Route 37.   ELEV. 4400'
MID-POINT: -Middle Trailhead-Forest Route 34.   ELEV. 4000'
TRAIL ENDS: -Lower Trailhead- Forest Road 3775/690
              near South Fork Dam.   ELEV. 3400'
DISTANCE: -Upper section (Road 37 to Road 34) 5.3 miles,
              hiker only.
              Lower section(Road 34 to Rd.3775/690)appx. 6.8 mi.
              mountain bike/hiker.

SEASON: -Spring, summer, fall. Mosquitos can be very bad in
              late spring and early summer. They should be vir-
              tually absent by the first of July.
BRING MAPS: -Butte Falls Ranger Dist.-Rogue River Ntl. Forest.

ACCESS: From Butte Falls, Oregon, travel east one mile to
              the county road leading north to the town of Pros-
pect. Turn onto this road and go 8.7 mi. to the junction of Forest Route 34. Turn right onto 34 and go 8.1 miles. The MID-POINT
TRAILHEAD is on the right just before reaching the junction with
Forest Route 37 and Road 3775.

UPPER TRAILHEAD. Continue on Route 34 to the junction with Route
37. Turn right (south) onto 37 and go 5.6 miles to a bridge that
crosses the Rogue River.The trailhead is on the right just before
you cross the bridge.

LOWER TRAILHEAD. From the mid-point trailhead on Route 34, take
Forest Road 3775 for 5.2 miles to the junction with Forest Road
3775/690. Turn left onto Road 3775/690 and go 0.5 mi. to the end
of the road where the trailhead is located.

FEATURES: Parking and turn-around is adequate at the trailheads.
The Lower South Fork of the Rogue River Trail follows the river
along its entire length. A car shuttle would be most helpful when
doing these trail sections. CARRY WATER!

CHAPTER 10 - PROSPECT AREA

MILL CREEK FALLS. (See map 5)

TRAILS BEGIN: -Mill Creek viewpoint parking area, 1 mile
                south of Prospect; and from the State Park at
                the south town limits of Prospect.
DIFFICULTY: -Easy. USE: hikers only.
SEASON: -All year except for occasional winter snows.

ACCESS: From Medford, take Crater Lake Highway (Hwy. 62)
                    to the community of Cascade Gorge (milepost 38).
Mill Creek Drive junctions on the right (east). Follow mileposts
on Mill Creek Drive, 5.4 miles   to the Mill Creek viewpoint parking area on the right. A large sign-map is erected here; giving
directions to the Avenue of the Giant Boulders, and viewpoints of
Barr Creek Falls and Mill Creek Falls. The trail to these points
begins from the south end of the parking area. While hiking these
trails note the signs that are posted to alert visitors:

"DANGER: POWER DAM SPILLWAY UPSTREAM. WATCH OUT FOR ANY FAST RISE
OF WATER AT ANY TIME AND WITHOUT WARNING.   BE SURE THAT YOU CAN
REACH SHORE SAFELY."

AN OREGON STATE PARK, WITH RESTROOMS, is located one mile further
north on Mill Creek Drive, just at the south town limits of Prospect. THE TRAIL TO PEARSONY FALLS begins here.   Metal posts indicate the names of the various trees. After about one mile, the
trail descends to the Rogue River bed, sometimes dry due to water
diversion from a power company dam upstream.   DANGER SIGNS WARN
THAT WATER COULD SUDDENLY BE RELEASED FROM THE DAM, and should be
taken seriously.

These trails were designed for public use by BOISE CASCADE TIMBER
AND WOOD PRODUCTS GROUP.

SUGAR PINE TRAIL #1080. (See map 4)

TRAIL BEGINS:	–Forest Road 6610/050.	ELEV. 2000'
TRAIL ENDS:	–Coalmine Creek.	ELEV. 2400'
DISTANCE:	–3.1 miles, easy, some creek crossings.	
	¬June–October. Stream crossings difficult during periods of heavy stream flow. USE: hiker/horse.	
BRING MAPS:	–Prospect Ranger Dist.–Rogue River Ntl. Forest.	
	–USFS Rec. Opportunity Guide–Sugar Pine Trail.	

ACCESS: From the town of Trail, Oregon, travel northeast on State Highway 62, 3.3 mile to Elk Creek Road. Turn left and continue northeast on Elk Creek Road, 11.1 miles to the junction with Sugar Pine Road. Turn left on Sugar Pine Road, and continue 2 mi. to the junction with Road 6610(Route 31). Turn right and continue on 6610 for 1 mile to Forest Road 6610/050 on the right. Road 6610/050 is not passable for passenger cars. The trailhead is 1/4 mile down this road.

"The trail follows Sugar Pine Creek for 3.1 miles to its confluence with Coalmine Creek. Dogwoods and rhododendrons can be observed in early summer. Old–growth Douglas fir, western hemlock, Pacific yew, and vine maple provide shade in the hot summer days. Sugar Pine Creek pools in many places, providing cool refreshment for wading. The natural arrangement of the bedrock in this creek is a spectacular sight!" (USFS Quote)

FEATURES: This hike should not be attempted during early spring or late fall months when stream crossings are difficult.   It is difficult for small children at any time. Hot summer months are best, but this is also a good trail for observing fall colors.

129

Upper Rogue Trails

UPPER ROGUE RIVER TRAIL #1034-CRATER RIM VIEWPOINT TO HAMAKER
MEADOWS. Segment 1 (See map 2)

DISTANCE: -9.3 miles, easy to moderate. USE: hikers only.
SEASON: -June to October. Wildflowers until mid-August.
CONNECTING TR.-Boundary Springs Trail 1057.
BRING MAPS: -Prospect Ranger District-Rogue River Ntl. Forest.
 -USFS Rec. Opportunity Guide-Upper Rogue River Tr.

ACCESS TO CRATER RIM VIEWPOINT, ELEV. 5200'.
Just north of the Union Creek Resort, at the junction with State
Hwys. 62 and 230, follow mileposts northeast on 230, 18.6 miles
to the viewpoint parking area and trailhead. Hike 0.6 mile to the
junction with Boundary Springs Trail 1057, that begins a 7.2 mile
hike to the Pacific Crest Trail. KEEP RIGHT at this junction onto Trail 1034, which reaches Hamaker Campground in 9.3 miles.

FEATURES: Starting from Crater Rim Viewpoint, the trail travels downstream. After 1/2 mile, it drops to the
river's edge, crosses a small creek before climbing to 200 foot
cliffs of compacted pumice. The next two miles offer impressive
sights, Ruth Falls can be heard below but is hard to see. Rough
Rider Falls is 2 miles further. Another waterfall is located 1.5
mile downstream. The trail leaves the river and winds 2.5 miles
through the woods, crosses Forest Road 6530 and then returns to
the river's edge at Hamaker Campground on Forest Road 900. THIS
IS 1 OF 7 SEGMENTS OF THE 48 MILE UPPER ROGUE RIVER TRAIL.

ACCESS TO HAMAKER CAMPGROUND, see next page.

HISTORY: "The Upper Rogue River Trail is a National Recreational Trail. Some segments of the trail were
built by the Civilian Conservation Corps as access routes for
recreation and fire supression purposes. The construction of the
rest of the trail began in 1975 as a Volunteer Bicentennial com-
memorative project, and was completed in late 1977. Long range
plans envision the Upper Rogue Trail extending from the Pacific
Crest Trail to the Pacific Coast." (USFS quote)

131

UPPER ROGUE RIVER TRAIL #1034....HAMAKER CAMPGROUND TO NEW TRAIL-
HEAD FOREST ROAD 6530/070. Segment 2 (see map 2)

DISTANCE:	-About 7.5 miles, easy to moderate.
SEASON:	-June through October. USE: hiker/horse. Motor vehicles not allowed.
BRING MAPS:	-Prospect Ranger District-Rogue River Ntl. Forest. -USFS Rec. Opportunity Guide-Upper Rogue River Tr.

ACCESS: HAMAKER CAMPGROUND, ELEV. 4000'.
                From the junction of State Hwys. 62 and 230, fol-
low mileposts northeast on 230, 12.1 miles to the junction with
Forest Road 6530. Turn right onto Road 6530 and go 0.6 mi. to the
junction with Forest Road 6530/900.   Turn right onto 900, and go
0.8 mi. to Hamaker Campground at the end of the road. (Trail 1034
heading north is along the left side of the road just before you
reach the Rogue River bridge).

FEATURES: From Hamaker Campground, Trail 1034 begins right
                (south) just after crossing the bridge. It first
leads away from the river and rejoins it two miles later near the
confluence of Muir Creek and the Rogue River.   The trail follows
through grassy meadows, crosses Hurryon Creek, then rejoins Rogue
River near Highway Falls. Beyond Highway Falls, the trail climbs
to the top of a pumice cliff with views of the Rogue River below.
After descending to the river bank and then crossing National Cr.
on a footlog, the trail meets Forest Road 6530.   Hike across the
bridge and make a left turn to continue south along the west bank
of the river.   About 1/4 mile further, look for an access trail
leading to a NEW (1989) trailhead/parking area on Road 6530/070,
replacing the Foster Creek Trailhead on Hwy. 62 that was difficult to reach.
THIS IS ONE OF 7 SEGMENTS OF THE 48 MILE UPPER ROGUE RIVER TRAIL.

ACCESS TO FOREST ROAD 6530/070 TRAILHEAD, see next page.

UPPER ROGUE RIVER TRAIL #1034-ROAD 6530/070 TRAILHEAD TO BIG BEND
Segment 3 (See maps 2,5,and 6)

DISTANCE: -About 9.5 miles, easy to moderate.
SEASON: -June through October. USE: hiker/horse. Motorized
                   vehicles not allowed.
BRING MAPS: -Prospect Ranger District-Rogue River Ntl. Forest.
                   -USFS Rec. Opportunity Guide-Upper Rogue River Tr.

ACCESS: FOREST ROAD 6530/070 TRAILHEAD. ELEV. 3578'.
                   North of the Union Creek Resort, at the junction
of State Hwys. 62 and 230, follow mileposts on 230 to milepost 6
at the County line.Turn right onto Forest Road 6530 and go 0.7 mi.
to the junction with Road 070 on the right. Turn right and go 0.1
mile to the trailhead and parking area.   This new trailhead was
built in 1989 by Gregory Forest Products and USFS to replace the
old, difficult to reach, Foster Creek Trailhead.

FEATURES: An access trail leads to the Upper Rogue River
                   Trail. Turn right to continue south and after a
short distance the trail climbs away from the river, crosses Hwy.
230 two miles south, and continues 0.5 mile to the former Foster
Creek Trailhead.

Hiking south from Foster Creek,it is necessary to wade the creek.
In about 1 mile downstream, the trail leaves the Rogue River and
climbs a pumice cliff. It then continues through a series of wet
marshy areas.   5 miles downstream, on the south side of a footbridge, Trail 1034 passes the abandoned 0.5 mile trail that went
to the Brown's Cabin Trailhead. Continuing south along the river,
the trail climbs and traverses a pumice bluff. It then follows
the river's edge as it winds around Big Bend and terminates on
Forest Road 6510, 3/4 mile north of its junction with Hwy. 230.

THIS IS ONE OF 7 SEGMENTS OF THE 48 MILE UPPER ROGUE RIVER TRAIL.

ACCESS TO BIG BEND, see next page.

133

UPPER ROGUE RIVER TRAIL #1034-BIG BEND TO NATURAL BRIDGE CAMP-GROUND AND VIEWPOINT. Segment 4 (See map 5)

DISTANCE: -7 miles, moderate grades, must ford Flat Creek.
SEASON: -June through October.
USE: -Hiker only.
CONNECTING TR.   -Rogue Gorge Trail 1034A.
BRING MAPS: -Prospect Ranger District-Rogue River Ntl. Forest.
                 -USFS Rec. Opportunity Guide-Upper Rogue River Tr.

ACCESS: BIG BEND TRAILHEAD, ELEV. 3525'.
                 North of the Union Creek Resort, at the junction
with State Hwys. 62 and 230, continue 0.9 mi. northeast on 230 to
the junction with Forest Road 6510. Turn left across Rogue River
bridge, and continue 3/4 mile to the crossing of the Upper Rogue
River Trail. Hiking north leads 7 miles to Foster Creek. Hiking
south leads 6 miles toward Natural Bridge Campground.

FEATURES: From Big Bend Trailhead, the trail climbs a rocky
                 embankment, and traverses a steep slope overlook-
ing the Rogue River. Fish Mountain to the north, becomes visible
through a brief opening in the trees. Further south, after frequent switchbacks, a steep forested slope overlooks Farewell Bend
Campground across the river. The trail then momentarily descends
to river level to view the water raging through the long, narrow
chute of a collapsed lava tube. South of Union Creek Campground,
the trail returns to a calm river and crosses Flat Creek, 4 miles
further south. The river regains its turbulent nature and Trail
1034 then reaches the first of 2 footbridges crossing to the east
bank of the river, at the junction with Rogue Gorge Trail 1034A,
1/4 mile north of Natural Bridge Campground. Traveling one mile
further along the west bank, leads one mile to the Natural Bridge
Viewpoint facility and footbridge. This area is 0.5 mile west of
Hwy. 62 accessible by Forest Road #300.

THIS IS ONE OF 7 SEGMENTS OF THE 47 MILE UPPER ROGUE RIVER TRAIL.

ACCESS TO NATURAL BRIDGE CAMP/VIEWPOINT FACILITY (See next page).

UPPER ROGUE RIVER TRAIL #1034-NATURAL BRIDGE CAMPGROUND/VIEWPOINT TO WOODRUFF BRIDGE. Segment 5 (See map 5)

DISTANCE: -3.5 miles, easy. USE: hikers only.
SEASON: -June through October.
CONNECTING TR.   -None.
BRING MAPS: -Prospect Ranger District-Rogue River Ntl. Forest.
                   -USFS Rec. Opportunity Guide-Upper Rogue River Tr.

ACCESS: NATURAL BRIDGE CAMPGROUND, ELEV. 3200'.
                   From the town of Prospect, follow mileposts north
on State Highway 62 to mile 54.8 at the junction with Forest Road
300. Turn left and go 1/2 mile to Natural Bridge Viewpoint parking lot. Follow a paved path to a footbridge. Do not cross the
footbridge if you are going toward Woodruff Bridge. Crossing the
bridge leads to the Natural Bridge Viewpoint facility interpretative stations, and then on further north to other segments of the
Upper Rogue River Trail.

FEATURES: From the above footbridge, continue downstream on
                   the east bank of the river, over a rough tread of
mossy lava rock which becomes slippery in wet weather. The trail
later climbs to view the river as it makes a sharp bend and rages
through a narrow chute of a collapsed lava tube. This rapids is
known as Knob Falls.

Several old skid roads are encountered, as trail 1034 approaches
Woodruff Bridge developed picnic area.   The U.S. Forest Service
advises, "The pools and river can be dangerous due to cold water
and a forceful current." THIS IS ONE OF 7 SEGMENTS OF THE 48 MI.
UPPER ROGUE RIVER TRAIL.

ACCESS TO WOODRUFF BRIDGE, see next page.

135

UPPER ROGUE RIVER TRAIL #1034-WOODRUFF BRIDGE TO RIVER BRIDGE
CAMPGROUND. Segment 6 (See map 5)

DISTANCE: -4.6 miles, easy, some moderate pitches. The
                   tread is rocky on the southern end.
SEASON: -June through October. USE: hikers only.
CONNECTING TR.   -None.
BRING MAPS: -Prospect Ranger District-Rogue River Ntl. Forest.
                   -USFS Rec. Opportunity Guide-Upper Rogue River Tr.

ACCESS: WOODRUFF BRIDGE, ELEV. 3000'.
                   From the town of Prospect, follow mileposts north
on State Highway 62 to mi. 51.3 at the junction with Forest Route
68. Turn left onto 68 and travel northwest 1.8 miles to Woodruff
Bridge.   Trailhead signs are on the east bank of the river indicating NORTH, 3.5 miles to Natural Bridge Campground; and SOUTH,
4.6 miles to River Bridge Campground.

FEATURES: From Woodruff Bridge Picnic Area, the trail heads
                   downstream along the east bank of the river, and
after about 1.5 miles, approaches the dark-colored cliffs of Takelma Gorge. The river drops through a series of rapids and turns
sharply to enter the gorge itself.   The narrow channel continues
for nearly 1.25 miles. The tread on this section of the trail is
quite rocky and the grades become steeper.

Below Takelma Gorge, the trail goes past the Upper Rogue Baptist
Church Camp, and then continues 1.4 miles to River Bridge Campground on Road 6210. (Excerpts USFS Recreation Opportunity Guide)

THIS IS ONE OF 7 SEGMENTS OF THE 48 MILE UPPER ROGUE RIVER TRAIL.

ACCESS TO RIVER BRIDGE CAMPGROUND, see next page.

UPPER ROGUE RIVER TRAIL #1034-RIVER BRIDGE CAMPGROUND TO PROSPECT
Segment 7 (See map 5)

DISTANCE:	-6.5 miles, easy. USE: hikers only.
SEASON:	-June through October.
CONNECTING TR:	-None.
BRING MAPS:	-Prospect Ranger District-Rogue River Ntl. Forest.
	-USFS Rec. Opportunity Guide-Upper Rogue River Tr.

ACCESS: RIVER BRIDGE CAMPGROUND, ELEV. 2900'
                 From the town of Prospect, follow mileposts north
on State Highway 62 to mile 49.2 at the junction with Forest Road
6210. Turn left and continue 1 mile to the trail crossing at the
near (east) end of the bridge. Trail signs are on the east bank
of the river and indicate 4.6 miles north to Woodruff Bridge, and
6.5 miles south to Prospect.

PROSPECT TRAILHEAD, southern terminus of the trail, ELEV. 2700'
On State Hwy. 62, travel to the northern edge of Prospect, 0.1 mi.
north of milepost 45. Turn left (west) onto the narrow dirt access road leading 1/2 mile to a picnic area and a power company
reservoir. Follow the road leading north along the east bank of
the river to the Upper Rogue River Trailhead. River Bridge Campground is 6.5 miles north.

FEATURES: From River Bridge Campground, the trail continues
                 south along the east bank of the river, crosses a
sandy beach, then enters a forest of tall sugar pines. Views of
the river occur where the trail nears the edge of 20 foot bluffs
bordering the river channel. The last four miles of trail leaves
the river, and the backwaters of the reservoir later become visible as the trail returns to the river bank. The trail joins and
follows an old road to the reservoir and a picnic area near Prospect. A 1/2 mile access road connects to Hwy. 62 from the dam.

THIS IS ONE OF 7 SEGMENTS OF THE 48 MILE UPPER ROGUE RIVER TRAIL.

ROGUE GORGE TRAIL #1034A (See map 5)

<u>TRAIL BEGINS:</u>	-Rogue Gorge Viewpoint, Highway 62. <u>ELEV.</u> 3363'
	-Also accessed from Farewell Bend Campground.
<u>TRAIL ENDS:</u>	-Near Natural Bridge Campground. <u>ELEV.</u> 3200'
<u>DISTANCE:</u>	-3.5 miles, easy grade. <u>USE:</u> hiker only.
<u>SEASON:</u>	-June through October-wildflowers through August.
<u>CONNECTING TR.</u>	-Union Creek Trail 1035.
	-Upper Rogue River Trail 1034.
<u>BRING MAPS:</u>	-Prospect Ranger Dist.-Rogue River Ntl. Forest.

<u>ACCESS:</u>   <u>ROGUE GORGE VIEWPOINT, ELEV. 3363'.</u>   From Union
Creek Resort,travel northeast on Highway 62, 0.3
mile to the Rogue Gorge viewpoint on the left. This viewpoint is
also reached from Farewell Bend Campground.Trail 1034A runs south
to Natural Bridge Campground on the east bank of the Rogue River.

<u>NATURAL BRIDGE VIEWPOINT, ELEVATION 3200'.</u> From the town of Pros-
pect, follow mileposts north on State Hwy. 62 to mile 54.8 at the
junction with Forest Road 300. Turn left onto 300 and go 0.5 mi.
to the viewpoint and campground. Trail 1034A runs north along the
east bank of the Rogue River.

<u>FEATURES:</u>   From the ROGUE GORGE VIEWPOINT,the trail reaches
Union Creek Campground, crosses a footbridge and
continues along the east side of the river.Downstream just before
Natural Bridge Campground is another footbridge that connects to
UPPER ROGUE RIVER TRAIL 1034.   The Rogue Gorge Trail stays along
the east bank to Natural Bridge Viewpoint.

The views of the Rogue River as it winds its way through the narrow channel of basalt lava, are very impressive. Autumnal color
may be enjoyed from mid-September through mid-October. The gorge
was formed by the erosive action of the river. The many pothole
formations were sculpted into solid rock by the continuous spin-
ning of small rocks, churned by the swift currents of the river.

<u>UNION CREEK TRAIL #1035.</u> (See maps 5 and 6)

<u>TRAIL BEGINS:</u>	-Union Creek Campground.	<u>ELEV.</u> 3200'
<u>TRAIL ENDS:</u>	-Forest Road 6200/610.	<u>ELEV.</u> 3767'
	-4.4 miles, easy. <u>USE:</u> hiker/fishermen/camping.	
<u>SEASON:</u>	-June through October.	
<u>CONNECTING TR.</u>	-Rogue Gorge Trail 1034A.	
<u>BRING MAPS:</u>	-Prospect Ranger District-Rogue River Ntl. Forest.	
	-USFS Rec. Opportunity Guide -Union Creek Trail.	

<u>ACCESS:</u>   <u>FROM UNION CREEK CAMPGROUND:</u>   At the confluence
                of Union Creek and the Rogue River, cross a foot-
bridge over Union Creek and follow the trail east to a point just
south of the Union Creek Resort on State Hwy. 62.

The trail crosses Hwy. 62, just south of the resort and then continues east along the north bank of the creek with a good view of
Union Falls in about 3 miles. The upper trailhead is 1 mile further.

By road, the <u>UPPER TRAILHEAD</u> is reached by travelling 1.3 miles
northeast of Union Creek Resort to the junction of State Highways
230 and 62. Continue northeast on 62, 2 miles to the junction of
Forest Road 6200/600. Turn right onto Road 600 and continue   0.2
mile to the junction with Forest Road 6200/610.   Turn left onto
Road 610 and go 0.1 mile to the trailhead on the right.

<u>HISTORY:</u>   "UNION CREEK, PEAK: Named in 1862 (the Civil War
                had begun the year before) by 'patriotic' pros-
pectors Chauncy Nye and Hiram G. Abbott.   (Pro-confederate feel-
ings, however, ran high among a large segment of the Jackson
County population.)"   (USFS quote)

SPHAGNUM BOG TRAIL #1038. (See map 2)

TRAIL BEGINS:	—Forest Road 6535 near milepost 5. ELEV. 5360'
TRAIL ENDS:	—West Boundary Crater Lake Ntl. Park. ELEV. 5572'
DISTANCE:	—1.1 mile. Easy grades. USE: hiker/horse.
SEASON:	—Usually snow-free July through September.
CONNECTING TR:	—Crater Springs Trail, Crater Lake Ntl. Park.
BRING MAPS:	—USFS Prospect Ranger Dist. Rogue River Ntl.Forest.
	—CRATER LAKE map/brochure-National Park Service.
	—USGS Crater Lake West, 7.5' series, 1985.

ACCESS: Just north of Union Creek Resort from the junction
              with State Highways 62 and 230, follow Hwy. 230 to
milepost 6 at the junction with Forest Road 6530. Turn RIGHT onto
Road 6530 and go 1.3 miles to the second junction with loop Road
6535. Follow Road 6535, 5.5 miles (just beyond milepost 5) to the
trailhead on the left. This trailhead was constructed in 1995 to
provide adequate parking and turn-around space for stock trailers
and other vehicles.

The trail begins its climb to a road gate at the upper end of Rd.
6535/660. The trail continues beyond the gate,1/2 mi. to the West
Boundary of Crater Lake Park, at the junction with Crater Springs
Trail. A sign reads; Sphagnum Bog 1.7 mi., PCT 4.7 mi., Boundary
Springs 7.9 mi.

Crater Springs Trail continues 1.2 mi. to the junction with Oasis
Butte Trail on the left, that leads 6.7 miles to Boundary Springs.
Keep right at the above junction and follow Crater Springs Trail,
0.5 mile south to Crater Springs, where a short spur leads south
to unmarked routes to SPHAGNUM BOG. Crater Springs Trail continues east from this spur to Pacific Crest Trail.

FEATURES: It is possible to continue south along unmarked routes
to Sphagnum Bog, thru wet meadows filled with bog dwelling plants
Care should be taken not to trample the fragile plant life or to
accidently step into deep, cold water pools.   Water is available
at Crater Springs. Camping is not allowed within a 0.5 mile rad-
ius of Sphagnum Bog. SEE BEGINNING OF CHAPTER 11 FOR CRATER LAKE
PARK BACKCOUNTRY USE REGULATIONS.

MINNEHAHA TRAIL #1039. (See map 2)

TRAIL BEGINS:	-Forest Road 6530/800.	ELEV.	3825'
TRAIL ENDS:	-Soda Springs.	ELEV.	4400'
DISTANCE:	-3.1 miles,easy. USE hiker,horse,mtn.& motorbikes.		
SEASON:	-Usually snow-free June through October.		
BRING MAPS:	-Prospect Ranger Dist. -Rogue River Ntl. Forest.		

ACCESS: From the Union Creek Resort, travel northeast on
                 Crater Lake Hwy. 62, 1.3 miles to the junction
with State Hwy. 230.   Follow mileposts on 230, 12.1 miles to the
junction with Forest Road 6530. Turn right onto 6530 and go 1.0
mile to Road 800. Turn right onto Road 800 and go 0.1 mi. to the
Minnehaha Trailhead on the left, near the old Minnehaha Camp.

FEATURES: The route begins as an old road that diminishes
                 to a trail, then follows Minnehaha Creek to Soda
Springs. Along the way, the trail passes at the edge of a large,
grassy meadow from where there are good views of Minnehaha Creek
with its beautiful waterfalls.

HISTORY: "MINNEHAHA CREEK, CAMP: The date of this name is
                 unknown; probably post-1900. The term is an In-
dian name from the eastern United States, made famous in Long-
fellow's poem 'Song of Hiawatha'." (USFS quote)

SHERWOOD CREEK TRAIL #1041 (See map 2)

TRAIL BEGINS:	-State Hwy. 230 near milepost 15. ELEV. 4634'
TRAIL ENDS:	-Three Lakes Camp, Road 3703. ELEV. 6000'
DISTANCE:	-4.5 miles, MORE DIFFICULT, stream crossings.
SEASON:	-June thru Oct. Snow often till Aug. on Road 3703.
USE:	Hiker/horse.
CONNECTING TR.	-Beaver Meadows Trail (Abandoned)
BRING MAPS:	-USFS Rec. Opportunity Guide-Sherwood Creek Trail.
	-Prospect Ranger District-Rogue River Ntl. Forest.

ACCESS: LOWER END OF TRAIL: Just north of the Union Creek Resort, at the junction of State Highways 62 and 230, go northeast on Hwy. 230, 0.2 mile beyond milepost 15. Turn left to a parking area and trailhead.

UPPER END OF TRAIL: Continue east on Hwy. 230 following mileposts to mile 20.6 at the junction with Three Lakes Road 3703. Turn left onto 3703 and go about 5.7 miles to the junction with Forest Road 3703/400 at the far (west) end of Three Lakes Camp. Turn left onto 3703/400 for 0.2 mile to the parking area at the west end of the lake. Follow blazes along an old road, 0.8 mile to the beginning of the trail.

FEATURES: FROM THE LOWER TRAILHEAD: The trail rises through a series of small meadows and high elevation forests. Stream crossings can be difficult even in late summer. In a few places the trail may be hard to follow when it passes thru meadows and stream crossings, as cattle trails can look like the main trail. Watch carefully for blazes and trail signs and note your route for the return trip. TRAIL LOG IS AS FOLLOWS:

.25 mile: Junction with ABANDONED Beaver Meadows loop trail, keep left.

1.25 mile: Junction with upper end of the Beaver Meadows Trail. Keep left.

1.5 mile SHERWOOD MEADOW: CAUTION:About half way along the west edge of the meadow, look for trail signs on trees.What looks like the continuation of the trail is an informal trail to a forest road. FROM SIGNS,THE TRAIL LEADS AT RIGHT ANGLES ACROSS THE MEADOW. LOOK FOR A ROCK DUCK AT THE FAR END OF THE MEADOW.The trail continues about 3 miles to Three Lakes Camp.

MUIR CREEK TRAIL #1042. (See map 2)

TRAIL BEGINS:	–State Hwy. 230 near milepost 10.	ELEV. 3825'
TRAIL ENDS:	–Buck Canyon Trail 1046.	ELEV. 4100'
DISTANCE:	–3.9 miles, easy. USE: hiker/horse.	
SEASON:	–June through October.	
CONNECTING TR.	–Buck Canyon Trail 1046.	
BRING MAPS:	–Prospect Ranger Dist. –Rogue River Ntl. Forest.	
	–USFS Rec. Opportunity Guide–Muir Creek Trail.	

ACCESS: Just north of the Union Creek Resort, at the intersection of State Highways 62 and 230, follow mileposts on 230, 10.4 miles just before crossing the bridge at Muir Creek. Muir Creek Trailhead is on the left (west) side of the road at the site of a horse unloading ramp and hitching rail.

FEATURES: Muir Creek Trail winds along the west bank of the creek, passing Muir Creek Falls in about 2.5 miles, and ends at Buck Canyon Trail 1046. Turning RIGHT onto Trail 1046 leads 0.5 mile to Forest Road 6560. This is a popular trail for fishermen.

I Think We Should Have Checked
The Map Sooner.

BUCK CANYON TRAILS

1046   Buck Canyon
1046A Hummingbird
      Meadows trail.
1047   Hole In The Ground Trail.

1046B Wiley Camp Trail
1044   Meadow Creek Tr.

BUCK CANYON TRAIL #1046 (See map 2)

TRAIL BEGINS:	-Forest Road 6560.	ELEV. 4160'
TRAIL ENDS:	-Hole In The Ground Camp.	ELEV. 5300'
DISTANCE:	-10.7 mi. plus 3 miles of access trails. High-point ELEV. about 6000 feet. USE: hiker/horse.	
	-Usually snow-free June through October.	
CONNECTING TR.	-Muir Creek Trail 1042.	
	-Hummingbird Meadows Trail 1046A. (Access #2)	
	-Wiley Camp Trail 1046B. (Access #3)	
	-Meadow Creek Trail 1044. (Access #4)	
	-Hole In The Ground Trail 1047. (Access #5)	
BRING MAPS:	-Prospect Ranger Dist. -Rogue River Ntl. Forest.	
	-USFS Rec. Opportunity Guide-Buck Canyon Trail.	

ACCESS #1 BUCK CANYON TRAILHEAD, ELEV. 4160'.   MORE DIFFICULT.
From the junction of Highways 62 and 230 just north of Union Cr.
Resort,follow mileposts northeast on Highway 230 to mile 12.1, at
the junction with Road 6560 on the left. Follow Road 6560,one mi.
and turn left onto Road 6560-190. Follow this road 0.5 mi. to the
trailhead. Distance: 0.25 mi. to Muir Creek Trail and 10.5 mi. to
Hole-In-The-Ground.

ACCESS #2 HUMMINGBIRD MEADOWS TRAIL 1046A, ELEV. 4000'.   EASIEST.
Continue 0.8 mi. north on Road 6560 to the junction with Forest
Road 6560/400 on the left. Follow Road 400 1.2 mi. to the trailhead at the end of the road. A sign indicates: "Hershberger Mtn.
13 miles".   This 1/2 mile access trail passes through Hummingbird Meadows and then fords Muir Creek.   There is no bridge, the
crossing may be difficult early in the season. The junction with
the Buck Canyon Trail is just beyond. ELEV. about 4400'.

Good hikers always leave a
trail cleaner than they
find it.

145

BUCK CANYON TRAIL #1046, page 2. (See map 2)

ACCESS #3 WILEY CAMP TRAIL 1046B, ELEV. 5200'. Near milepost 12 on State Hwy. 230 at the junction with Forest Road 6560, turn and travel northwest on Road 6560, 4 miles to the Rogue-Umpqua Divide where the road number changes to Forest Route 37. Continue on 37 for 1/2 mile to Forest Road 3700/800. Turn left and follow Road 800, 2.3 mi. to the junction with Forest Road 3700/870. Turn left and follow 870, 2.5 mi. to the trailhead on the left side of the road. The 1 mile Wiley Camp Trail descends from the Rogue-Umpqua Divide,and crosses Muir Creek. Wiley Camp is located at the south east side of the creek. This trail, rated DIFFICULT, joins Buck Canyon Trail at appx. ELEV. 4800'.

ACCESS #4 MEADOW CREEK TRAIL 1044, ELEV. 4900'. Follow mileposts on State Highway 230 to mile 9.2 at the second junction with loop Road 6540. Turn left onto 6540 and go 3 miles to the junction of Road 6540/700. Turn right onto 700 and go about 1.0 mi. WATCHING CAREFULLY ON THE LEFT for the trailhead sign. This steep 1 mile trail passes Bear Camp in about 0.5 mi. through a series of meadows before joining the Buck Canyon Trail.ELEV. about 5360'. Rated DIFFICULT.

ACCESS #5 HOLE-IN-THE-GROUND TRAIL 1047, ELEV. 5200'. From State Highway 230, near milepost 9 (mile 9.2), at the northern turnoff for loop Road 6540, turn left on Road 6540 and continue 4.5 miles (at milepost 6) to the junction with Forest Road 6540/500. Turn right onto Road 500, and continue 1.5 mi. to the trailhead at the end of the road. The trail leads 0.5 mi. across Log Cr. and joins Buck Canyon Trail and Rogue Umpqua Divide Trail 1470 at the edge of a small meadow. Hole in the Ground Camp is east of the meadow just inside the trees. ELEV. about 5600'. Rated DIFFICULT.

(See map 2)

FEATURES: The views along the way, north to south direction, include Buckneck Mtn., the knob of Devil's Slide, the Rogue-Umpqua Divide, the Foster Creek and Rogue River drainages, Mt. McLoughlin, Mt. Shasta, Buck Canyon Rim, Fish Mountain, Mt. Thielsen, the Crater Lake Rim and Union Peak. In early June when wildflowers are at their best, numerous hummingbirds feed on red horsemint at Hummingbird Meadow.

The Buck Canyon Trail ends at Hole In The Ground, a marshy meadow that at one time was a shallow, glacial lake at the head of Foster Creek. While passing through the high elevation meadows and glacial valleys, there is sometimes confusion between recreation trails and stock trails, created by summer grazing. Watch carefully for tree blazes and signs.

Most of the Buck Canyon Trail System lies within the Rogue-Umpqua Divide Wilderness Area. It is advised to obtain maps and Recreation Opportunity Guides from the Prospect, or Tiller Ranger Stations, before attempting any of these trails. "HORSE/PACK SADDLE users are encouraged to enter via ACCESS # 1, the main Buck Canyon Trailhead." (Quote: USFS Recreation Opportunity Guide)

The Rogue-Umpqua Divide Wilderness was created by the Oregon Wilderness Act of 1984. Wilderness regulations include:

PACK OUT ALL LITTER, especially foil packaging that doesn't burn.
BURY HUMAN WASTE 6 to 8 inches deep 200' or more from open water.
CAMPFIRES only in safe spots, keep small. Best to carry stoves.
CAMP IN TENT SITES, no drainage ditches, leave area as found.
MOTORIZED and MECHANICAL EQUIPMENT- prohibited in wilderness.

NATIONAL CREEK FALLS TRAIL #1053. (See map 2)

TRAIL BEGINS:	-Forest Road 6530/300.	ELEV. 4000'
TRAIL ENDS:	-National Creek Falls.	ELEV. 3760'
DISTANCE:	-0.4 mile, moderate, USE: hiker only.	
SEASON:	-June through October.	
BRING MAPS:	-Prospect Ranger Dist.-Rogue River Ntl. Forest.	
	-USFS Rec. Opportunity Guide-National Creek Falls.	

ACCESS: Just north of the Union Creek Resort, at the in-
                tersection of State Highways 62 and 230, follow
mileposts on 230 to milepost 6, at the junction with Forest Road
6530.   Turn right onto Road 6530 and go about 4 mi. to the junction with Road 6530/300. Turn right onto Road 300 and proceed to
the National Creek Falls parking lot and trailhead.

FEATURES: This short trail drops down through a mixed con-
                ifer forest to the base of the falls.   National
Creek is fed by springs in Crater Lake National Park.

HISTORY: "NATIONAL CREEK, FALLS, CAMP: The date of this
                name is unknown;   it may have been given to the
creek by members of the Forest Service road building crew in
1910." (USFS quote)

148

BOUNDARY SPRINGS TRAIL #1057. (See map 2)

TRAIL BEGINS:	-Near Crater Rim Viewpoint, Hwy. 230. ELEV. 4900'
TRAIL ENDS:	-Boundary Springs, Crater Lake Park. ELEV. 5060'
DISTANCE:	-About 2 miles, easy grade. USE: hiker only.
SEASON:	-Usually snow-free June to October.
CONNECTING TR:	-Upper Rogue Trail 1034.
BRING MAPS:	-Prospect Ranger Dist. -Rogue River Ntl. Forest.
	-USFS Rec. Opportunity Guide-Boundary Springs Tr.

ACCESS: Just north of Union Creek Resort, at the junction with State Highways 62 and 230, follow the mileposts northeast on 230, 18.6 miles to Crater Rim Viewpoint on the right.

Starting from the parking area, take the Upper Rogue River Trail 0.6 mi. to the junction with the Boundary Springs Trail. Turn to the left (southeast) on the Boundary Springs Tr. and hike about 2 miles to Boundary Springs. Along the way, the trail comes out to Lake West Road and crosses the Rogue River at a bridge. The trail resumes south immediately after crossing the bridge.

FEATURES: This trail begins a 7.2 mile link with the PCNST (Pacific Crest Trail). Hikers are advised to use special care to protect this sensitive environment....do not camp here and do not walk on the moss. Boundary Springs has been added to Crater Lake National Park, where DOGS NOT ALLOWED.

"The springs form the origin of the Upper Rogue River; named subsequent to 1905 because of their location at the boundary between Crater Lake National Park and Rogue River National Forest."
(USFS quote)

149

<u>VARMINT CAMP TRAIL #1070.</u> (See map 5 and 6)

<u>TRAIL BEGINS:</u> –Milepost 10 Forest Road 6205.   <u>ELEV.</u> 3600'
<u>TRAIL ENDS:</u>   –Forest Road 830.   <u>ELEV.</u> 5400'
<u>DISTANCE:</u>   –3.1 miles, moderate grades. <u>USE:</u> hiker/horse/mtn.
              bike/motorbike. Seasonal motorized closure March
              1 to June 30.
<u>SEASON:</u>   –June through October.
<u>BRING MAPS:</u>   –USFS Prospect Ranger District, Rogue River N.F.
              –USFS Recreation Opportunity Guide (this trail).

<u>ACCESS:</u>   From the town of Prospect, Oregon, drive east on
               County Route 992 leading toward Butte Falls, 1.1
mile to the junction with Red Blanket Road.   Follow Red Blanket
Road 0.3 mile to Forest Road 6205. Turn left onto Road 6205 and
continue 10.5 mi. to Varmint Camp Trailhead on the left. There is
parking for 1 or 2 vehicles across the road from the trailhead. <u>A
Sign at milepost 4 of Road 6205 indicates the road is closed beyond that point December 1 to April 15.</u>

<u>FEATURES.</u>   From Road 6205 Trailhead, the trail climbs grad-
                ually for about 1 mi.,crosses Varmint Creek then
climbs steeply for 1.5 miles through a dense conifer forest. The
trail crosses a mountain meadow lined with wild onion.   Look for
wildflowers in mid-summer.

Caution should be exercised if using a motorcycle on this trail.
The tread is narrow and rocky in places. The trail ends on Forest
Road #830.

<u>HISTORY:</u>   "Varmint Creek,Camp: A turn-of-the-century hun-
                ters' and sheepherders' camp,probably named af-
ter the presence of coyotes or other varmints. (USFS quote)

COLD SPRINGS TRAIL #1073. (See map 6)

TRAIL BEGINS:	–Forest Road 6205/100.	ELEV. 6200'
TRAIL ENDS:	–Cold Springs.	ELEV. 5940'
DISTANCE:	–2.6 miles, moderate.	
SEASON:	–May through October.	
USE:	–Hiker, horse, mountain bike.	
BRING MAPS:	–Prospect Ranger Dist.–Rogue River Ntl. Forest.	
	–USFS Rec. Opportunity Guide–Cold Spr. Tr. 1073.	

ACCESS: From Prospect, travel east on County Route 992
                 leading toward Butte Falls, and go 1.1 mile   to
the junction with Red Blanket Road.   Follow Red Blanket Road 0.3
mile to Road 6205. Turn left onto Road 6205 and go 4.0 miles to
the junction with Road 6205/100. Turn left onto Road 6205/100 and
go about 7 miles to the trailhead on the right. Parking space is
provided directly across the road.

FEATURES: The trail begins its journey,and after about 1.0
                 mile reaches "Paul Bunyan's Grave" on the north
side of the trail. Look for a hill with loose rocks, and a nearby metallic Forest Service sign tacked to a tree. The trail later
crosses a road, and resumes directly beyond, before ending at the
springs. CARRY WATER, as the springs are muddied and may be dried
up.

The route is sometimes hard to follow when passing through meadows. Rock Cairns, tree blazes, and diamond-shaped markers can be
followed fairly easily. Elk may be seen, or their sounds may be
heard in the thickets below the trail. There is an abundance of
wildflowers in season.

GEYSER SPRINGS TRAIL #1087. (See map 11)

TRAIL BEGINS:	-Forest Road 3795/300.	ELEV. 4080'
TRAIL ENDS:	-Middle Fork of the Rogue River.	ELEV. 3240'
DISTANCE:	-1.1 mile, difficult. USE: hiker.	
SEASON:	-Summer months. LIMITED MAINTENANCE.	
BRING MAPS:	-Prospect Ranger Dist.-Rogue River Ntl. Forest.	
	-USFS Rec. Opportunity Guide-Geyser Spr. Trail.	

ACCESS: From the town of Prospect, Oregon, drive east on County Road 992 leading toward Butte Falls, for 2.5 miles to the junction with Forest Route 37. Turn left onto 37 and go 2.8 miles to the junction with Forest Road 3795. Continue on 3795, 2.7 miles to Forest Road 3795/300. Follow Road 300, 1.2 miles to the trailhead on the right. Road 300 is gated from Nov. 1 to June 15.

FEATURES: After the first 1/3 mile, Geyser Springs can be seen about 25 feet below the trail. There is no established trail leading to the springs from this point, so care must be taken to get there and back. The main trail continues to the Middle Fork of the Rogue River. This is a steep trail dropping about 800 feet from the road to the river. Native rainbow and brook trout are popular with fishermen.

Geyser Springs is one of the headwater springs that feed the Middle Fork of the Rogue River.

HISTORY: The Geyser Springs Trail was once part of an old Forest Service trail system and telephone line that ran from the Imnaha Guard Station, down the Middle Fork Canyon, up to Bessie Rock Guard Station, and ended at Bessie Rock Lookout. Used for fire watch communications in the 1920's, the telephone line and much of the trail were abandoned in the 1960's. (USFS information)

152

GOLDEN STAIRS TRAIL #1092,(See map 5)

TRAIL BEGINS:	-Near Forest Road 68/550.	ELEV. 3750'
TRAIL ENDS:	-Rogue-Umpqua Divide Trail 1470.	ELEV. 5350'
DISTANCE:	-4.3 mi., moderately steep.	
SEASON:	-June through Oct. USE: hiker/horse/motorcycle.	
CONNECTING TR.	-Rogue-Umpqua Divide Trail 1470.	
BRING MAPS:	-Prospect Ranger Dist.-Rogue River Ntl. Forest.	
	-USFS Rec. Opportunity Guide-Golden Stairs Trail.	

ACCESS: LOWER TRAILHEAD: From the Prospect Ranger Sta-
                 tion (north end of Prospect Oregon), go north on
State Hwy. 62, 6 miles (just beyond milepost 51), to the junction
with Forest Route 68.   Turn left onto 68 and follow mileposts to
mile 5 at the junction with Forest Road 550.   Turn right onto 550
and continue one mile to an unsigned junction.   Keep left and go
2 miles, passing the junction with Road 557, and continue 0.1 mi.
further to the signed trailhead on the right.

UPPER TRAILHEAD: From the junction of State Hwy. 62 and Forest
Route 68, turn left and continue on 68, 2.5 miles to the junction
with Forest Road 6510.   Keep right onto 6510 and travel 2.0 miles
to the junction with Forest Road 6510/500.   Turn left onto Road
500 and travel about 4.0 miles to the junction with Roads 700 and
770. Continue straight ahead onto Rd.700, 1.1 mi. to Yellowjacket
Camp.   The Rogue Umpqua Divide Trail passes by this point. Follow
this trail 1.0 mile west to the upper end of Golden Stairs Trail.

FEATURES: The lower end of the trail begins through stands
                   of fir before continuing along the southern, ex-
posed ridge of Falcon Butte.   Along the way, there are good views
of the Rogue River, Elk Creek and Woodruff Creek drainages.   Further on toward the Rogue-Umpqua Divide, the face of Elephant Head
and the slopes of Abbott Butte will be seen. The upper end of the
trail junctions with the Rogue-Umpqua Divide Trail about 1.0 mile
west of Forest Road 6510/700.   NO WATER

HISTORY: Golden Stairs Trail was "named in part from the Abbott
           brothers alleged gold mine in the area." (USFS quote)

ROGUE-UMPQUA DIVIDE TRAIL #1470. (See maps 5,1B and 2)

TRAIL BEGINS:-Junction of Forest Routes 68 and 30 at Rogue-Umpqua
　　　　　　　Divide, at milepost 30 on Route 68.
TRAIL ENDS:　-Three Lakes Camp, Forest Road 3703.
DISTANCE:　　-31.4 miles USE: hiker/horse. SEASON: summer/fall.
BRING MAPS:　-USFS Rogue-Umpqua Divide, Boulder Creek and Mt.
　　　　　　　Thielsen Wildernesses.
　　　　　　　-USFS Tiller, Diamond Lake and Prospect Ranger Dis-
　　　　　　　tricts-Umpqua and Rogue River National Forests.

FEATURES:　This National Recreation Trail is the primary route
through the Rogue-Umpqua Divide Wilderness. The trail offers ex-
ceptional views both east and west as it weaves across the crest
of the divide.　To the west, lies the irregular and deeply dis-
sected terrain of the Umpqua Drainage;while to the east the trav-
eler sees the broad, open Rogue Basin, with the peaks of the high
Cascades rising above. In addition to the fine vistas,the divide
features a spectacular display of wildflowers in its many meadows
from mid-June until mid-August.

The Divide Trail begins from the southern end of the wilderness.
In places, the trail parallels the old CCC road to Abbott Butte.
Due to a steep and narrow section of trail, horse users are advised to take the old road at one point and loop back into the
trail, avoiding a potential hazard.

The trail passes below Abbott Butte Lookout and descends to a
small pond below a rock cliff called Elephant Head. The old lookout is still standing, but it is unsafe to climb up to the building.

Traveling east, the trail is joined by Golden Stairs Trail #1092,
three miles beyond Abbott Butte. This steep trail leads to the
Rogue River National Forest Road #6800-550. One mile past this
junction, the trail enters Yellowjacket Camp. From here,the trail
follows an old skid road for 1/2 mile. A live creek crosses the
trail just below the road. The trail then climbs the south slope
of Anderson Mountain and opens to a gigantic sub-alpine meadow.
Here,Sandstone trail #1436 joins the divide trail from the Umpqua
side. From the Rogue side of the divide,Anderson Camp Trail #1075
reaches the ridgetop and joins the divide trail.

154

-continued

From Anderson Mountain, the Divide Trail travels northerly on the crest of a rocky ridge, offering fine views of Crater Lake Rim and Mt. McLoughlin to the east; Highrock Mountain to the west and Abbott Butte to the southwest. Pup Prairie Trail #1434 intersects the Divide Trail just before the trail meets Road 6515-530 at its junction with Road 6515. Here, a spring can be found in the meadow south of this junction. Road 6515-530 becomes the route for the Divide Trail for about 1.5 miles to the junction of Acker Divide Trail #1437. At this intersection the road leads another 1/2 mile to Hershberger Lookout. The Divide Trail however, continues north at this junction, along the route known as the Log Pile Trail. Fish Lake Trail #1570 intersects the Rogue-Umpqua Divide Trail 3/4 mile down this section of trail.

About 1/4 mile further, the Rocky Rim Trail #1572 intersects to the west. The Divide Trail then passes through a saddle onto the eastern face of Weaver Mountain where vistas open to the north and east. The trail then descends to the edge of an ancient shallow glacial lake, now a marshy meadow called Hole-in-the-ground. After passing along the southeast edge of the meadow, the trail forks. The Divide Trail continues on the northerly fork, crossing the meadow to Hole-in the Ground Camp. Here, Buck Canyon Trail #1046 intersects and the Divide Trail heads north for a strenuous one mile climb to Road #3700-870.

This road, at the end of Fish Creek Valley serves as a connecting route between segments of the Divide Trail. To return to the Rogue-Umpqua Divide Trail, follow this road for about 1 mile to Happy Camp. 1/10 of a mile further down the road, the trail continues off to the left of the road. Take this trail to the intersection with the Whitehorse Meadow Trail #1477, and proceed northeast on this trail down the valley. About 3/4 of a mile down the valley, the Whitehorse Meadow Trail turns right and climbs out of the valley. The Divide Trail continues down the valley. This segment of trail passes the Fish Creek Shelter before it climbs out of the valley and crosses Road #3700-870.

The Divide Trail continues up the ridge with some steep stretches and then down the east slope, across Forest Route #37, and on to Buck Camp. Clear Camp lies about 1 mile further down the trail, and the Rogue-Umpqua Divide Trail terminates at THREE LAKES CAMP, on Forest Road #3703. (From Tiller Ranger Dist. Recreation Guide)

155

ACCESS TO ROGUE-UMPQUA DIVIDE TRAIL.

SOUTHERN END OF ROGUE-UMPQUA DIVIDE TRAIL.-Abbott Butte Trailhead
From the town of Prospect, go north on Hwy. 62 just beyond mile-post 51 at the junction with Forest Route 68. Turn left onto 68 and go 13 miles to the Rogue-Umpqua Divide at the junction with Forest Route 30. The trailhead is on the right.

Via Golden Stairs Trail #1092.
North of Prospect on Hwy. 62, just beyond milepost 51, turn left onto Forest Route 68 and follow mileposts to mile 5 at the junction with Forest Road 550.Turn right and go 1 mi. to an(unsigned) junction. Keep left and go 2 miles, passing the junction with Rd. 557, and continue 0.1 mile further to the signed trailhead on the right. This steep trail continues 4.3 miles to the Rogue-Umpqua Divide Trail, about 1 mile west of Forest Road 6510-700.

YELLOWJACKET CAMP.
North of Prospect on Hwy. 62, just beyond milepost 51, turn left on Forest Route 68 and go about 2.5 miles to Forest Road 6510. Turn right and follow 6510, 2 miles to Road 6510/500. Follow Road 500 about 4 miles to the junction of Roads 700 and 770. Continue straight ahead onto Road 700, 1.1 mi. to Yellowjacket Camp.

VIA ANDERSON CAMP TRAIL #1075. (LIMITED MAINTENANCE)
North of Prospect on Hwy. 62, just beyond milepost 51, turn left onto Forest Route 68 and go about 2.5 miles to Forest Road 6510. Turn right and follow 6510, 5.8 miles to Forest Road 6515. Turn left onto 6515 and go 6.3 miles, looking carefully for the trail head on the left. Anderson Camp Trail reaches the Rogue-Umpqua Divide Trail after 3/4 mile. To reach Anderson Mountain Summit, turn left (south) to a sign posted at a short, faint trail to the summit.

VIA HERSHBERGER ROAD.
North of Prospect on Hwy. 62, just beyond milepost 51, turn left onto Forest Route 68 and go about 2.5 miles to Forest Road 6510. Turn right and follow 6510, 5.8 miles to Forest Road 6515. Turn left onto 6515 and go 9.6 miles to the junction of Roads 525 and 530. A spring is located in the meadow south of this junction, along the east bank of Flat Creek. The trail follows along Road 530 for about 1.5 miles before continuing as a trail to points north. -continued

ACCESS TO ROGUE-UMPQUA DIVIDE TRAIL-continued.

VIA HOLE-IN-THE-GROUND TRAIL #1047.
North of Union Creek Resort, at the junction of Hwys. 62 and 230, follow mileposts on 230 to mile 9.1 (the northern end of loop Rd. 6540.) Turn LEFT and go about 4.8 miles (at milepost 6) to the junction with Forest Road 6540/500. Turn RIGHT onto Road 500 and go 1.5 miles to the trailhead at the end of the road. ELEV. 5200' Trail 1047 travels along Log Creek and joins Rogue-Umpqua Divide Trail at the edge of a small glacial meadow. Hole-in-the-Ground Camp is east of the meadow, just inside the trees. The junction with Buck Canyon Trail #1046 appears at this camp ELEV. 5600'.

TO WHERE THE DIVIDE TRAIL CROSSES FOREST ROUTE 37.
Follow mileposts on State Highway 230 to mi. 12.1 at the junction with Forest Road 6560. Turn LEFT onto Road 6560 and go 4 miles to the Rogue-Umpqua Divide, where the route number becomes Route 37. Follow Route 37, 0.4 miles further and look carefully for a sign far to the left, indicating the Divide Trail leading southwest. On the right side of Route 37, look just beyond for a road track from where the Divide Trail leads northeast to Three Lakes Camp.

ALONG FISH CREEK VALLEY ROAD 870.
Continue 0.1 mi. further on Route 37 to the junction with Forest Road 800. Turn LEFT onto Road 800 and go 3 miles to Fish Creek Valley Road 870. Turn LEFT onto Road 870 and go 0.9 mile to where the Divide Trail crosses LEFT from Road 37 and RIGHT toward the Fish Creek Shelter.

Fish Creek Valley Road continues about 3 miles to where the Divide Trail merges from the RIGHT (from Fish Creek Valley) to follow Road 870, about 1.1 mi. to its end. A sign reads: "Hole-in-the-ground 1 mile, Hershberger Lookout 5 miles, Abbott Butte 19 miles".

FROM THREE LAKES ROAD 3703.
North of Union Creek Resort, follow mileposts on Hwy. 230 to mile 20.6 Turn LEFT onto Three Lakes Road 3703 and go 5.7 mi. to the junction of Road 3703/400. Turn LEFT on Road 400 and go 0.2 mile to a parking area at the west end of the lake. Follow blazes on an old road, 0.8 mi. to the beginning of the trail.

157

The Rogue-Umpqua-Divide Trail 1470 lies within the Rogue-Umpqua Divide Wilderness, created by the Oregon Wilderness Act of 1984.

WILDERNESS REGULATIONS INCLUDE:

- -PACK OUT ALL LITTER, especially foil packaging that doesn't burn.

- -BURY HUMAN WASTE 6 to 8 inches deep, 200 feet or more from open water.

- -CAMPFIRES only in safe spots, keep small. It is best to carry stoves.

- -CAMPING: Pitch your tent so no drainage ditch is required. Replace rocks and other materials removed from sleeping areas.

- -MOTORIZED and MECHANICAL equipment, including bicycles, are prohibited in the wilderness.

  (EXCERPTS: "New Wilderness on the Umpqua National Forest" brochure)

As You Hike Under The Forest
Canopy These Guys Will dispute Your
Passage.

158

ROCKY RIM TRAIL #1572. (See map 1B)

TRAIL BEGINS:	-UPPER TRAILHEAD: Rogue Umpqua Divide Trail 1470, 1 mile north of Hershberger Mtn. ELEV. 5680'
TRAIL ENDS:	-LOWER TRAILHEAD: Beaver Swamp Trailhead, Umpqua Forest Road 2840/400 near Fish Lake. ELEV. 4000'
DISTANCE:	-6.8 miles, moderate. USE: hiker/horse.
SEASON:	-Upper end snow-free July to October.
CONNECTING TR.:	-Rogue-Umpqua Divide Trail 1470.
	-Rocky Ridge Trail 1571, (partially abandoned).
BRING MAPS:	-Tiller Ranger District-Umpqua National Forest.
	-USFS -Rogue Umpqua Divide, Boulder Creek and Mt. Thielsen Wildernesses.
	-USFS Recreation Opportunity Guide Rocky Rim Tr.

ACCESS: -UPPER END: North of Prospect on Hwy. 62 just be-
            yond milepost 51, turn left onto Forest Route 68
and go about 2.5 miles to Forest Road 6510. Turn right and follow
6510, 5.8 miles to Forest Road 6515.   Turn left onto 6515 and go
9.6 miles to the junction of Roads 525, 530 and the Rogue-Umpqua
Divide Trail 1470.A spring is located in the meadow south of this
junction along the east bank of Flat Creek. Follow Road 530 about
1.5 miles to where the Divide Trail continues.   Take the Divide
Trail 1 mile north to the beginning of Rocky Rim Trail.

FEATURES: This description uses only the 4 mile portion of
            Rocky Rim Trail from its upper end near Hershber-
ger Mountain to the junction with the Rocky Ridge Trail and return, a very attractive day hike.   From the Rogue-Umpqua Divide
Trail, Rocky Rim Trail travels northwest through timber and sub-
alpine meadows before meeting the narrow backbone of Rocky Ridge.
The trail features a birdseye view of Fish Lake, the Castle Creek
drainage, and of the high Cascade Mountains. Wildflowers usually
are in great numbers, well into the summer months.

CHAPTER 11 - CRATER LAKE AREA

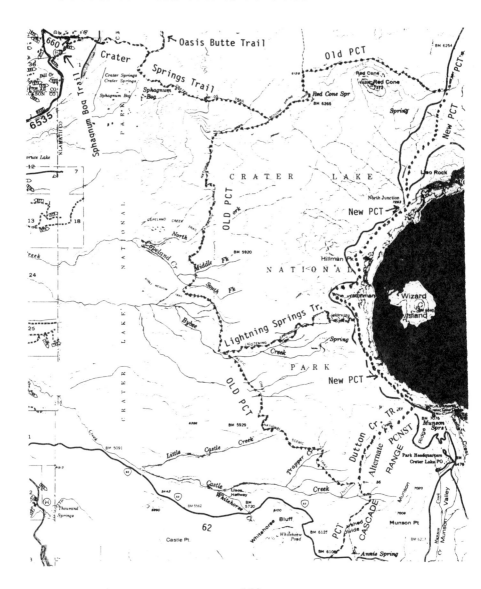

CRATER LAKE NATIONAL PARK BACKCOUNTRY USE REGULATIONS.

BACKCOUNTRY USE PERMITS ARE REQUIRED FOR ALL OVERNIGHT STAYS. The only exception is for overnight hikers who enter on the Pacific Crest Trail and exit the PCT at the opposite boundary. Free permits are available at entrance stations, information and visitor centers, from park rangers (after hours) or by mail. OTHER REGS:

1. CAMPING AND CAMPFIRES Open campfires allowed where not specifically prohibited.. Use only dead and down wood. No cutting or damaging living or standing vegetation, or collecting wood above 6900 ft. Use established fire rings at existing sites.In un-designated sites, remove all signs of fire by scattering rocks and churning the soil. Prior to leaving the campsite, make sure the fire is out and cold.
CAMPING AND OPEN FIRES are prohibited between Rim Drive and Crater Lake; on Phantom Ship; Wizard Island; on Mt. Scott or its summit trails; within any meadow; within one mile of any paved road, nature trail or developed area; within 1/4 mile of Boundary Springs or Sphagnum Bog; within 100 ft. of any water source, trail or other camping party except when using a designated campsite.
2. PARTY SIZE(overnight trips) Limit 8 persons, 12 head of stock.
3. STAY ON TRAILS: NO HIKING OR CLIMBING INSIDE THE RIM except on the Cleetwood Trail.
4. PETS ARE NOT ALLOWED ON ANY PARK TRAIL, NOR ANYWHERE ELSE IN THE BACKCOUNTRY.
5. FIREARMS, bicycles, and motorized vehicles ARE NOT PERMITTED IN THE BACKCOUNTRY.
6. HORSES/PACK ANIMALS permitted only on designated trails. Horse Regulation handouts are available at park visitor centers.
7. SANITATION: Pack out all litter and leave clean campsite. Use privies where available, otherwise make your toilet in a shallow slit trench and cover when finished, away from camp and over 100 feet from any water source. BOIL OR TREAT ALL WATER.
8. PROTECTION FROM BEARS: Suspend food items from a tree branch, at least 10 ft. above ground and 4 ft. horizontally from the trunk. Store and prepare food away from sleeping areas. Food is defined as any packaged, bottled or canned consumables, drinks, toiletries, perfumes, soaps, etc. (Excerpts "Crater Lake Backcountry Use" leaflet).

161

<u>UNION PEAK TRAIL, CRATER LAKE NATIONAL PARK.</u> (See map 7)

<u>TRAIL BEGINS:</u>   -Pacific Crest Trail, about 3 miles southwest of
                State Highway 62.   <u>ELEV.</u> 6550'
<u>TRAIL ENDS:</u>   -Union Peak summit.   <u>ELEV.</u> 7709'
<u>DISTANCE:</u>   -About 2.5 miles, moderate to steep grades.
<u>USE:</u>   -Hikers only.
<u>SEASON:</u>   -Usually snow-free July through September.
<u>CONNECTING TR.</u> -Pacific Crest National Scenic Trail.
<u>BRING MAPS:</u>   -USFS Pacific Crest Trail-Oregon Central Portion.
                -CRATER LAKE map/brochure-National Park Service.

<u>ACCESS:</u>   Just north of Union Creek Resort, at the inter-
                    section of State Hwys. 230 and 62, travel north-
east on 62,   15.7 miles to a point where the Pacific Crest Trail
(PCNST) crosses the highway. ELEV. about 6200'.   After parking,
go southwest on the PCNST about 3 miles to the junction with the
Union Peak Trail. Follow the Union Peak Trail about 2.5 miles to
the summit of Union Peak. CARRY WATER.

To the south you can see Mt. McLoughlin. Diamond Peak, Mt. Bailey
and Mt. Thielsen are to the north. The Crater Lake Rim, with its
lofty peaks, appears in the northeast.

<u>NOTE:</u> PLEASE OBSERVE CRATER LAKE NATIONAL PARK BACKCOUNTRY USE
REGULATIONS LISTED AT THE BEGINNING OF THIS CHAPTER.

<u>HISTORY:</u>   "UNION PEAK (7709 feet), located in the southwest
                    corner of the park, was so-named during the Civil
War by Northern sympathizers in the Rogue River Valley."
(USFS quote)

162

DUTTON CREEK TRAIL- CRATER LAKE NATIONAL PARK. (See Map page 160)
(Southern leg of a Pacific Crest Trail alternate route).

TRAIL BEGINS: -Pacific Crest Trail (PCNST).   ELEV. 6100'
TRAIL ENDS: -Park Headquarters Road, 200 feet south of its
                   junction with the Rim Drive.   ELEV. 7100'
DISTANCE: -2.5 miles one way. Steep grades.
SEASON: -Usually snow-free July through September.
CONNECTING TRAIL: -Pacific Crest National Scenic Trail.
BRING MAPS: -USGS Crater Lake West, 7.5' series, 1985.
                  -Pacific Crest Trail, Oregon Central Portion.
                  -CRATER LAKE map/brochure-National Park Service.

ACCESS: LOWER TRAILHEAD: North of Union Creek Resort
                  at the junction of State Highways 62 and 230,
go 15.7 miles on Hwy. 62 to where the Pacific Crest Trail crosses
the highway. Park at this location and hike north, 1.7 miles to
the junction with the lower end of the Dutton Crk. Tr.(the southern leg of the new PCT alternate route). After leaving this older
section of the PCT, the Dutton Creek Trail leads 2.5 miles to its
upper trailhead on Park Headquarters Road near West Rim Drive.

UPPER TRAILHEAD: From the south entrance station of Crater Lake
National Park, travel beyond the Park Headquarters, and continue
north to within 200 feet of the junction with the West Crater Lk.
Rim Drive. Dutton Creek Trail leads downhill left (southwest).

Travelling further north,the PCT alternate route crosses West Rim
Drive and follows 6 miles along the west rim of Crater Lake.After
crossing the East Rim Drive at North Junction, the route descends
from Llao Rock and, after 2 miles, reaches the intersection where
this alternate route meets the older section of the PCT.

HISTORY: Captain Clarence E. Dutton   commanded a U.S.
                  Geological Survey party to sound the depth of
Crater Lake from their boat, the Cleetwood.   Their deepest wire
soundings indicated the lake depth at 1996 feet, amazingly close
to sonar measurements of 1932 feet officially recorded in 1959.
(From "Crater Lake National Park" brochure). PLEASE SEE BEGINNING
OF THIS CHAPTER FOR BACKCOUNTRY USE REGULATIONS   IN CRATER LAKE
PARK.

<u>LIGHTNING SPRINGS TRAIL.</u> (See map 7)

<u>TRAIL BEGINS:</u>	-Crater Lake Rim Drive.	<u>ELEV.</u> 7170'
<u>TRAIL ENDS:</u>	-Pacific Crest Trail.	<u>ELEV.</u> 5850'
<u>DISTANCE:</u>	-4 miles, steep grades.	
<u>SEASON:</u>	-Usually snow-free July through September.	
<u>CONNECTING TR.</u>	-Pacific Crest National Scenic Trail.	
<u>BRING MAPS:</u>	-USGS Crater Lake West, 7.5' series, 1985.	
	-USFS Pacific Crest Trail-Oregon Central Portion.	
	-CRATER LAKE map/brochure-National Park Service.	

<u>ACCESS:</u>   The Lightning Springs Trail begins from the west
                portion of Crater Lake Rim Drive, about 2.3 miles
northwest of Rim Village.   (This point can also be reached from
Highway 238 at the junction with the North Rim Access Road.   Take
the North Rim Access Road to the Crater Lake Rim Drive and turn
right for about 3.5 miles to Lightning Springs Trailhead.)

<u>FEATURES:</u>   The trail switchbacks sharply downhill,   reaching
                Lightning Springs in less than 1 mile.   Water is
available here,   but should be boiled before drinking.   From the
springs, a stream follows the trail as it continues to the Pacific Crest Trail (PCNST) near Bybee Creek.   Travelling south on the
PCNST leads 6.3 miles to State Highway 62. <u>BACKCOUNTRY USE REGU-
LATIONS IN CRATER LAKE PARK ARE LISTED   AT THE BEGINNING OF THIS
CHAPTER.</u>

Build Campfires only in safe
places, and make small fires.

CHAPTER 12 - DIAMOND LAKE AREA

MT. THIELSEN TRAIL #1456. (See map 1A)

TRAIL BEGINS:	-State Highway 138 near milepost 81.	ELEV. 5400'
TRAIL ENDS:	-Mt. Thielsen Summit.	ELEV. 9182'
DISTANCE:	-4.9 miles, more difficult.	
SEASON:	-Summer and fall; hiker,horse. Winter skiing.	
CONNECTING TR:	-Spruce Ridge Trail 1458, Pacific Crest Trail.	
BRING MAPS:	-USFS Recreation Guide, Diamond Lake Ranger Dist.	
	-Mt. Thielsen Wilderness information-USFS Diamond Lake, Chemult, Crescent Ranger Districts.	
	-USFS Pacific Crest Trail-Central Oregon Portion.	
	-USGS "Diamond Lake" and "Mount Thielsen", 7.5' series 1985.	

ACCESS: Near the southeast corner of Diamond Lake, State Highways 230 and 138 intersect. From this point, go 1.5 miles north on 138 to Mt. Thielsen Trailhead on the right (east) side of the road between mileposts 81 and 82.

FEATURES: The trail leads upwards 1.6 miles to the junction with Spruce Ridge Trail 1458, and 1.3 miles further to the Pacific Crest Trail.

After crossing the Pacific Crest Trail, a 2 mile scramble begins a steep climb along a ridge to the east side of the summit pinnacle. The route up to the pinnacle must be well chosen to allow for proper hand and foot placements. This portion is steep. The use of a climber's rope is not absolutely necessary, but could be set in place as guidance and support to others in your party who may need it. Views from the summit extend north to Mt. Hood and south to Mt. Shasta.

HISTORY: Mt. Thielsen has been referred to as the "Lightning Rod of the Cascades," and was named for Hans Thielsen, a prominent railroad engineer and builder. The peak is one of several old volcanoes formed by lava flow about 2 million years ago when geologic forces folded and fractured the High Cascades. (USFS Information)

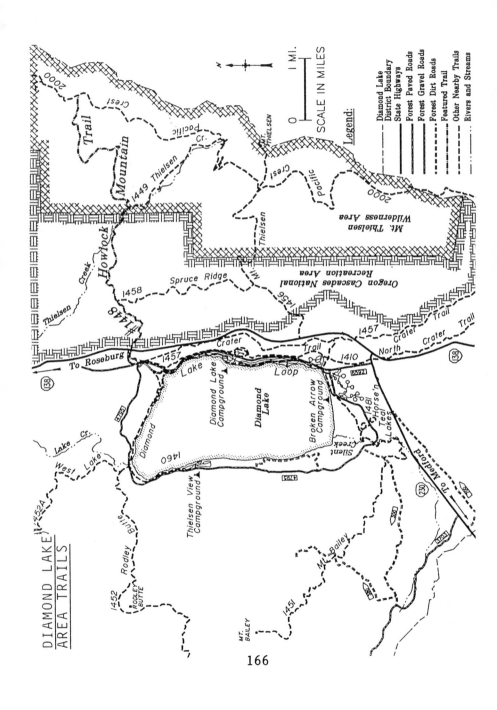

DIAMOND LAKE
AREA TRAILS

Legend:

Diamond Lake District Boundary
State Highways
Forest Paved Roads
Forest Gravel Roads
Forest Dirt Roads
Featured Trail
Other Nearby Trails
Rivers and Streams

SCALE IN MILES

0   1 MI.

N

166

HOWLOCK MTN. TRAIL #1448. (See map 1A)

TRAIL BEGINS: -Forest Road 4795 near Diamond Lake. ELEV. 5390'
TRAIL ENDS: -Pacific Crest Trail (PCNST). ELEV. 7220'
DISTANCE: -7 miles, difficult. USE: hiker/horse/skiers.
SEASON: -Hikers, July through September. Winter skiing.
CONNECTING TR. -Spruce Ridge Trail 1458, Thielsen Creek Trail
1449 and Pacific Crest National Scenic Trail.
BRING MAPS: -USFS Recreation Guide, Diamond Lake Ranger Dist.
-Mt. Thielsen Wilderness information-USFS Diamond
Lake, Chemult, Crescent Ranger Districts.
-USFS Pacific Crest Trail-Oregon Central Portion.

ACCESS: Just north of the Union Creek Resort at the junc-
                 tion with Highways 62 and 230, follow mileposts
on 230, 23.9 mi. to the junction with State Hwy. 138. Turn left
and go north on 138, 4.3 miles to the junction of Road 4795, the
north entrance to Diamond Lake Recreation Area. Turn south onto
Road 4795 and go 0.3 mile to the Howlock Mtn. Trailhead parking
area on the left.

FEATURES: From the Howlock Mtn. Trailhead, the Spruce Ridge
                 Trail is 1.2 miles, Timothy Meadows about 3 mi.,
Thielsen Creek Trail 3.5 miles(the last source of water along the
Howlock Mtn. Trail), and Pacific Crest Trail 7 miles. This point
on the Pacific Crest Trail is nearly 1 mile northwest of and 1000
feet lower elevation than Howlock Mountain.

From the upper Howlock Mtn. Trailhead, Windego Pass is 19 miles
north along the PCNST and the PCNST Trailhead on Hwy. 138 is 11.0
miles south.

The views of Howlock Mountain, Mt. Thielsen, Mt. Bailey and of
open meadows are outstanding. A loop hike using the Howlock Mtn.
Trail 1448 can be made by hiking right (south) along the Pacific
Crest Trail 3 miles to the Thielsen Creek Trail junction. Turn
right onto Thielsen Creek Trail 1449 and go about 2 1/4 miles to
the Howlock Mountain Trail. Keep left and follow the Howlock Mtn.
Trail 3 1/2 miles back to its trailhead. The total loop distance
is nearly 16 miles.

167

<u>THIELSEN CREEK TRAIL #1449.</u> (See map 1A)

<u>TRAIL BEGINS:</u> -(LOWER END): Howlock Mtn. Trail.   <u>ELEV.</u> 5600'
<u>TRAIL ENDS:</u>   -(UPPER END): Pacific Crest Trail.   <u>ELEV.</u> 6500'
<u>DISTANCE:</u>   -2.1 miles, more difficult. <u>USE:</u> hiker and horse
                in summer and fall. Winter skiing.
<u>CONNECTING TR.</u> -Howlock Mtn. Trail 1448 and Pacific Crest Trail.
<u>BRING MAPS:</u>   -USFS Recreation Guide, Diamond Lake Ranger Dist.
                -Mt. Thielsen Wilderness information USFS Diamond
                Lake, Chemult, Crescent Ranger Districts.
                USFS Pacific Crest Trail-Oregon Central Portion.

<u>ACCESS:</u>   Follow the directions to Howlock Mtn. Trailhead
                on the previous page. Take the Howlock Mtn. Trail
3.5 mi. to the LOWER END of the Thielsen Creek Trail. Turn right
and go 2.1 miles southeast to the Pacific Crest Trail.

From the upper Thielsen Creek Trailhead, Windego Pass is 22 miles
north along the PCNST and the North Crater Trailhead on Hwy. 138
is 8 miles south.

<u>FEATURES:</u>   Thielsen Creek Camp is along the upper end of the
                Thielsen Creek Trail about 1/8 mile below the Pa-
cific Crest Trail. Water is available. A 16 mile loop trip back
to the Howlock Mtn. Trailhead could be made by using the Thielsen
Creek Trail, taking the Pacific Crest Trail 3 miles north to the
Howlock Mtn. Trail, then turning left and following Howlock Mtn.
Trail 7 miles back to its trailhead.

Always take extra clothing
along. You may need some
dry things to put on.

<u>MT. BAILEY TRAIL #1451.</u> (See maps 1A or 3)

<u>TRAIL BEGINS:</u>   -Forest Road 4795/300.   <u>ELEV.</u> 5200'
<u>TRAIL ENDS:</u>   -Mt. Bailey summit.   <u>ELEV.</u> 8363'
<u>DISTANCE:</u>   -5 miles, moderate grades. <u>USE:</u> hiker only.
<u>SEASON:</u>   -Hikers July to October.
<u>BRING MAPS:</u>   -Diamond Lake Ranger Dist.-Umpqua Ntl. Forest.
                -USFS Rec. Opportunity Guide-Mt. Bailey Trail.
                -USGS Diamond Lake, 7.5' series, 1985.

<u>ACCESS #1.</u>   From the southeast corner of Diamond Lake, go about
2 miles west on Road 4795 to the junction of Road 4795/300. Turn
left onto Road 300 and go 0.4 mile to the trailhead parking lot.
Mt. Bailey Trail begins on the right of the parking area.   ELEV.
about 5200'.

<u>ACCESS#2.</u>   INTERCEPTS THE MT. BAILEY TRAIL, 2-1/4 MILES HIGHER
ON THE MOUNTAIN SLOPES, ELEV. ABOUT 6075'.   Near milepost 21 on
State Highway 230, find the junction with Forest Road 3703.   Turn
onto Road 3703 and travel northwest, about 2 miles to the junction with Forest Road 4795/300. Turn right onto 300 and go about
0.1 mi. to Forest Road 4795/380 on the left. Road 380 is narrow,
rocky and undriveable. It is a 1.5 mile hike up Road 380 to the
point where Mt. Bailey Trail crosses and climbs to the summit.

<u>FEATURES:</u>   No technical ability is required to reach the summit.
          The last 0.5 mi. is quite steep and rocky and may be
too difficult for small children.   Mt. Thielsen and Diamond Lake
are in the foreground.   To the north you can see Mt. Jefferson,
Three Fingered Jack, Mt. Washington, the Three Sisters,   Broken
Top, Diamond Peak, Bachelor Butte and nearby Cowhorn Mountain.

To the south you can see the Crater Lake Rim, Union Peak, Mt. Mc-
Loughlin and Mt. Shasta.

Rogue River National Recreation Trail

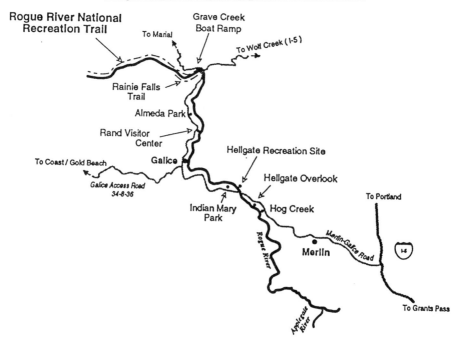

CHAPTER 13 - LOWER ROGUE AREA

LOWER ROGUE RIVER TRAIL #1160-Grave Creek to Foster Bar.

TRAIL BEGINS: -Grave Creek Trailhead, Merlin-Galice Road, 27
    miles northwest of Grants Pass.   ELEV. 650'

TRAIL ENDS: -Foster Bar near Illahe.   ELEV. 207'

DISTANCE: -40 miles, moderate grades. USE: hiker only.

SEASON: -Open all year, canyon very hot in summer months.

BRING MAPS: BLM/USFS "The Wild and Scenic Rogue River".

ACCESS: From Interstate Highway 5, Merlin exit, take the
Merlin-Galice Road, 27 miles northwest to the
Grave Creek boat landing just after crossing the Rogue River. The
last commercial facilities are located at Galice (store/restau-
rant, gas and car shuttle services that will arrange to have your
car at the Foster Creek landing at your designated time).

DAY HIKING: From the boat landing;hike to Rainie Falls (mile
2.0), Whiskey Creek cabin (mile 3.3), Big Slide
(mile 3.7) or Russian Creek (mile 5.8) and return. The cabin at
Whiskey Creek is a Registered National Landmark maintained by the
BLM. To find it, cross the bridge over Whiskey Creek and take the
side trail immediately to the right. OVERNIGHT CAMPING is available at Whiskey Creek, Big Slide and Russian Creek campsites.

40 MILE TRIP: The 40 mile trip is comfortably hiked in 5 days.
The BLM/USFS map/brochure gives a detailed log
for hikers and boaters, as well as trail tips and precautions
concerning heat, ticks, poison oak, rattlesnakes, etc. Information about Federal agencies, river guides, motels, lodge accom-
modations, fishing and hunting regulations, USGS topo maps, vegetation, animals, fish, and birds; is also given.

The upper 24 miles are administered by the Medford District Bur-
eau of Land Management, and the lower 16 miles by USFS, Siskiyou
National Forest. FOR MORE INFORMATION CONTACT:
-Medford Dist. B.L.M., 3040 Biddle Road, Medford, OR. 97504
-Siskiyou Ntl. Forest, 200 N.E. Greenfield Rd., Grants Pass 97526
-Galice Ranger Dist., 1465 N.E. 7th, Grants Pass, OR 97526
-Gold Beach Ranger Dist.,1225 S. Ellensburg, Gold Beach OR, 97444

CHAPTER 14 - PACIFIC CREST TRAIL ROAD ACCESS

<u>COOK AND GREEN PASS-FOREST ROAD 1055.</u> (See map 26)

<u>TEMPORARY REPAIRS HAVE BEEN MADE TO STORM-DAMAGED ROAD 1055,</u> and
<u>the permanent repairs are scheduled. Check with USFS for updates!</u>

<u>SEASON:</u>   -Usually snow-free July through October.
<u>CONNECTING TR.</u> -Cook and Green Trail 959, Horse Camp Trail 958.
<u>BRING MAPS:</u>   -USFS Rogue River and Klamath National Forests.
                          -USFS Pacific Crest Trail-Oregon Southern Portion.
                          -USFS brochure-Red Buttes Wilderness.

<u>ACCESS:</u>   From the town of Ruch, Oregon, follow mileposts
                          south on Upper Applegate Road, 18.8 miles to the
junction with Carberry Creek Road (County Route 777).   Keep left
and go beyond milepost 20 to the California-Oregon border, at the
signed junction with Forest Roads 1040 and 1050.   Turn left onto
Road 1050 and go 0.9 mi. to the junction with Forest Road 1055 on
the right. Travel south on Road 1055 to Cook and Green Pass near
milepost 10. The Pacific Crest Trail comes in on the left (east),
and then follows south along the undriveable Kangaroo Road about
3.5 miles.   Near Lily Pad Lake, look left for the junction where
the Pacific Crest Trail continues as a trail to points south.

<u>FEATURES:</u>   WATER is located from a spring near the Cook and
                          Green Pass.   Hike down Cook and Green Trail less
                          than 1/4 mile.

<u>HISTORY:</u>   "COOK AND GREEN PASS, CAMPGROUND: Robert Cook and
                          the two Green brothers were partners in several
mining ventures in this vicinity during the 1870's and 1880's and
the name undoubtedly resulted from their activities."
(USFS quote)

PACIFIC CREST TRAIL ACCESS, FOREST ROAD 2025. (See map 27)

SEASON: -Usually snow-free July through October.
BRING MAPS: -USFS Rogue River and Klamath National Forests.
              -USFS Pacific Crest Trail-Oregon Southern Portion.

ACCESS: From the the town of Ruch, Oregon, follow mileposts
              south on Upper Applegate Road to mile 9.3, at the
junction with Beaver Creek Road (Forest Route 20). Turn left onto
20 and follow mileposts to mile 14.1 at the junction with Forest
Road 2025.

Turn right onto 2025 and follow mileposts to:
-Mile 4.3 Pacific Crest Trail crosses the road, look for signs.
-Mile 5.1 Pacific Crest Trail crosses the road at the junction
           with Forest Road 40-S-01. Look for signs.

Forest Road 2025 can also be reached via Forest Route 20 from the
east, but portions of the road could be bumpy and not recommended
for passenger cars.

FEATURES: Watch carefully for trail signs, as road spurs and
              other evidence of timber harvesting can add confu-
sion. For water sources along the trail, check with Star Ranger
Station near milepost 7 on Upper Applegate Road.

ALWAYS READ THE POSTED SIGNS
AT THE TRAILHEAD.

173

PACIFIC CREST TRAIL ACCESS, FOREST ROUTE 22. (See maps 20 and 28)

SEASON: -Usually snow-free July to October. Wildflowers in
                 abundance throughout the summer months.
BRING MAPS: -USFS Rogue River and Klamath National Forests.
              -USFS Pacific Crest Trail-Oregon Southern Portion.

ACCESS: From Talent, Oregon, at the intersection of Talent
                 Avenue and Main Street, go south on Main St., which
becomes Wagner Creek Road in about 1 mile.   Follow mileposts on
Wagner Creek Road to the following mileage points:

-Mile 4.5 Pavement ends.
-Mile 7.1 Bald Mt. Road junction, keep left.
-Mile 9.1 Wagner Gap (three-way junction) keep left on Forest
           Route 22.

Continue on Forest Route 22, approx. 8 miles to the junction with
Forest Route 20 on the Siskiyou Crest. Turn right on Forest Route
20 and go 0.1 mi. to the junction of Forest Roads 2040 and 40S16.
Look to the left where the Pacific Crest Trail crosses 40S16.

FEATURES: Forest Route 22 is unpaved, and there are some curves
            at its lower elevations.   It is best to be cautious.
Otherwise, this road provides a good access to the Pacific Crest
Trail as it continues along the Siskiyou crest. For other access
points along Forest Route 20, see details on the following page.

PACIFIC CREST TRAIL ACCESS-ALONG FOREST ROUTE 20 and Hwy. 99S.
(Maps 24,27,28)

SEASON: -Usually snow-free by late July at higher elevations
                 (Mt. Ashland and Dutchman Peak areas).
BRING MAPS: -USFS Pacific Crest Trail-Oregon Southern Portion.
                 -USFS Rogue River and Klamath National Forests.
                 -BLM Medford District, Pacific Crest Trail Log.

ACCESS: From Interstate Highway 5,Ashland Exit 14, continue
                 9 miles to Mt. Ashland Exit 6 leading to a junction
with Old Highway 99 South. Keep right and go 0.6 mile to a hiker
trail sign on the right indicating the Pacific Crest Trail leading west toward Mt. Ashland and California. Continue 0.1 mile to
Mt. Ashland Access Road, and follow this road to mile readings:

Mile 7.0   PCNST crosses the road at the National Forest Boundary,
            FROM THIS POINT THE ROAD BECOMES FOREST ROUTE 20.
Mile 11.1   Grouse Gap, PCNST parallel to road on the left(south).
Mile 16.1   Junction with Forest Roads 40S16 and 40S20, look left
            to where the PCNST crosses.
Mile 16.9   PCNST crosses Route 20 at Siskiyou Gap.
Mile 19.9   Wrangle Gap, Jnc. Road 2030, PCNST on right (north).
Mile 20.1   PCNST crosses Route 20.
Mile 21.9   Track on left (south) leads about 0.1 mile to Sheep
            Camp Springs.
Mile 22.3   Jackson Gap.(To reach the PCNST turn left onto Road
            40S01 and go 0.6 mile to where the PCNST crosses).
Mile 23.7   (Appx.) Junction with Forest Road 2025. (To reach the
            PCNST, turn left and go 4.3 miles to where the PCNST
            crosses.)

FEATURES: Food and a pay telephone are located at Callahan's
            Restaurant on Old Highway 99S just east of Interstate
5 Mt. Ashland exit. Route 20 between Grouse Gap and Road 2025 may
be too rough for passenger cars. Water is scarce along this portion of the trail.ORVs including bicycles-NOT ALLOWED on the PCT.

PACIFIC CREST TRAIL ACCESS-PILOT ROCK ROAD. (See map 29)

SEASON: -Usually snow-free by early May.
BRING MAPS: -USFS Pacific Crest Trail-Oregon Southern Portion.
                 -BLM Medford District-Pacific Crest Trail Log.

ACCESS: From Ashland Exit 14, continue southeast on Inter-
                 state Hwy. 5, 9 miles to Mt. Ashland Exit 6.   The
off-ramp leads to a junction with Old Highway 99 South. Keep to
the right at this junction and go 1.9 miles to the junction with
Pilot Rock Road 40-2E-33. ALONG THE WAY, THE PACIFIC CREST TRAIL
FOLLOWS OLD HIGHWAY 99S FOR A DISTANCE OF 1/2 MILE SOUTH OF THE
FREEWAY OVERPASS.   LOOK ON THE LEFT FOR A TRAIL SIGN NAILED TO A
TREE WHERE THE PCNST LEAVES THE ROAD AND HEADS TOWARD PILOT ROCK.

Turn left (east) onto Pilot Rock Road using your odometer to note
the following Pacific Crest Trail (PCNST) crossings:

Mile 1   PCNST crosses road in a saddle, look for trail signs.
Mile 2.1 Keep left downhill at a junction. (A right turn would
          lead 0.8 mile to the base of Pilot Rock and an access
          to the PCNST.)
Mile 2.9 Road junction, stay uphill to the right.
Mile 3.8 Road junction, stay right.
Mile 3.9 PCNST crosses at the crest of a ridge near a road gate
          in a recent logging area. Look for trail signs. From
this point, the PCNST LEADS RIGHT passing the base of Pilot Rock
and reaches Old Highway 99S in about 5.8 miles OR The PCNST LEADS
LEFT (northeast) to State Hwy. 66 (Greensprings Hwy.) in 11 mi.,
passing the slopes of Soda Mtn. and Hobart Bluff. CARRY WATER.

HISTORY: "PILOT ROCK, a volcanic plug so named because of its
                 prominence as a landmark to early travelers on the
Oregon-California Trail. Although the chute on the north face of
the rock can be scaled without special equipment, climbers should
be cautious of loose rock." (USFS quote)

PACIFIC CREST TRAIL ACCESS, BALDY CREEK ROAD 40-3E-5.(Maps 22,29)

SEASON: -Usually snow-free late May to October.
BRING MAPS: -USFS Pacific Crest Trail-Oregon Southern Portion.
             -BLM Transportation Map-Medford District-Klamath
             Resource Area.
             -BLM Medford District-Pacific Crest Trail Log.

ACCESS: From Ashland Interstate Highway 5 Exit 14, travel
             14.8 miles (southeast) on State Highway 66. Turn
right onto Tyler Creek Road and go 1.4 miles to the junction with
Baldy Creek Road 40-3E-5. Take 40-3E-5, 5.7 miles to the crest of
a ridge at the junction with Road 40-3E-30. The PCNST crosses the
road (40-3E-5) just before reaching a cattle guard.

TURNING RIGHT (SOUTH) onto the PCNST leads 9.4 mi. to Interstate
Hwy. 5 (passing Porcupine Mtn. at mile 2.6 and Pilot Rock at mile
5.3)

TURNING LEFT (NORTH) onto the PCNST leads 7.4 mi. to Hwy 66 (passing the western slopes of Soda Mountain at mile 1.5 and crossing
Soda Mountain Road near mile 3.0).

FEATURES: The Baldy Creek Road provides access to the Pacif-
             ic Crest National Scenic Trail, southwest of Soda
Mountain Lookout, at the near mid-point of the Highway 66-Inter-
state Highway 5 section of the trail. CARRY WATER when hiking in
this area. The Pacific Crest Trail passes through BLM and private lands. Watch carefully for the trail as it travels through
areas of timber harvesting. Numerous roads and cattle trails can
add to the confusion. Wildflowers are abundant from May to July.

177

PACIFIC CREST TRAIL ACCESS, STATE HIGHWAY 66.

SEASON: -Usually snow-free late May through October. Wildflowers abundant May to July.

BRING MAPS: -USFS Pacific Crest Trail-Oregon Southern Portion.
-BLM Transportation Map -Medford District -Klamath
Resource Area.
-BLM Medford District-Pacific Crest Trail Log.

USE: CLOSED TO MOTORIZED/MECHANICAL VEHICLES, INCLUDING
BICYCLES.

ACCESS: From Interstate Hwy. 5, Ashland Exit 14, follow the
mileposts east on State Hwy. 66, 15.7 miles to the
highway summit at Soda Mtn. Road. The Pacific Crest Trail crosses Hwy. 66 just beyond.

From this point the trail leads RIGHT, south and west, 16.8 miles
to Interstate Highway 5. Hobart Bluff, Soda Mountain Road, Soda
Mountain, and Pilot Rock are landmarks along the way.

Leading from the LEFT of Highway 66, the PCNST travels 4.6 miles
to Little Hyatt Reservoir then approx. 1.5 miles further to Hyatt
Prairie Road.

FEATURES: In this area of the Pacific Crest Trail, there are
views of the Rogue River Valley, Mt. Shasta in northern California and the Klamath Basin. The trail passes through
mixed private and BLM administered lands. Watch for trail insig-
nias. The trail may be hard to follow due to timber harvesting,
cattle trails, and numerous roads. CARRY DRINKING WATER, as on-
route supplies are very limited. Check with Ashland Ranger Station or Medford BLM office for exact locations.

HISTORY: "State Highway 66.......Known locally as the Greensprings Highway, this road parallels the 'Old Applegate Trail' which was used during the 1840's by pioneers who
branched off the main Oregon Trail at Fort Hall Idaho and crossed
the sagebrush desert of northern Nevada." (USFS quote)

HYATT LAKE RESERVOIR. (See map 22)

From Interstate Hwy. 5, Ashland Exit 14, follow mileposts east on State Hwy. 66, 17.5 mi.to the junction with East Hyatt Lake Road. Turn left onto this road and travel 3.1 mi.north to the south end of Hyatt Lake at the junction with West Hyatt Lake Road. A hikers camp at nearby Hyatt Lake Campground provides showers. Hyatt Lake Resort (across the lake) has food, phone and a maildrop.

The Pacific Crest Trail crosses the above road junction and leads southwest 1.5 mi. to Little Hyatt Lake, and 4.6 miles further to Greensprings Hwy 66. Leading northeast from Hyatt Lake, the trail goes along the east shore of Howard Prairie Lake and points north.

KENO ACCESS ROAD 39-7E-31. (See map 23)

From Interstate Hwy. 5, Ashland Exit 14,travel east on State Hwy. 66, 0.6 mi.to the junction with Dead Indian Memorial Road (County Route 722).Turn left onto this Route and follow mileposts to mile 18.5 at the junction with Keno Access Road 39-7E-31. Turn right onto 39-7E-31 and go 5.0 miles to where the Pacific Crest Trail crosses. Hiking northeast from this point, leads 3 miles to Big Springs at Griffin Pass and points north. Hiking southwest leads 3 miles to the southern shore of Howard Prairie Lake and BLM Road 38-4E-32. Willow Lake Campground is located 1.8 miles northwest along this road, on the southwest shore Of Howard Prairie Lake.

GRIFFIN PASS, ROAD 2520. (See map 23)

From Interstate Hwy. 5, Ashland Exit 14,travel east on State Hwy. 66, 0.6 mi. to the Junction with Dead Indian Memorial Rd. (County Route 722).Turn left onto this route and follow mileposts to mile 23.7 at the junction with Forest Road 2520. Turn right onto 2520 and continue 4.0 mi. to Griffin Pass, where the Pacific Crest Tr. crosses. 600 feet further on Road 2520 leads to a faint trail on the left leading to a spring (metal storage container). The water needs to be treated. Hiking northeast, the PCNST climbs to the eastern slopes of Old Baldy Mountain and on to Dead Indian Memorial Road. Hiking southwest,the trail descends to Keno Access Rd. and on toward Howard Prairie Lake and other points south.

FOREST MAP: Pacific Crest Trail-Oregon Southern Portion.

OLD BALDY MOUNTAIN. ROAD 2520/600. (See map 23)
From Interstate Hwy. 5, Ashland Exit 14, travel east on Hwy. 66,
0.6 mi. to the junction with Dead Indian Memorial Road. Turn left
onto this road and go 23.7 mi. to Road 2520, on the right.   Turn
onto Road 2520 and go 2.4 mi. to the junction with Road 2520/640.
Turn left onto Road 640 and go 0.6 mi. and merger with Road 600.
Follow Road 600,passing junctions with Roads 680 and 650, 1.0 mi.
to roads end (where a log blocks a Jeep track leading to the summit of Old Baldy Mountain, a good sidetrip.)
-There are no signs giving directions to the Pacific Crest Trail.
From the above log at roads end,follow a faint path 200 feet east
to the PCNST. It would be well to mark the path for your return
trip to Road 600. TURNING RIGHT onto the PCNST leads past a Forest service gate, 2.0 mi. to Griffin Pass and points south. TURN-
ING LEFT onto the PCNST leads downhill 1.7 miles to where Burton
Flat Road crosses and 1.9 mi. further to Dead Indian Mem. Road.

DEAD INDIAN MEMORIAL ROAD: (See map 23)
From Interstate Hwy. 5, Ashland Exit 14,follow State Hwy. 66, 0.6
mi. to Dead Indian Memorial Road. Turn left onto this road and go
27.2 mile to a PCNST parking area on the right. The PCNST LEADS
SOUTH, 3.6 mi. to Old Baldy Mtn. and southern points. THE PCNST
LEADS NORTH 11 mi.,passing Brown Mtn. Shelter (WATER PUMP), Road
700, west slopes of Brown Mtn., and High Lakes Trail Jnc. before
reaching Highway 140.

STATE HIGHWAY 140. (See map 16)
From WHITE CITY, follow mileposts east on Hwy. 140 to mile 32.5
at the Pacific Crest Trail Summit Parking Area on the left. The
PCNST South from Highway 140 crosses the Highlakes Trail in 0.5
mile, travels along the western slopes of Brown Mtn. It then passes the forks of Little Butte Creek,the Brown Mtn.Trail junction,
Road 700 at the 9.2 mile point, Brown Mtn Shelter(WATER PUMP) and
it is 2.0 miles further to Dead Indian Memorial Road.

The PCNST north from highway 140 enters Sky Lakes Wilderness in
2.0 mi., and crosses Mt. McLoughlin Trail in another 1.5 mile. It
then continues through Sky Lakes Wilderness and on to State Highway 62 in Crater Lake Park.

PACIFIC CREST TRAIL ROAD ACCESS POINTS -cont.
FOREST MAP: Pacific Crest Trail, Oregon Central Portion.

STATE HIGHWAY 62, NEAR ANNIE SPRING. (SEE MAP ON PAGE 160)
North of Union Creek Resort at the junction of State Highways 230
and 62,go 15.7 mi.northeast on Hwy.62 to where the PCNST crosses.
This point is 0.8 mile west of Crater Lake Park south entrance.

The PCNST SOUTH FROM HIGHWAY 62 passes Union Peak before continuing through Sky Lakes Wilderness, with good views of many lakes
and Mt. McLoughlin just north of State Highway 140.

GOING 1.7 miles NORTH on the PCT leads to a junction with DUTTON
CREEK TRAIL. The route for pack stock/hiker continues 15.2 miles
to a Pacific Crest Trail Parking Area on North Rim Access Road,
and 9 mi. more to Highway 138. A SHORTER, HIKER ONLY SCENIC ROUTE
co-locates with the DUTTON CREEK TRAIL, 2.5 miles to Park Headquarters Road at Rim Village. The Alternate PCT continues about
6.0 miles, skirting the west rim of the lake to North Rim Drive.
After crossing North Rim Drive,the trail descends about 2.5 miles
along the west slopes of Llao Rock to rejoin the original section
of the PCT at the PCT parking area on North Rim Access Road. It
is 9.0 trail miles further to State Highway 138.

STATE HIGHWAY 138. (See map 1A or 3)
From the southeast corner of Diamond Lake,at the intersection of
Highways 230 and 138, travel 4 mi. southeast on Hwy.138 to where
the Pacific Crest Trail crosses the highway.This crossing is 3/4
mile east of the north entrance to Crater Lake National Park.

IF TRAVELING SOUTH through Crater Lake National Park, please see
the previous description.

The Pacific Crest Trail NORTH FROM HIGHWAY 138 passes the junctions of North Crater Trail 1410, Mt. Thielsen Trail 1456,Thiel-
sen Creek Trail 1449 and Howlock Mtn.Trail 1448. These 4 trails
offer sidetrips to Diamond Lake Resort.

NOTES

ALPHABETICAL INDEX OF TRAILS

1A

See map 3

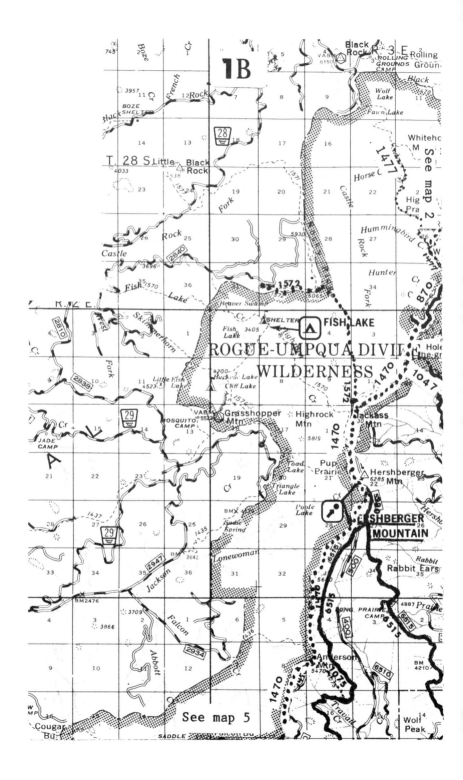

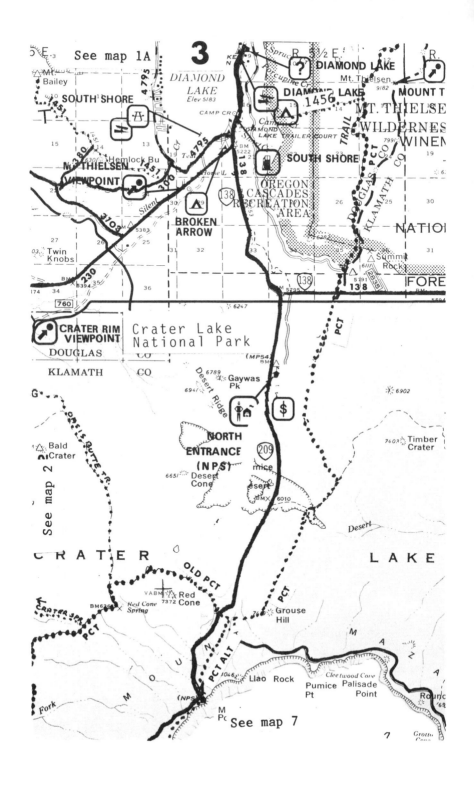

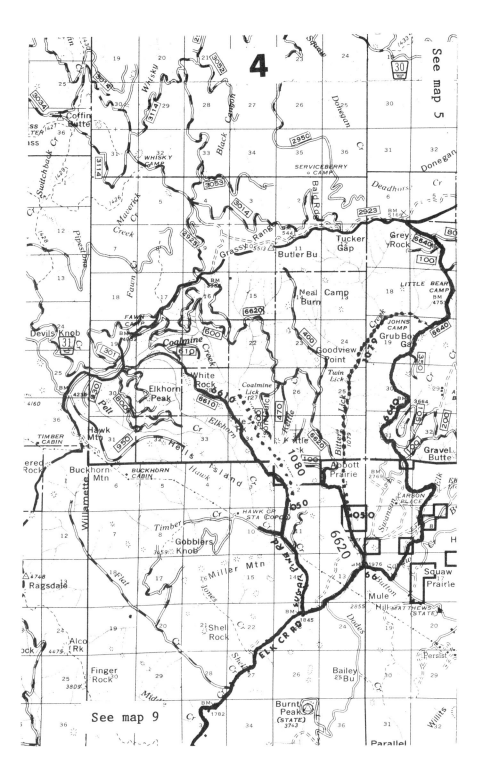

See map 5

See map 9

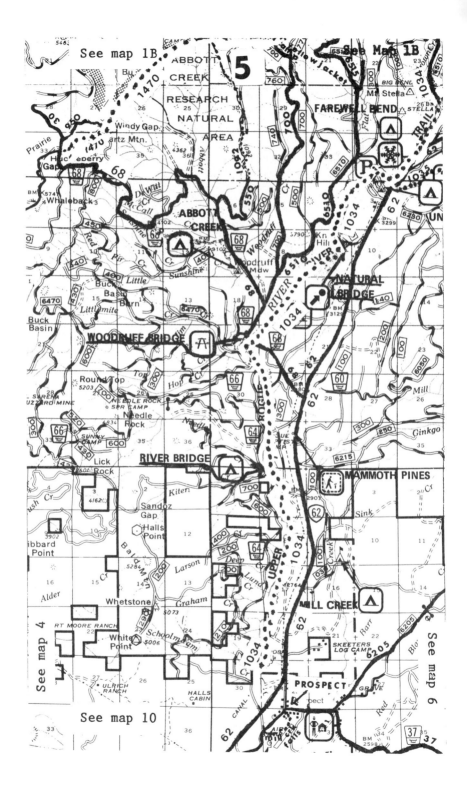

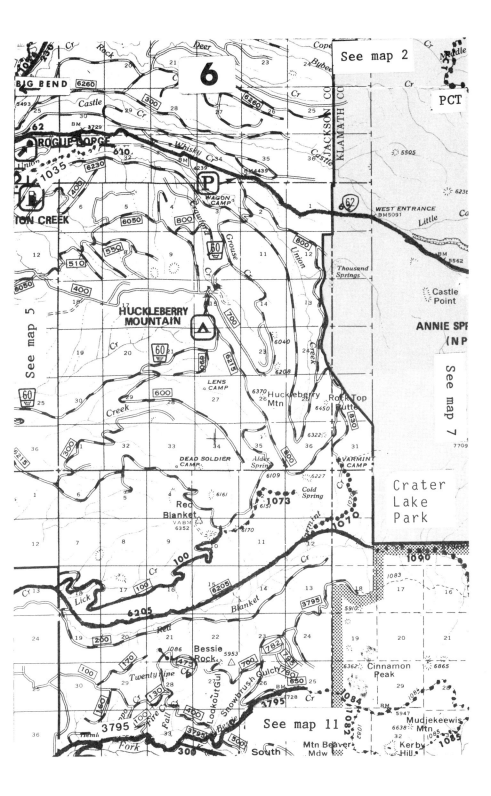

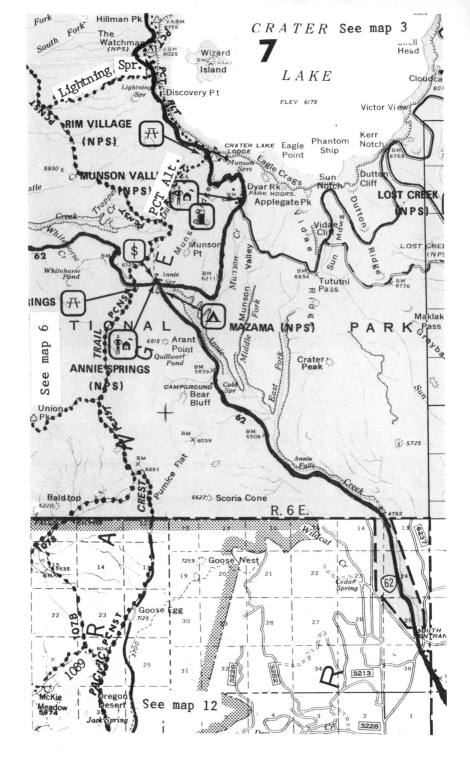

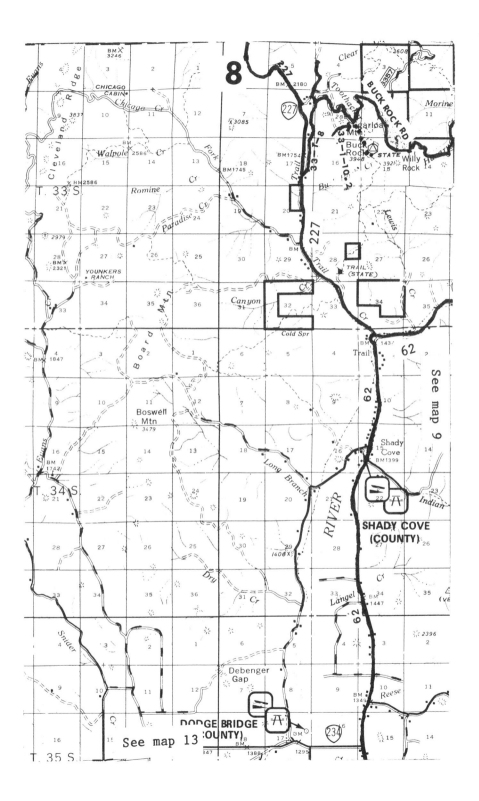

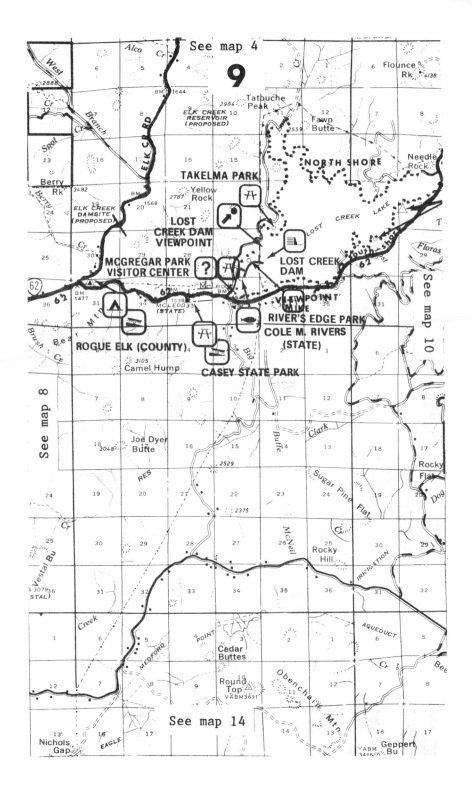

See map 4

9

Alco Cr

West

Cr
12

Spot
13

Berry
Rk

Berry
24

ELK CREEK RD

Branch
Cr

6   5   4   2   Cr   1   6   Flounce 5
                                                    Rk   4138

BM 1644

Tatouche
Peak
2984
ELK CREEK 10
RESERVOIR
(PROPOSED)   2559

12
Fawn
Butte

18   17   16   15   **NORTH SHORE**   Needle
                                                            Rock

3482   BM   Yellow
             20 1568 Rock   21   2787   LOST CREEK LAKE   T
ELK CREEK   **TAKELMA PARK**
DAMSITE
(PROPOSED)   Floras
Cr   30   29   28   29

25   South Shore   62

**LOST
CREEK DAM
VIEWPOINT**

**MCGREGAR PARK
VISITOR CENTER**   **?**   🏕   **LOST CREEK
                              DAM**

62   BM   McLeod BM
      1477 67 BM 33
36 62 31   30 McLEOD33 **VIEWPOINT
                    (STATE)**   MI   36   31

Brush Cr   🏕   **River's Edge Park**
                         COLE M. RIVERS
ROGUE ELK (COUNTY)   **(STATE)**   1   6

3105
Camel Hump   **CASEY STATE PARK**

7   8   9   10   11   12

18 3048 Joe Dyer   16   15   14   Clark 13   18   17   Rocky
         Butte   Flat
RES   2529

24   19   20   21   22   23   Sugar Pine Flat 19   20 Dog

Cr
25   30   29   28   27   26 McNeil 25   30   29
                                         Rocky
                                         Hill
Vestal Bu
3079 36 31   32   33   34   35   36   31   32
STAL)

Creek   AQUEDUCT
1   6   5   MEDFORD POINT 3   2   1   6   5
                         Cedar
                         Buttes   Cr   Bee

12   7   8   Round 19   Obenchain 12   7   8
                     Top ABM3691   Mtn

See map 14

13   16   17   EAGLE   14   13   18   17
Nichols   Geppert
Gap   Bu
                                          ABM
                                          3466

See map 8

See map 10

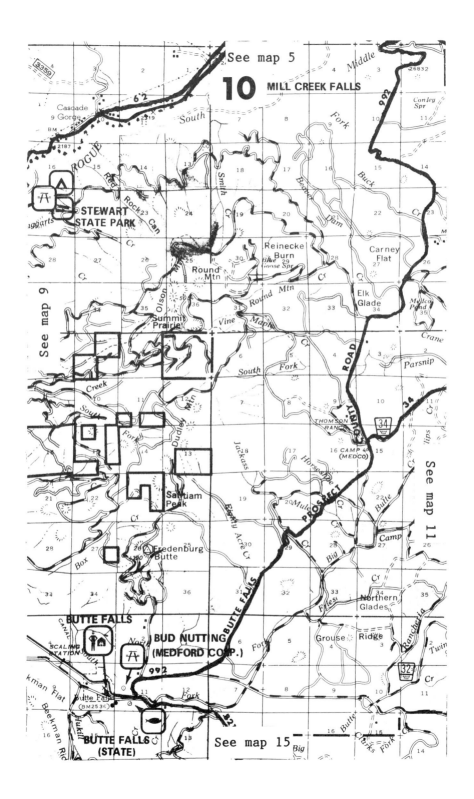

See map 5

10 MILL CREEK FALLS

See map 9

See map 11

STEWART STATE PARK

ROGUE

Cascade
9 Gorge

Reinecke Burn

Round Mtn

Summit Prairie

Carney Flat

Elk Glade

THOMSON RANCH

CAMP 46 (MEDCO)

Saltiam Peak

Fredenburg Butte

BUTTE FALLS

BUD NUTTING (MEDFORD CORP.)

Northern Glades

Grouse Ridge

BUTTE FALLS (STATE)

See map 15

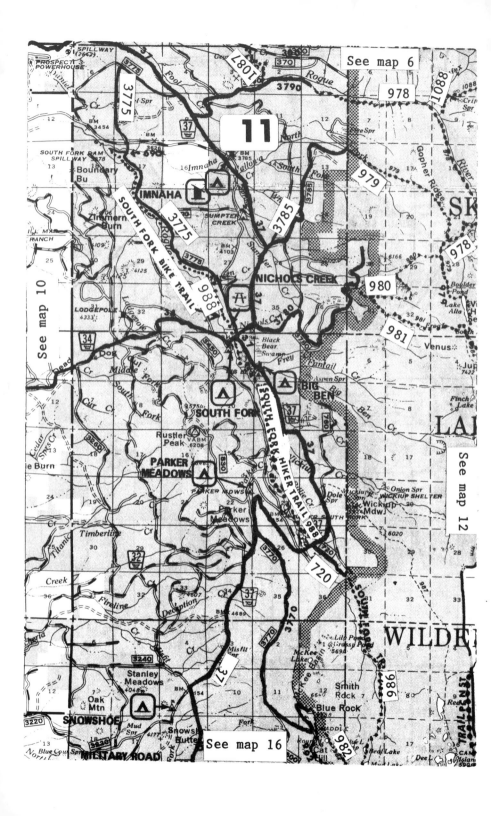

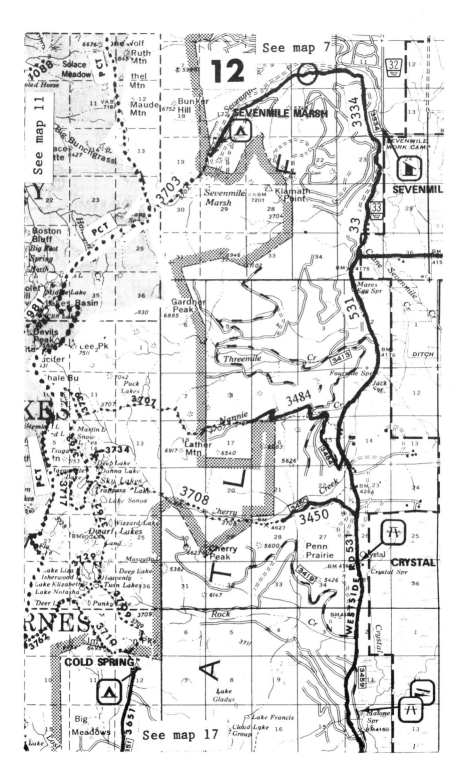

See map 7

12

SEVENMILE MARSH

See map 11

SEVENMILE
WORK CAMP

SEVENMIL

Solace
Meadow

One Wolf
Ruth
Mtn

thel
Mtn

Maude
Mtn

Bunker
Hill

Sevenmile
Marsh

Klamath
Point

Boston
Bluff

Big Foot
Spring
North

Gardner
Peak

Mares
Egg Spr

Devils
Peak

Lee Pk

Threemile

Fourmile Spr

Jack
Cr

Puck
Lakes

Nannie

Lather
Mtn

Martin L
Snow
Lakes

Deep Lake
Donna Lake
Sky Lakes
Trappers Lake
Lake Sonya

Wizzard Lake

Dwarf Lakes
J. Land

Cherry

Cherry
Peak

Creek

Penn
Prairie

Crystal
Spr

CRYSTAL

Lake Liza
Isherwood
Lake Elizabeth
Lake Notasha

Deep Lake
Heavenly
Twin Lakes

Mosquito

Deer L

Punky Lake

Rock

Cr

Crystal

COLD SPRING

Big
Meadows

Lake
Gladys

Lake Francis
Cloud Lake
Group

Malone
Spr

See map 17

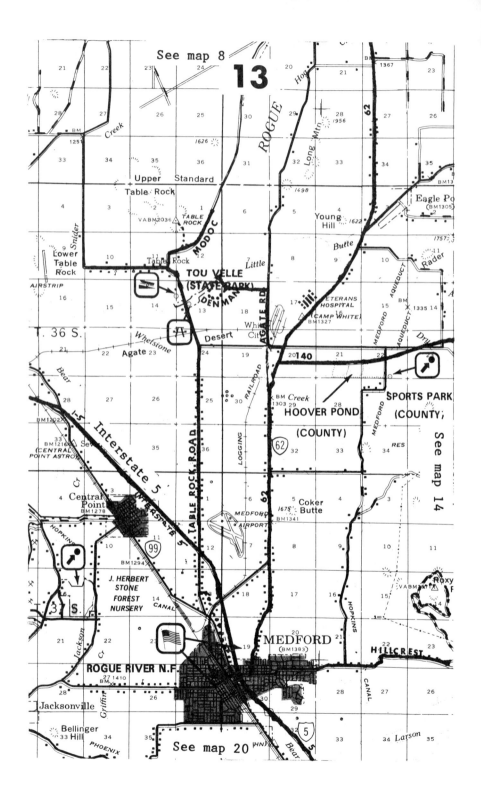

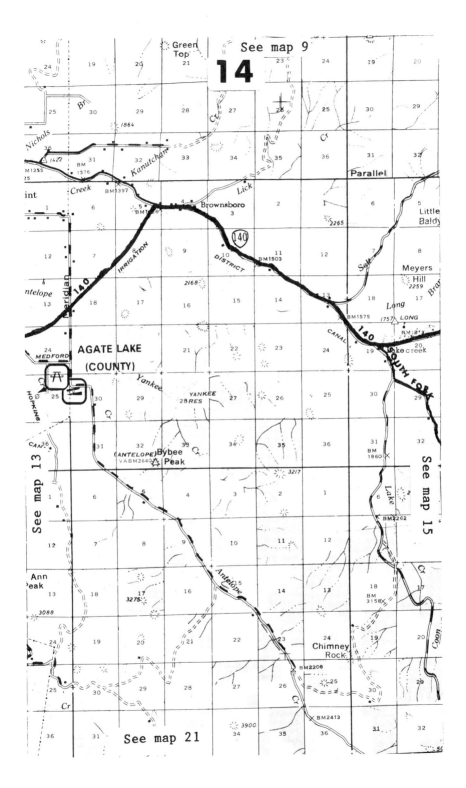

Green Top

23   24   19   20

19   20   21

24   25   30   29   28   27   26   25   30   29

Br

1864

Nichols   Cr

36   31   32   33   34   35   36   31   32

1422   BM 1376   Kanutchan   Parallel

M1355

25   Creek   BM1397   Lick   Little

int   1   6   5   4   Brownsboro   2   1   6   5   Baldy

BM1   3   2265

140

12   7   8   9   10   11   12   8

DISTRICT   BM1503   Meyers

2168   Salt   Hill

IRRIGATION   2259

ntelope   13   18   17   16   15   14   13   18   17   Long   Br

BM1575   LONG   140

24   AGATE LAKE   21   22   23   24   19   lakecreek   20

MEDFORD   (COUNTY)   Yankee   CANAL   SOUTH FORK

25   30   29   YANKEE   27   26   25   30   29

28 RES

HOPKINS   Cr

CAN 36   31   32   39   34   35   36   31   32

(ANTELOPE)Bybee   Cr   BM

VABM2640   Peak   1860

3217

Lake

See map 13   1   6   5   4   3   2   1   6   2   See map 15

BM2262

12   7   8   9   10   11   12

Ann   Antelope   5   18   Cr

Peak   13   18   17   16   14   13   BM   17

3275   3156

3088

24   19   20   21   22   23   24   19   20   Coon

Chimney

Rock

BM2208

25   30   29   28   27   26   25   30   29

Cr

3900   BM2413

36   31   34   35   36   31   32

See map 21

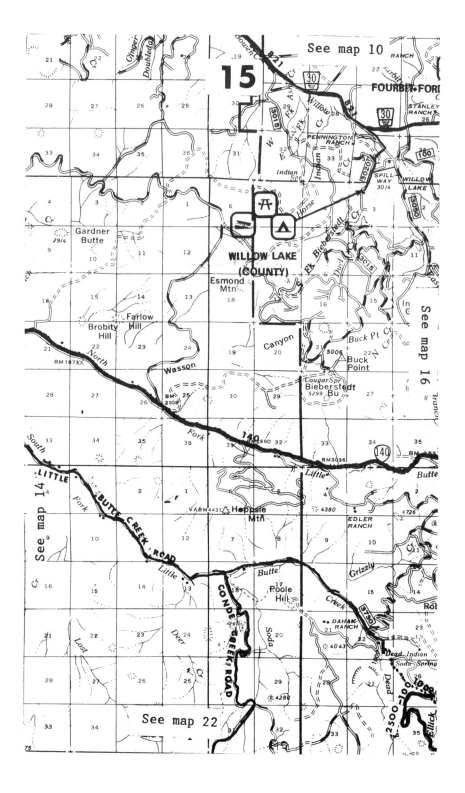

See map 10

15

FOURBIT FORK

See map 16

See map 14

See map 22

WILLOW LAKE
(COUNTY)

STANLEY RANCH

PENNINGTON RANCH

SPILL WAY 3014

WILLOW LAKE

Gardner Butte

Esmond Mtn

Farlow Hill

Brobity Hill

Wasson

Canyon

Buck Point

CougarSpr
Bieberstedt Bu

Hoppie Mtn

EDLER RANCH

Butte

Poole Hill

Grizzly

DAHAK RANCH

Dead Indian Soda Spring

BUTTE CREEK ROAD

CONDE CREEK ROAD

Soda

Deer

Lost

75

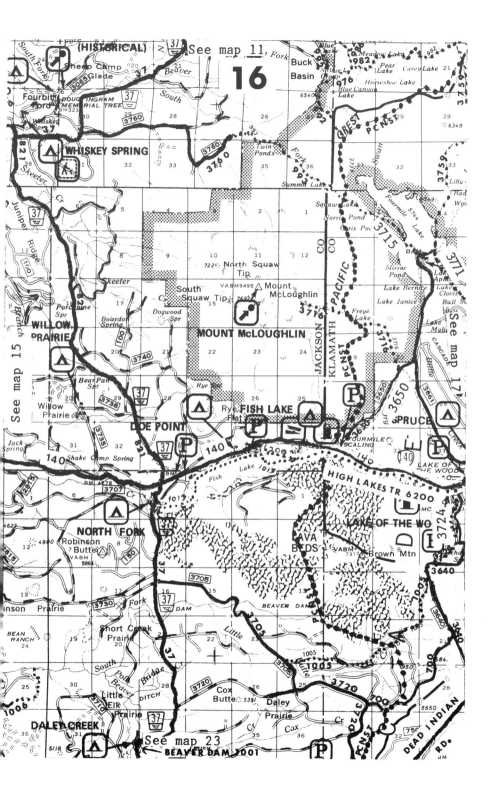

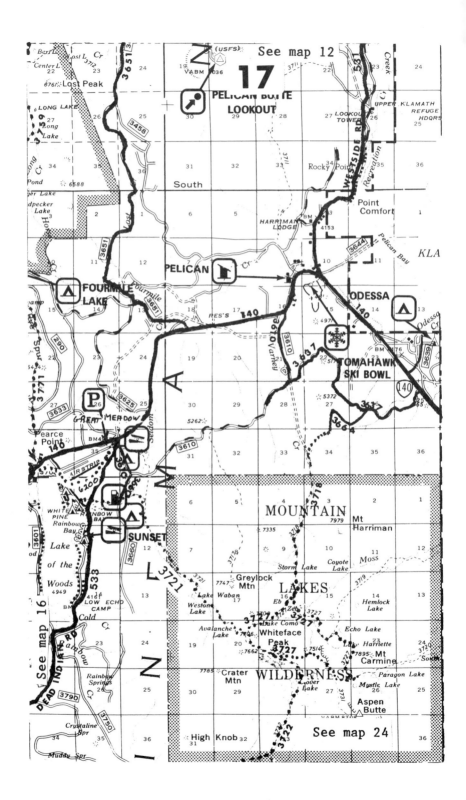

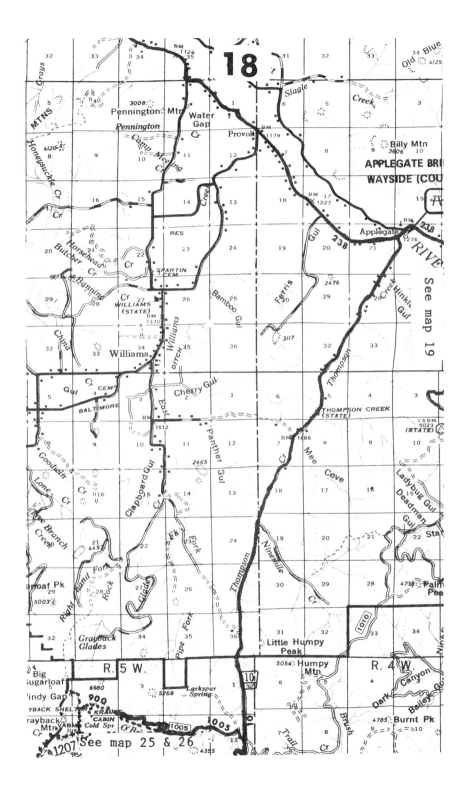

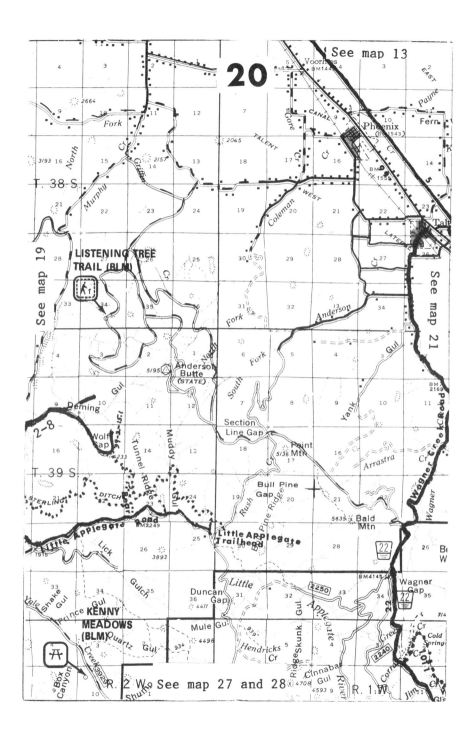

20

See map 19

See map 21

Voorhees
BM 1444

Phoenix
BM 1543

Fern

Talent

T. 38 S.

Fork

North

Murphy

Griffin Cr.

TALENT

Coleman

WEST

Cr.

BM 1555

LISTENING TREE
TRAIL (BLM)

Fork

North Cr.

Anderson

Anderson
Butte
(STATE)

South Fork

Fork

Section
Line Gap

Point
Mtn

Yank Gul.

Arrastra

Wagner Creek RD.

Wagner

Deming

Gul.

Wolf
Gap

Tunnel Ridge

Muddy Gul.

2-8-

T. 39 S.

STERLING

DITCH

Bull Pine
Gap

Rush Cr.

Pine Ridge

Bald
Mtn
5635

Little Applegate

Pond
BM 2249

Lick

Little Applegate
Trailhead

22

Be
W

Yale Snake Gul.

Prince Gul.

Gulch

Duncan
Gap
4411

Little

2250

BM4145

Applegate

Wagner
Gap

22

KENNY
MEADOWS
(BLM)

Quartz Gul.

Mule Gul.

Hendricks
Cr.

RidgeSkunk Gul.

River

Three Cr.

Cold
Spring

2240

Box
Canyon

Creek

R. 2 W. See map 27 and 28

Cinnabar
Gul.
4708

R. 1 W.

Jim

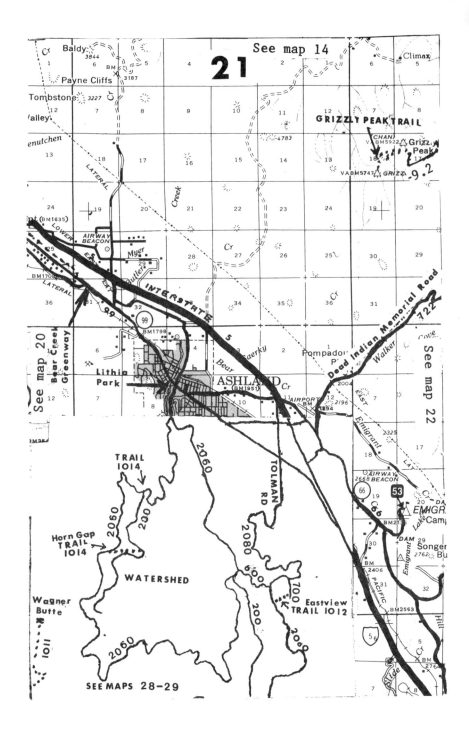

See map 14

21

See map 20

See map 22

Baldy
3844
BM
Payne Cliffs 3187
Tombstone 3227
Valley
enutchen

GRIZZLY PEAK TRAIL
CHAN
BM5922 Grizz
Peak
VABM5747 GRIZZ 9.2

4783

AIRWAY BEACON
Myer

BM1635
LOWER
BM1708
LATERAL
INTERSTATE
99
BM1798

Cr
Cr

Bear Creek Greenway
Lithia Park
ASHLAND
BM1951
Cr
Baerky
Pompadou
Dead Indian Memorial Road
Walker
Cove
722
AIRPORT
BM
2196
1894
2004
2325
AIRWAY BEACON
2668
66
66
53
EMIGR.
Lake Camp
DA
BM213
DAM
BM
2406
Songer
2762 Bu
EMIGRANT
PACIFIC
BM2563
5
5
Cr
BM
276

TRAIL 1014
2060
200
Horn Gap TRAIL 1014
2050
WATERSHED
Wagner Butte
1011
2060
2080
600
700
200
Eastview TRAIL 1012
2060
TOLMAN RD
EAST

SEE MAPS 28-29

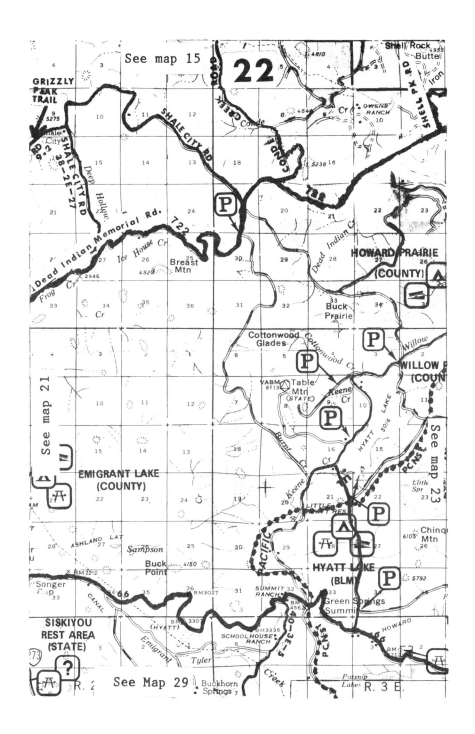

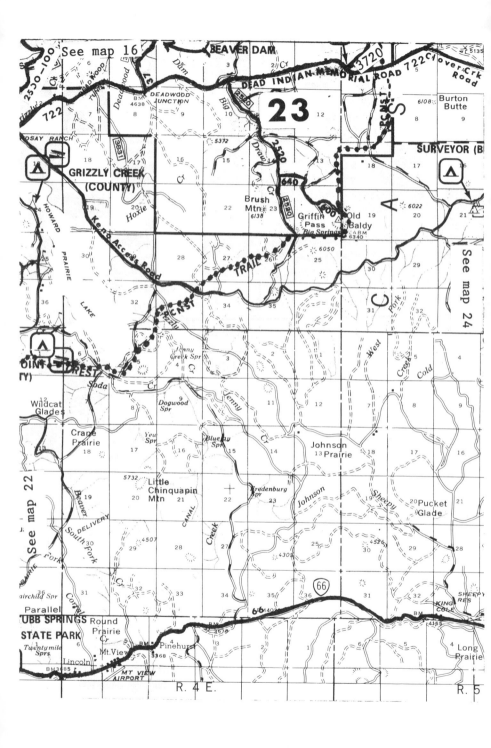

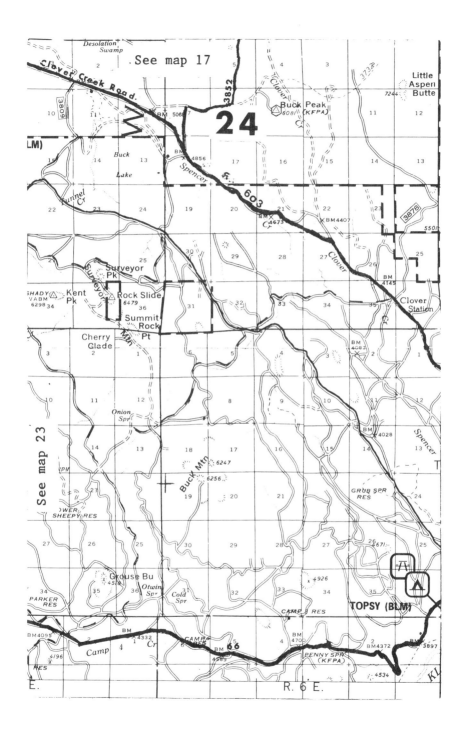

See map 17

Desolation Swamp

Clover Creek Road.

Little Aspen Butte

24

Buck Peak (KFPA)

Buck Lake

Tunnel Cr

Spencer

603

Clover

Surveyor Pk

SHADY VABM 6298

Kent Pk

Rock Slide

Summit Rock Pt

Surveyor Mtn

Cherry Glade

Clover Station

See map 23

Onion Spr

Buck Mtn

GRUB SPR RES

WER SHEEPY RES

Grouse Bu

Otwin Spr

Cold Spr

PARKER RES

CAMP RES

TOPSY (BLM)

BM4095

Camp Cr

66

PENNY SPR (KFPA)

RES

KL

E.

R. 6 E.

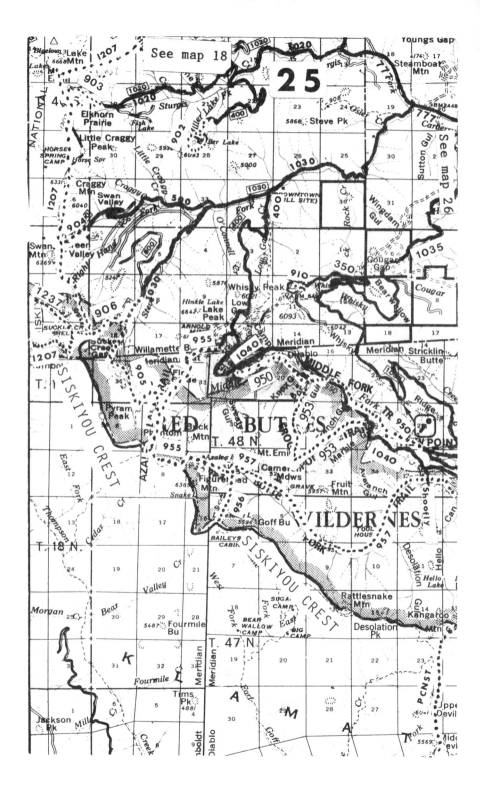

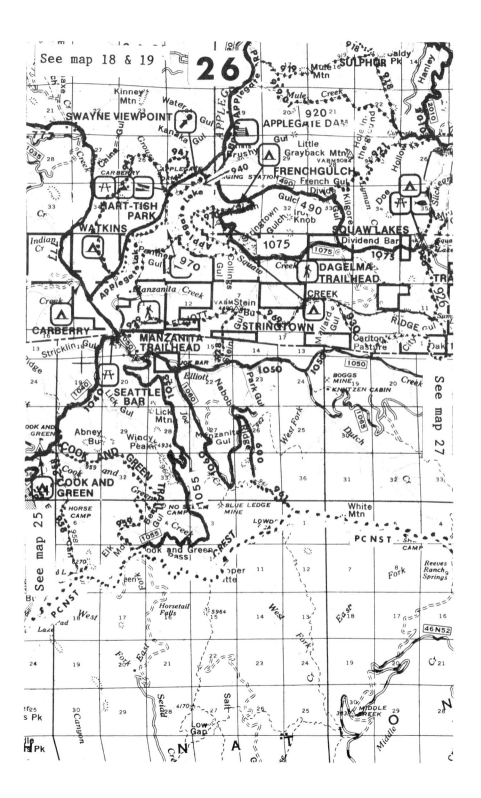

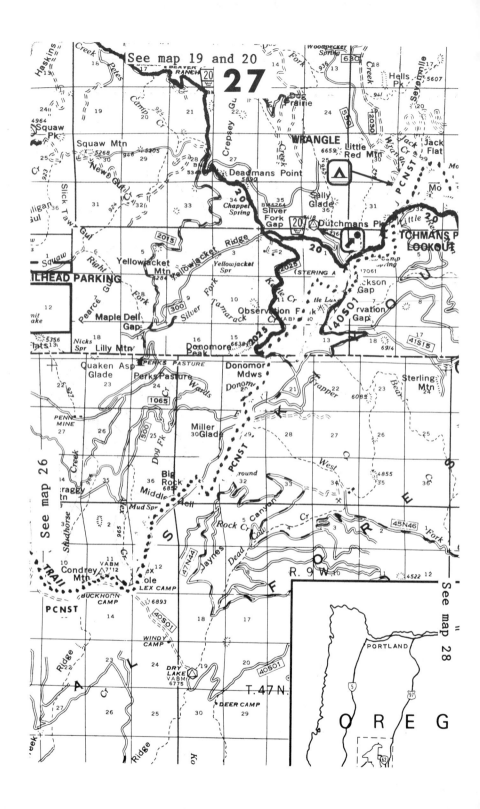

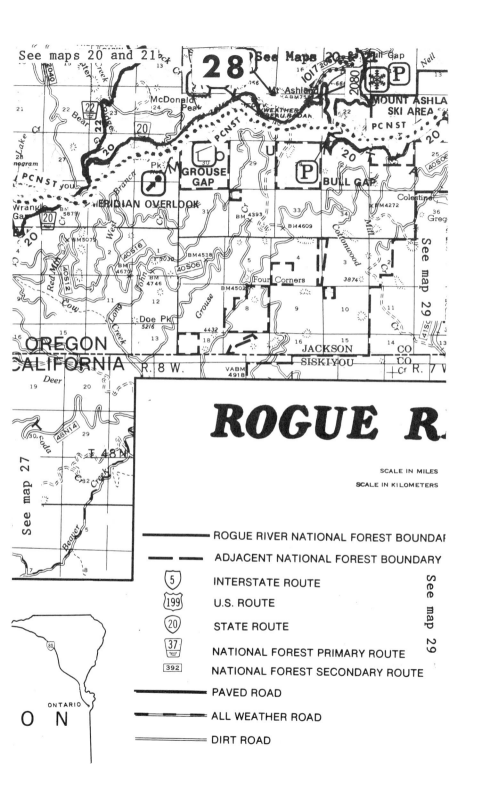

MOUNT ASHLAND
SKI AREA

PCN ST

PCN ST

GROUSE
GAP

BULL GAP

Colestine

MERIDIAN OVERLOOK

BM 4393

BM 4609

Wrangle
Ga.

20

BM 5879

BM 5075

40516

40506

BM 4538

40512

BM
4670

BM
4746

BM 4502

Four Corners

3874

Doe Pk
5216

Grouse

4432

See map 29

OREGON

CALIFORNIA   R. 8 W.

JACKSON   CO

SISKIYOU   CO

VABM
4918

R. 7 W.

Deer

48N14

T. 48 N.

See map 27

Soda

Creek

Beaver

ROGUE R.

SCALE IN MILES

SCALE IN KILOMETERS

———————— ROGUE RIVER NATIONAL FOREST BOUNDAR.

— — — ADJACENT NATIONAL FOREST BOUNDARY

(5) INTERSTATE ROUTE

(199) U.S. ROUTE

(20) STATE ROUTE

37 NATIONAL FOREST PRIMARY ROUTE

392 NATIONAL FOREST SECONDARY ROUTE

———————— PAVED ROAD

———————— ALL WEATHER ROAD

———————— DIRT ROAD

See map 29

ONTARIO

O   N

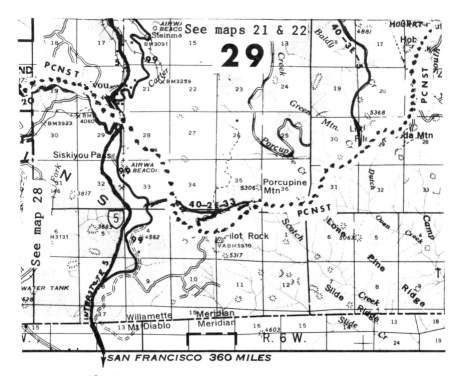

29

PCNST

Siskiyou Pass

Porcupine Mtn.

PCNST

ilot Rock

Willamette
Mt. Diablo

Meridian
Meridian

R. 6 W.

SAN FRANCISCO 360 MILES

IVER National Forest

LEGEND

☐ ROGUE RIVER NATIONAL FOREST	△ CAMPGROUND
☐ ADJACENT NATIONAL FOREST	� PICNIC AREA
☐ BUREAU OF LAND MANAGEMENT	🐟 FISHING
☐ STATE LANDS	⛵ LAUNCHING RAMP
⚑ FOREST SUPERVISOR HEADQUARTERS	❄ WINTER RECREATION A
🏠 RANGER STATION	🚶 NATURE TRAIL
⛽ FOREST SERVICE STATION	⌂ TRAIL SHELTER
— — — PACIFIC CREST NATIONAL SCENIC TRAIL (Closed to Motorized Vehicles)	P WINTER PARKING (FEE AT SOME AREAS)
	🔭 POINT OF INTEREST

See Map 28